I0042230

Psychological Borders in Europe and the United States

Psychological Borders in Europe and the United States

Contemporary Nationalism, Nativism, and Populism

Maria del Mar Fariña

LEXINGTON BOOKS
Lanham • Boulder • New York • London

Rowman & Littlefield
Bloomsbury Publishing Inc, 1359 Broadway, New York, NY 10018, USA
Bloomsbury Publishing Plc, 50 Bedford Square, London, WC1B 3DP, UK
Bloomsbury Publishing Ireland, 29 Earlsfort Terrace, Dublin 2, D02 AY28, Ireland
www.bloomsbury.com

Published by Lexington Books
An imprint of The Rowman & Littlefield Publishing Group, Inc.
4501 Forbes Boulevard, Suite 200, Lanham, Maryland 20706
www.rowman.com
86-90 Paul Street, London EC2A 4NE

Copyright © 2023 by The Rowman & Littlefield Publishing Group, Inc.

All rights reserved. No part of this publication may be: i) reproduced or transmitted in any
form, electronic or mechanical, including photocopying, recording or by means of any
information storage or retrieval system without prior permission in writing from the
publishers; or ii) used or reproduced in any way for the training, development or
operation of artificial intelligence (AI) technologies, including generative AI technologies.
The rights holders expressly reserve this publication from the text and data mining
exception as per Article 4(3) of the Digital Single Market Directive (EU) 2019/790.

British Library Cataloguing in Publication Information available

Library of Congress Cataloging-in-Publication Data

Names: Fariña, Maria del Mar, author.
Title: Psychological borders in Europe and the United States : contemporary
nationalism, nativism, and populism / Maria del Mar Fariña.
Description: Lanham, Maryland : Lexington Books, [2023] | Includes
bibliographical references and index.
Identifiers: LCCN 2023032567 (print) | LCCN 2023032568 (ebook) | ISBN
9781793610614 (cloth) | ISBN 9781793610638 (paperback) | ISBN 9781793610621 (ebook)
Subjects: LCSH: Political psychology–Europe. | Political psychology–United States. |
Collective memory–Political aspects. | Nationalism and collective memory. | Nativism. |
Populism. Classification: LCC JA74.5 .D447 2023 (print) | LCC JA74.5 (ebook) |
DDC 320.01/9–dc23/eng/20230803
LC record available at https://lccn.loc.gov/2023032567
LC ebook record available at https://lccn.loc.gov/2023032568

Contents

PART I: NATIONALISM, NATIVISM, AND POPULISM: WHAT'S THE DIFFERENCE?   1

Chapter One: Nationalism, Nativism, and Populism: What's the Difference?   3

Chapter Two: Nationalism   7

Chapter Three: Nativism   21

Chapter Four: Nativism, War, the Ku Klux Klan, and White Power Movements   33

Chapter Five: Populism   51

PART II: CONSTRUCTION AND SOCIOPOLITICAL MOBILIZATION OF LARGE-GROUP IDENTITIES: THE INTEGRATED SOCIOPOLITICAL AND PSYCHOLOGICAL ANALYSIS MODEL   67

Chapter Six: Mobilization of Large-Group Identities: The Case of the Identitarian Movement   69

Chapter Seven: Integrated Sociopolitical Analysis: Individual and Collective Identity Constructions   83

PART III: POLITICAL PSYCHOLOGY, BORDERS, AND IDENTITY WARS   109

Chapter Eight: Integrated Psychological Analysis: Political Psychology, Borders, and Identity Wars in Europe and the United States   111

**PART IV: AN INTEGRATED SOCIOPOLITICAL
AND PSYCHOLOGICAL APPROACH TO
CONTEMPORARY IDENTITY-DRIVEN CONFLICT
AND HISTORICAL COLLECTIVE TRAUMAS**   133

Chapter Nine: An Integrated Sociopolitical and Psychological
Approach (ISPA) to Identity-Driven Conflict and Historical
Collective Traumas   135

Chapter Ten: Historical Collective Traumas and Resistance
to Identity Transformation and Mourning: American
Immigration Policy   141

Chapter Eleven: Russia and Ukraine: The Development of a New
Identity and Thwarted Mourning   161

References   167

Index   193

About the Author   203

PART I

Nationalism, Nativism, and Populism: What's the Difference?

Chapter One

Nationalism, Nativism, and Populism

What's the Difference?

The sociopolitical landscape has changed significantly over the last decade in both Europe and the United States. Whereas in the past, most of the major ruling parties in the United States and Europe fell somewhere between the traditional right, center, and left ideological spectrum, this is no longer the case. While centrist and moderate parties have seen a sharp electoral decline, far right, radical right, populist (whether left or right leaning), nationalist and nativist parties and movements now seem to pervade the sociopolitical arena in Europe, as well as in the United States (Biswas, 2020; Gostoli, 2019; Inglehart & Norris, 2016). Many of these terms are used interchangeably, or in tandem, whenever a particular politician or political group uses divisive, xenophobic, anti-Semitic, and/or Islamophobic rhetoric, to delineate who belongs and who doesn't to a particular society and nation-state (Fariña, 2018; Kienpointner, 2017; Reisigl, 2017; Wodak, 2017). Such rhetoric aims to explain existing social and economic inequality through binary constructions (Derrida, 2001, 2016), where those constructed as "other" are directly responsible for the increasing economic and "moral" decline experienced by a particular society and its "dominant group"—obscuring the destructive and violent effects of the capitalist global economic system and in particular of neoliberalism (Reisigl, 2017; Wodak, 2017a). Yet, the influx of undocumented immigration and refugee and asylum seekers fleeing armed conflict or severe poverty and the rise of terrorist acts—whether foreign or domestic—have pervaded media headlines in European countries and the United States alike.

Debates have thus shifted to national identity politics (BBC, 2019), where uttered discourses either seek to strengthen or subvert sociopolitical constructions that define the identity of the nation-state, who "the real national citizens are" and therefore, who "the nation-state belongs to." These discourses, whether articulated by politicians or social groups, exert pressure and influence the nature of the socioeconomic policies implemented by European nations, as well as the United States (Mudde, 2016). Many of these recent policies, restrictive and exclusionary in nature, especially in immigration, refugee, and asylum policy, have gained support by mobilizing and/or intensifying existing, country- specific racial, ethnic, cultural and religious divides. Examples of these discursive, group mobilization efforts are easily found in statements made by now "mainstream" political party leaders, such as Geert Wilders—Party for Freedom (PVV) in the Netherlands, or by President Donald Trump in the United States; as much as by leaders and members of previously marginalized, and/or new far-right or radical right groups, such as Markus Willinger from the Generation Identity movement (Valencia-Garcia, 2018). These identity-based dynamics are easily observable when some of their public statements are compared concurrently (Kienpointner, 2017). For example, Wilders states

> Our history compels us to fight a battle that is not an option but a necessity. After all, this is a battle for the . . . survival of the Netherlands as a recognizable nation; a country that is about to say goodbye to its ancient roots in exchange for multiculturalism, cultural relativism, and a European super state, all under the leadership of a self-satisfied political elite that has long lost the plot. (Wilders, 2005)

Similarly, President Trump in 2016, when running for the US presidency on an immigration control platform, stated "When Mexico sends its people, they're not sending their best; they're not sending you. They're sending people that have lots of problems, and they're bringing those problems with us. They're bringing drugs. They're bringing crime. They're rapists. And some, I assume, are good people" (as quoted by LoGiurato, 2016). And, Markus Willinger, when discussing cultural identity in *A Europe of Nations* (1992)—one of three books written for the Generation Identity movement—argued that

> A person's cultural identity is nearly unchangeable. Every person is molded in early childhood, and this process can only occur again . . . in absolutely exceptional cases. . . . How should millions of people from the Global East suddenly become Europeans? They can't. . . . Our continent and our culture can't survive if millions of non-Europeans live here. We can't preserve our identity under these conditions. (as quoted by Valencia-Garcia, 2018)

In all these discursive instances, identity emerges as a construct that delineates and defines who the real members of a particular society are. The "racial, ethnic, cultural or religious others" emerge as undesirable invaders, whose presence will corrupt the cultural history of the dominant group, leading to the inevitable transformation of their nation-state (Fariña, 2018). Such identity-based constructions seem to suggest that said cultural history and nation-state has existed throughout time as a fixed and stable reality. The mythical and temporal nature of that cultural history, central to the delineation of the current nation-states and borders in Europe and the United States is not only "forgotten," but also effectively dissociated from social awareness and history itself (Gellner, 2006; Leerssen, 2006; Volkan, 2017; Wodak, 2017b). The newly formed Identity and Democracy party, ID—union formed in 2019 between ten far-right European parties, including the Rassemblement National Party in France, the Freedom Party in Austria (FPÖ), and Lega per Salvini Premier in Italy—is perhaps the best political expression of these dynamics. Under a platform based on national identity and sovereignty that rejects supranational bodies, such as the European Union, ID pledges to preserve "the identity of the peoples and nations of Europe, in accordance with the specific characteristics of each people. The right to control and regulate immigration is thus a fundamental principle shared by the members of the ID Party" (Identity and Democracy Party n.d.).

Given the centrality of identity-based claims to contemporary sociopolitical processes and debates, and the conflation of the various political ideologies and movements that seek to mobilize particular groups to "protect their nation," it is first necessary to establish some conceptual clarity (Bonikowski, Halikiopoulou, Kaufmann, & Rooduijn, 2018; Duyvendak & Kesic, 2018; Freeden, 1998; Macshane, 2019; Riedel, 2018); to then, examine how certain political actors mobilize existing sociopolitical constructions to reinforce national physical and psychological borders.

This book attempts to establish this conceptual clarity through an integrated sociopolitical and psychological analysis model informed by historiography, critical discourse historical analysis, and psychodynamic individual and collective identity formation processes (Fariña, 2018; Volkan, 2018, 2020; Wodak, 2015, 2017, 2020, 2021). The model is described and applied to the study of contemporary rising ideologies in Europe and the United States—specifically nationalism, nativism, and populism. The processes involved in the construction and sociopolitical mobilization of large-group identities are also presented and explored.

Part I engages in a sociopolitical analysis of nationalism, nativism, and populism, while exploring the connection between nativism, white power groups and war. The sociopolitical analysis applies a historiographic and critical discourse historical analysis approach to the study of these contemporary social and political processes. Part II introduces and explains the integrated sociopolitical and psychological model and examines the processes involved in the construction and sociopolitical mobilization of large-group identities. Part III engages in an integrated psychological analysis of contemporary political processes, by first introducing political psychology to then explore the formation of national and psychological borders and their implications—including dynamics of identity driven aggression. The integrated psychological analysis is then applied to the cases of France and the Rassemblement National (The National Rally Party), and Spain and VOX. Part IV examines the connection between the rise of subjugatory ideologies such as nativism and unprocessed historical collective traumas. The application of the integrated sociopolitical and psychological analysis model highlights the role of trauma, social reenactments, transformation, and large collective mourning to contemporary sociopolitical processes. The integrated sociopolitical and psychological approach is then presented as a useful conflict management and resolution approach to identity-driven conflict and historical collective trauma. The role of immigration and asylum policy in maintaining, changing, and transforming existing large collective identities is discussed, to then examine the war between Russia and the Ukraine. The book includes specific integrated case application to European countries where nationalism, nativism, and populism have been growing, as well as the United States.

Chapter Two

Nationalism

The definitions of nationalism are quite varied and contested. While some political science scholars question whether or not nationalism is even a political ideology (Ball, Dagger, O'Neill, 2019; Heywood, 2021), arguing that the many forms nationalism can take, prevent it from being classified as an established political ideology—such as liberalism, conservatism, or socialism (Freeden, 1998); others focus on its conceptual structure (see Freeden, 1998), while others state that nationalism "is one of the dominant [political ideologies] of the last two centuries" (Leerseen, 2006, p. 13). Given the many definitions and conceptualizations, it may be helpful instead to begin with nationalism's main focus, the nation-state and its construction—also shared by nativism and populism, albeit in a different manner.

EUROPE: THE NATION-STATE AND NATIONALISM

Breuilly (2006) and Leerssen (2006), when discussing nationalism and the nation-state, define the nation in modernist terms as "the most natural, organic collective aggregate of humans, and the most natural and organic subdivision of humanity" (p. 14). However, others such as Kedourie (1960), after the rise and fall of fascism, began to offer a postmodernist understanding of nationalism, where its mythical nature and thus, that of the nation-state, emerged as "invented in Europe at the beginning of the nineteenth century" (Kedourie, 1960, p. 9). For Kedourie (1960), nationalism constructed and legitimized the nation-state as a natural and stable entity, which, once created, legitimized nationalism itself. That is,

> [Nationalism is a] doctrine that. . . pretends to supply a criterion for the deter-
> mination of the unit of population proper to enjoy a government exclusively its
> own, for the legitimate exercise of power in the state, and for the right organiza-
> tion of states. (Kedourie 1960, p. 9)

7

The question is therefore, how does nationalism provide the criteria to identify who "the people" are? And, how has it influenced the creation of the various European nation-states that are now understood as historically stable units?

"WE THE PEOPLE": CIVIC COMMITMENT AND CULTURAL "BELONGING"

Nationalism rests on two essential principles to identify and define the national, physical borders of a people: civic commitment—the voluntary commitment of a people to live together under a social contract; and cultural belonging—access to a shared, historical culture (ethnic nationalism) (Gellner, 2006).

Democracy and civic commitment—fundamental to democracy—are a product of the Enlightenment era, as Leerssen (2006) aptly describes in *National Thought in Europe: A Cultural History*. During the eighteenth century, as European absolute monarchies began to weaken, Enlightenment philosophers such as Locke, Montesquieu, and Rousseau started to examine different forms of government, all resting on the premise of a social contract—while disagreeing on whether this contract should be with, or between, "the people" and a monarch or a tripartite government (see Passmore, 2009; Leerssen, 2006). Yet, it was Rousseau, with the publication of the *Contrat Social*, who introduced the notion of *volonté générale* or collective/voluntaristic will, providing the conceptual foundation for what is now referred to as civic commitment. Rousseau posited that people could only coexist in a society if they shared a voluntaristic will to live together, under a government that ruled according to the will of the people (Gellner, 2006; Leerssen, 2006). Rousseau's writings were not only instrumental to the French Revolution but also influenced the US social contract—the Constitution. Rousseauian ideals can be easily heard in its preamble:

> We the People of the United States, in Order to form a more perfect Union, establish Justice, insure domestic Tranquility, provide for the common defense, promote the general Welfare, and secure the Blessings of Liberty to ourselves and our Posterity, do ordain and establish this Constitution for the United States of America. (U. S. Const. pmbl.)

Culture, and therefore cultural belonging, are more elusive concepts; the significance of "culture" to nationalism can be traced to the Romantic period, and specifically to Johann Gottfried Herder—often considered the precursor of German Romanticism (Steinby, 2009). Herder focused on language and its diversity, linking a people's identity to their shared language and its manifestations—in the form of popular folk songs, tales, art, and traditions. Culture, as argued by Herder, was not "something" that belonged to the elites, intellectuals, or higher classes—high culture, as defined during the Enlightenment Era. For Herder, it was the "real people," those belonging to the lower classes, who had access to the "true culture" of the group, or nation. Herder advocated for a return to popular culture, away from cosmopolitanism, strongly criticizing the French hegemony that had marked the Enlightenment era, as can be seen when he stated, "We do not have a fatherland, no sense of our own that we live for, but we are philanthropists and cosmopolitan citizens of the world. All rulers of Europe already speak the French language, soon we shall all speak it! . . . Oh national characters, where have you gone?" (Herder, 1795, p. 66). For Herder, language and a people's culture were inevitably interconnected. Language ensured the survival of each people as a distinct group and maintained cultural distinctiveness and diversity among nations (Benner, 2016).

Herder's and Rousseau's ideas provided the conceptual foundation for nationalism. Their ideas created a mechanism to differentiate between, and legitimize the existence of distinct ethnic groups and thus nations and nationalities—nationality, understood as a "marker" of belonging to a specific society with a shared, historical common language and culture. The social contract, on the other hand, provided the political and governmental structure for a distinct "people" to assert their right to live together in a territory occupied by their ethnic group—the nation (Benner, 2016).

The Romantic period expanded nationalist thought. For Romantic writers, collective history played an essential role in defining and maintaining a people's identity. Frieder Schlegel (1988) among others, not only emphasized history's centrality, but also argued that literature was the most effective vehicle for its excavation and transmission. In other words, literature was essential to the creation of a collective, national identity. A people's identity and desire to live together as one, could only emerge if a shared common past, linked to the group's spoken language and traditions, could be established (Gellner, 2006). Only upon such recognition, could people be mobilized to demand to be acknowledged as a unit, with access to self-governance—the nation. National-cultural consciousness raising was therefore essential to the mobilization of a people, and literature provided the mechanism through which *historicity* could be both produced and intergenerationally transmitted until it was unquestionably accepted without further investigation—what critical discourse historical analysis refers to as common-sense normalization processes (Wodak, 2017, 2021).

HISTORICITY, NATIONAL IDENTITY,
AND TERRITORIAL BORDERS

Although as Herder argued, it was the "real, lower class working people" that had access to a group's true culture, it was instead the elites and intellectuals who were tasked with the national-cultural consciousness-raising enterprise, producing and documenting the historical, sociocultural life of particular "collectives" for popular dissemination (Gellner, 2006). As Leerssen (2006) states,

> Early cultural nationalism often coincides with the discovery of the nation's identity, something which might even be called its "invention" or "construction" . . . and amounts in many cases to self-invention. . . . What is required . . . is an act of articulation, *naming.* (pp. 166–67)

From this point on, nationalism sought to articulate and disseminate the shared sociohistorical and ethnic culture of a people, inventing and legitimizing existing and new nation-states, as well as the need for territorial borders (Gellner, 2006). For nationalism, territorial borders were essential; they delineated the nation-state, which enabled the development of a political and governmental structure for the protection of the ethnic group and the territory it had historically inhabited and/or occupied. As Gellner (2006) states, "Nationalism is primarily a political principle, which holds that the political and the national unit should be congruent" (p. 1). In this manner, nationalism facilitated the centralization and consolidation of a people's self-governance efforts, or fostered separatist movements—shifting the territorial borders of nation-states for new ones to emerge (Gellner, 2006; Leerseen, 2006). As Leerssen (2006) states, "the ideology of nationalism sets out . . . to fix in politics the profile of culture" (p. 175).

While the Romantic period constructed language and historicity as essential to the preservation of ethno-culturally diverse identities and nations, the emergence of the scientific paradigm and in particular Darwinism introduced a new marker of distinctiveness, race.

NATIONALISM AND THE RACIAL PARADIGM

The rise of the scientific paradigm provided nationalism with another element to further delineate who belonged to a particular nation-state. As anthropologists attempted to organize the various ethno-cultural and linguistic groups that existed through racial, pseudoscientific methodology, language, nationality, ethnicity, and race began to be conflated and intertwined with each other.

Languages were named after the country they were spoken in, and races after specific ethnic groups and their languages. Races such as the Celtic, Slavic, and Germanic were birthed and hierarchically organized according to particular biological and phenotypical attributes ascribed to each racial-ethnic group (Benner, 2016; McMahon, 2016). The implications were significant for nationalism; nation-states were no longer defined by the shared history, language, and culture of their people, but rather by the "shared descent, [and] common inheritance passed along a physical bloodline," which was inextricably linked to the peoples' sociohistorical ethnic culture (Leerseen, 2006, p. 209). Racial purity was thereby necessary, to preserve a people's national-cultural identity, as not all races were equally endowed (Benner, 2016; Leerseen, 2006; McMahon, 2016).

Although Herder and Prichard's monogenist explanation of human diversity had initially provided the basis for ethno-cultural-linguistic nationalism—all human variations share a common origin with various adaptations; at the end, it was the scientific, Darwinian paradigm, emphasizing polygenism—all human variations reflect racial differences and distinct origins—that prevailed. With polygenism, fears of racial-ethnic-cultural degeneration due to miscegenation took center stage and became nationalism's primary concern.

Count Arthur de Gobineau's *Essay sur l'inégalité des races humaines* (1853–1855) was particularly instrumental to this project, providing the basis for the hierarchical organization of the races, according to their perceived higher achievements and intellect. Miscegenation, therefore, not only threatened the racial purity of particular racial-ethno-cultural groups, but could lead to the degeneration of the group. It is at this juncture that nationalism shifts from a revolutionary, anti-cosmopolitan, political movement, to a conservative, right-leaning one. With this shift, nationalism begins to display authoritarian undertones, as well as a preoccupation with the regeneration of "the people," and with leaders who demonstrate the superiority of their "peoples"—establishing the foundation for the 1930s fascist leaders that were to emerge. Whereas initially, nationalism sought to preserve the linguistic, ethno-cultural human variations that existed from cosmopolitan hegemony, it now became how politicians and governments alike sought to achieve "state hegemony" (Leerssen 2006, p. 216). A new ethno-geopolitical nationalism had emerged (Gellner, 2006).

ETHNO-GEOPOLITICAL NATIONALISM AND WORLD WAR I

By 1914, the nation-states across Europe had formed a number of strategic political alliances. Britain, France, and Russia had formed the Triple

Entente coalition, while Germany, Austria-Hungary, and Italy joined forces through the Triple Alliance (Wilde, 2020). Tensions between the European nation-states had existed during the last century and had intensified in the years prior to World War I, coming to a head in 1914. In Sarajevo, on June 28, 1914, Gavrilo Princip, a Serbian nationalist, assassinated Archduke Franz Ferdinand—heir to the Austria-Hungarian Empire—igniting existing tensions between the two European coalitions and detonating World War I.

Germany, Austria-Hungary, the Ottoman Empire, and Bulgaria—the Central Powers—united against Great Britain, France, Russia, Italy, Romania, Japan, and the United States—the Allied Powers. The war ended in November 1918 with the victory of the Allied Powers. By 1919, nationalism had become a dominant political ideology. The Allied Powers, seeking to end the European historical tensions that led to World War I, saw in nationalism a possible solution. The work of Leon Dominian (1917), who published *The Frontier of Language and Nationality in Europe,* was particularly influential to this endeavor (Leerssen, 2006). Dominian (1917) argued that "to separate the idea of language from that of nationality is rarely possible. To say that a man's accent betrays his nationality is another way of stating that every language has a home of its own upon the surface of the earth" (p. 1).

Meanwhile, in the United States, Madison Grant had published *The Passing of the Great Race* (1916). Although Grant's ideas emphasized the primacy of race in a similar and yet dissimilar context to that of Europe, he agreed with Dominian in that language stood as a proxy measure for race in Europe and as such, produced national unity and nationality itself. As Grant (1917) states:

> The prevailing lack of race consciousness in Europe compels us to disregard it as a basis for nationality. In the existing nations, races are generally scattered throughout the map, and are nearly always grouped in classes, as originally race was the basis of all class, caste, and social distinctions. Race therefore being not available as a test of nationality, we are compelled to language. As a matter of fact, language is the factor in the creation of national unity, because aspirations find their best expression through language. (p. xvii)

Ethno-geopolitical nationalism, influenced by Grant and Dominian, provided the Allied Powers a mechanism to legitimize the geographical redistribution of European nation-states at the Treaty of Versailles in Paris in 1919, under the principle of "voluntaristic will" of the people, or self-governance (Breuilly, 2013). Through ethno-geopolitical nationalism, new territorial borders were delineated to encapsulate presumed ethno-cultural-linguistic collectivities. While some nation-states saw their territorial borders expand, others had to cede some territory to ethnic minority groups who were now asserting their right to live as one, in their own nation-state (Breuilly, 2013; Gellner, 2006; McMahon, 2016).

PRE–WORLD WAR II NATIONALISM, FASCISM, AND POST-1945 NATIONALISM

Although ethno-geopolitical nationalism had been held as a possible solution to the tensions leading up to the interwar period, it failed to accomplish this goal. Instead, the redrawing of many territorial boundaries and the creation of new nation-states contributed to the tensions that culminated in World War II and the rise of fascism. As Brubaker (1996) states, "In interwar Europe, one of the most dangerous fault lines was that along which domestic nationalism of ethnically heterogeneous nationalizing states collided with the transborder nationalism of neighboring 'homeland' states, oriented to co-ethnics living as minorities in the nationalizing states" (p. 107). For example, during the Treaty of Versailles, Germany was required to cede some of its territory to Poland and Czechoslovakia. Poland's and Czechoslovakia's new territorial boundaries transformed ethnic Germans who had previously lived as an ethnic majority in these territories into an ethnic minority that remained tied to its German ethno-historical-cultural roots—Deustches Volk (Zimmer, 2013). The post–World War I and pre–World War II period was marked by a nationalism that focused on the subjugation of ethnic minorities living in multiethnic nation-states; the racio-ethno-cultural-linguistic homogenization of the nation-state took center stage and with it, the oppression of those constructed as ethnic minorities (Gellner, 2006; Leerssen, 2006; Zimmer, 2013). Over time fascist movements, capitalizing on ethno-racial nationalist claims and tensions within and between nation-states, rose to power in Italy, Germany, and Spain, eventually leading to World War II—the most deadly and devastating period in European history.

After the end of World War II, or post-1945, "Western Europe . . . faced the dual task of anti-totalitarianism and the defense of individuals and minorities against the authority of the state" (Leerssen, 2006, p. 234). Ethno-racial-cultural-linguistic nationalism largely receded into the background, although continuing to manifest through regional, ethnic separatist movements, such as the Basque (ETA) and Irish (IRA) nationalist independence movements. The Holocaust's and World War II's death toll and dehumanization, as well as the humanitarian crisis caused by the mass number of displaced people in Europe, were vividly present in the memory of all nation-states (Arendt, 1966). Nationalism's emphasis on ethno-racial nation-statehood and its link with authoritarianism could no longer be embraced. Although nationalism as a separatist political movement continued to exist, overall nationalist thought shifted its attention to the preservation of nation-states, through the principle of civic commitment to the nation; nationhood and the identification of a people with its nation became the central enterprise of civic and banal nationalism (Billig, 1995)—national, civic commitment to the nation rests on banal nationalism to maintain the daily sense and performance of nationhood. As during the Romantic period, nationalism needed to find a mechanism to create, nurture and support an individual's identification with its nation—national ideology, its associated discourses and the symbolization of nationhood were essential tools for this endeavor.

FROM BANAL NATIONALISM TO A NEW ETHNO-RACIAL-CULTURAL-LINGUISTIC NATIONALISM: A RETURN TO THE PAST?

Billig (1995) defined banal nationalism as "the ideological habits which enable the established nations of the West to be reproduced. . . . Daily, the nation is indicated, or 'flagged,' in the lives of its citizenry. Nationalism, far from being an intermittent mood in established nations, is the endemic condition" (p. 7). For Billig, one cannot understand nationalism's influence on daily life and in a person's individual and collective identity formation process, if one does not examine everyday social discourses—such as those presented verbally or in text by the media. These discourses, when accepted as "facts" or common-sense truths, are reproduced by individuals, and become part of what it means to belong to a particular nation-state—forming the person's sense of nationhood and national identity (Leerssen, 2006; Wodak, 2021). Although national belonging is largely a cognitive process, it is also an affective one, as it requires an affective/emotional attachment—identification—to the nation-state and what it represents.

Banal and civic nationalism are only effective in preserving the nation-state and its identity inasmuch as they can foster a social, cognitive, and affective/emotional link between the people and its nation. National identity when defined from a national ideological and socio-psychological perspective, is best understood as a complex, "affective and sociocognitive [identification] process that links [the] individual to [that particular] large group"—the nation (Fariña, 2018, p. 65; Renan, 1882; Stern, 1995; Ross, 1997; Tajfel, 1982; Volkan, 2013, 2018). The national identification process that civic and banal nationalism foster starts early in life, largely out of conscious individual awareness, and is mediated by familial, social, and environmental contexts embedded in nationalist symbols that are "unnoticed" or "taken for granted" in daily life—flags, traditional foods, music, language (Fariña, 2018; Ross, 1997; Skey & Antonsich, 2017; Volkan, 2020). The very early nature of these group-nationalist attachments explains "why people are willing to make great personal sacrifices" in the name of their national identity and for their nation (Ross, 1997, p. 22), as well as the significance of individual and collective national identifications to civic and banal nationalism and the nation-state. Individual, national identification processes not only result in an individual sense of national belonging but also support and reinforce the national ideology that fosters them (Fariña, 2018; Renan, 1882; Wodak, 2020).

However, civic and banal nationalism depend on the intergenerational transmission of the nation-state's group-specific nationalist symbols—historical and cultural in nature—to preserve the nation-state's character/nature—historical, cultural, ethno-racial, and linguistic character. With globalization, the creation of the European Union (EU) facilitated the exchange and mobility of European nationals between belonging nation-states (Habermas, 2001; Leerssen, 2006). Along with the increased mobility of people between the various nation-states, the European Union also sought to achieve an economic and monetary union, to facilitate commerce and achieve greater competitive leverage in the global capitalist market (European Union n.d.; Habermas, 2001). In 2002, the euro was introduced and has since replaced the local currencies of the European Union nation-states (Ellyatt, 2020; European Union n.d.).

The gradual disappearance of the nation-states' original currency, as well as the increasing role of the EU as a supranational body to nation-states' governments, was well received by some and strongly opposed by others, giving way to the Eurosceptic movement (Dijkstra, Poelman, & Rodriguez-Pose, 2018; Essletzbichler et al., 2018). For banal and civic nationalism, the late 1990s to early 2000s, with the loss of EU nation-states' original currencies and the loosening of border enforcement, herald the beginning of a gradual erosion of the nation-states it sought to protect; that is, the specific historic, ethno-racial, cultural, and linguistic roots of the nation-states were transforming—for example, the loss of original currencies was held as a symbol of identity loss due to cosmopolitanism and multiculturalism (Billig, 1995; Lucassen, 2005; Leerssen, 2006). As Leerssen (2006) states, "Eurosceptic rhetoric reflected a general, and growing, populist mistrust between citizens and government—a political malaise which has come to affect intra-national affairs" (p. 243). Identity and national identification processes began to shift, from an identification with the nation-state and associated nationality, to one with "Europeanness" and European citizenship (Habermas, 2001; Vergara, 2007).

By the 1990s, while individual, national and nation-symbolic identifications were weakening, globalization and its effects were intensifying in Europe. Many European nation-states were seeing higher immigration rates from African and Asian countries, alongside increasing rates of asylum-seekers and refugees (Doomernik & Bruquetas-Callejo, 2016; Leerssen, 2006). Amid rising immigration rates, anti-immigrant and anti-asylum/refugee sociopolitical discourses began to emerge in the late 1990s, intensifying by the mid 2010s, as European nation-states were confronted with the 2016 Middle Eastern and North African refugee and asylum-seeker crisis. The scope of the crisis, and the rapid influx of Middle Eastern and North African refugees, enabled anti-immigrant and xenophobic sociopolitical discourses to penetrate many nation-states' political mainstream, along with previously marginalized historical, ethno-racial, cultural, and linguistic nationalist rhetoric. Existing Euroscepticism, anti–European Union sentiment and mistrust increased, as many European nation-states' governments and the EU struggled to effectively manage the humanitarian crisis, setting the stage for the rise of ethno-racial nationalism in 2015—now emerging as neo-nationalism. As Dijkstra, Poelman, and Rodriguez-Pose (2020) discuss, in "2004, only 28% of the population aged 15 and over did not trust the EU. This share rose to 47% in 2012. . . . [Overall, between] 2004 and 2018, the share of population distrusting the EU increased by more than 20 percentage points in nine Member States" (p. 2).

Far-right nationalist parties, amid growing Euroscepticism, and shifting ethno-racial-cultural demographic patterns in European nation-states, seized the opportunity to mobilize the masses through ethno-racial nationalism, successfully entering the European political mainstream as of 2000. The far-right Austrian Freedom Party, AFP, secured 27 percent of the national vote during the 2000 elections, becoming part of the country's governing coalition, after forming an alliance with the People's Party—a neoconservative party. Many European nation-states' governments rejected the AFP and FPÖ coalition as a legitimate government, due to the AFP's ties with Nazism and its xenophobic platform. As Joschka Fischer, Germany's foreign minister, stated in 2000 "This is the first time an anti-European, xenophobic party with a very dubious relationship toward the Nazi past has come into the government of a member state" (Biswas, 2020). What was initially considered an isolated political event, marked instead the beginning of a new, far-right, ethno-racial nationalist political era, that has since expanded across many European nation-states (Biswas, 2020).

As of 2019, far-right, nationalist parties have integrated themselves in the political mainstream of nineteen European nation-states, and account for 3 percent to 49 percent of the national vote (Europe and Right-Wing Nationalism: A Country-By-Country Guide, 2019). Among them are Hungary (Fidesz, 49 percent; Jobbic, 19 percent); Austria (Freedom Party, 26 percent); Switzerland (Swiss People Party, 25.5 percent); Denmark (Danish People's Party, 21 percent in 2019); Belgium (New Flemish Alliance, 20.4 percent); Italy (Fratelli d'Italia, 29 percent, Lega, 9 percent); Spain (Vox,

15 percent); France (National Rally, 17 percent); Germany (Alternative for Germany, 17 percent).

Although there are a number of differences between the various, far-right parties that have emerged in Europe, they all share a number of commonalities. First, they are grounded on ethno-racial nationalism; second, they seek to protect the people's ethno-racial, cultural, linguistic, and national identity and that of the nation-state; third, they reject multiculturalism as it threatens to transform the historical essence of the nation-state and its people, and see immigration as a threat to the identity of the nation; fourth, they reject supranational governing entities such as the European Union, favoring national independence over national interdependence—in other words, are informed by and capitalize from the Eurosceptic movement. Yet, they differ, first on the degree of authoritarianism they incorporate within their political platform; and second, on the use of antiestablishment rhetoric—that is, the degree to which the party and its leader are positioned as defenders of the "common people" against the "corrupt elite-establishment."

While many of the contemporary far-right parties accept the democratic process and a peoples' right to self-determination and self-governance, such as the National Rally in France, and the Freedom Party in Austria; others use the democratic process to achieve governing power to gradually implement totalitarian policies and reforms designed to undermine the democratic process that brought them to power, such as those implemented in Hungary by the Fidesz Party (Arendt, 1966). For example, the amendments to Hungary's Fundamental Law, implemented in 2012, limit the power of the courts by prohibiting the courts from reviewing changes made to the Fundamental Law and from considering rulings prior to the enacted changes. Other restrictions have limited, "election campaign broadcasts . . . to only state media, . . . [as well as freedom] of expression in the interest of combating hate speech . . . [while also giving] Parliament the sole right to decide which religious organizations may be deemed churches" (Zeldin, 2013).

NATIONALISM: IN SUM

Nationalism, through national-cultural consciousness raising, created the mechanism whereby a people could come to discover and embrace the existence of a shared, group-specific, historical identity to then exercise their right to self-governance. Identity and identity politics are therefore as central to the history of the European nation-states as they are to nationalism—European nation-states could not have been birthed in their current form without nationalism. Furthermore, ethno-racial, geopolitical nationalism necessitates banal and civic nationalism, and together they are constitutive to the current European nation-states. That is, the daily symbolic performance of a nation-state's national identity supports the maintenance of the nation-state as a legitimate, sociopolitical, ethno-racial, cultural and linguistic, historical unit of self-governance. Territorial borders in turn enable the self-governing unit to physically materialize itself in the perceptual world, while tangibly inscribing the nation-state's *historicized* ethno-racial, cultural, linguistic difference to other nation-states, as real and legitimate. Yet, as Gellner states (2006), nationalism "Suffers from pervasive false consciousness. Its myths invert reality: it claims to defend folk culture, while in fact it is forging a high culture; it claims to protect an old folk society while in fact helping to build up an anonymous, mass society" (p. 119).

From a historical, sociopolitical perspective, nationalism is an ideology in that it shapes a people's understanding of who they are and of the society in which they live, as it produces and reproduces group, social, cognitive, and political constructions of who "we are" and who "we are not" (Fariña, 2018). These social and cognitive constructions support individual and large-group identity formation processes that become affectively meaningful and essential to the individual and large-group identity of a people (see chapter seven). Yet, nationalism does not explain, guide, or dictate the structure and form of a nation-state's government, unlike other long-established political ideologies—liberalism, socialism, etc. (Freeden, 1998), and in this manner it is an incomplete political ideology that needs to draw from other established ideologies; in most cases right-leaning political ideologies, although not exclusively. Gellner's (2006) definition and deconstruction of nationalism is therefore the simplest and yet most insightful:

> Nationalism—the principle of homogenous cultural units as the foundations of political life, and of the obligatory cultural unity of rules and ruled—is indeed inscribed neither in the nature of things . . . nor in the pre-conditions of social life in general, and the contention that it is so inscribed is a falsehood which nationalist doctrine has succeeded in presenting as self-evident. (p. 120)

Yet, the effects of the current capitalist, global, economic system and, in particular of neoliberalism, including transnational exchanges of labor, growing wealth inequality, and poverty, directly challenge *historical* homogenous national identity constructions that had legitimized the various European nation-states. The rise of neo-nationalism at a time of increasing economic inequality, mass forced transnational displacement, and increasing social unrest is not an anomaly, but rather an expectable reaction to the transformation of the nation-state and its people's identity as originally *created* (Branton, Dillingham, Dunaway, & Miller, 2007; Davis, Goidel, Lipsmeyer, Whitten, & Young, 2019; Kaufmann, 2019; Mudde, 2016a; Mudde, 2016b). What will happen, as Gellner (2006) states, may largely depend on "whether the rulers [and their people] are willing [to accept] and . . . run a mobile society, one in which rulers and ruled can merge and form a cultural continuum," or instead, chose to reaffirm their national, territorial, and identity boundaries (p. 123).

Chapter Three

Nativism

As with nationalism, there is much conceptual disagreement among scholars about what nativism is, and how it ought to be defined and understood (see Duyvendak & Kesic, 2018; Friedman, 2017; Guia, 2016; Kaufmann, 2019; Mudde, 2016b). For some, nativism is an American political movement linked to the Know Nothing party of the 1850s, also known as the American Party. Although party members referred to themselves as American natives, opponents saw them as intolerant narrow-minded nativists (Fariña, 2018; Higham, 1972; Kaufmann, 2019; Mudde, 2016b; Serwer, 2019; Young, 2017). Since then, this term and its usage has expanded to the European political arena—despite its distinctive American origins (Higham, 1972)—while resurfacing in the sociopolitical mainstream of the United States. Yet, the term nativist and nativism as a political movement or even ideology, as argued by some scholars, provides fertile ground for conceptual slippage and confusion (Guia, 2019; Serwer, 2019). It is therefore essential to trace its origins and evolution, to clarify its meaning and contemporary sociopolitical implications.

NATIVISM: AMERICAN WHITE NATIONALISM?

Although nationalism was previously discussed as a European phenomenon, sparked by the French Revolution, and inextricably tied to the formation of the European nation-states, some scholars disagree, arguing instead that "the new [independent] American nations served as 'creole pioneers' for the modern age of nationalism" in Europe (Doyle & Van Young, 2013). What scholars can agree on is that

> Whether American independence movements inspired or followed European nationalist movements is less important than our understanding that all were part of a broad trans-Atlantic exchange of ideas, people, and state models that

marked the first epoch in the history of modern nationalism. (Doyle & Van Young, 2013)

Just as Madison Grant's writings were instrumental to European, ethno-geopolitical nationalism before World War II, so were Rousseauian notions of *volonté générale* and the social contract to the formation of the United States and its Constitution. Despite shared commonalities between nationalist separatist and independentist movements in Europe and the Americas, there are also essential differences from the formation of the new nation-states in the Americas, and in particular to that of the United States.

Whereas nationalism in Europe had sought to centralize, maintain, or promote the formation of new nation-states along specific shared, *historical*, ethno-racial, cultural and linguistic national identities, the United States came into existence as a nation-state on very different premises, after achieving colonial independence from Britain in 1776 (Grant, 2013). As its initial British colonial status implies, what is now accepted as the United States came into being as a British colonial settlement comprised of the thirteen original colonies. Later, French and Spanish colonial settlements in the Americas were incorporated into what is now the United States through purchase, annexations and wars, such as the French and Indian War—pre-independence—and, the Mexican-American War—post-independence (The European Competition for North America, The British & American Colonial Perspective: A Sampling, 1699–1763, 2009). Not only were the original colonizers of North America ethnically, culturally and linguistically diverse, but they also lacked a shared, large group historical past—an essential feature of nationalism.

More importantly, the United States sought independence from Britain on economic grounds and grievances, including taxation, and not based on ethno-geopolitical nationalistic claims. The well-known slogan "No taxation without representation" (Center for Systemic Peace, 2021; Grant, 2013) refers to one of the twenty-seven grievances against King George III that led to the American Revolution. These grievances, referenced in the US Declaration of Independence as "repeated injuries and usurpations," later informed "both the Articles of Confederation and the U. S. Constitution" (Grant, 2013; Trenchard & Peale, 2019). While "No taxation without representation" clearly speaks to Rousseauian thought and ideals, specifically to the social contract, and therefore to civic nationalism and commitment, it does not speak to nationalism's primary concern—the identification and preservation of a people as *historically* and *culturally* distinct from that of other nation-states (Herder, 1774/2010; Gellner, 2006; Grant, 2013; Leerssen, 2006). In fact, some scholars argue that the United States of America did not fully emerge as a nation-state until the end of the Civil War in 1877

(Piereson, 2020; Konh, 2017), since up to that point, the states comprising the United States had a primary attachment to themselves rather than to the nation-state as a whole. There was a lack of national culture or identity, which had traditionally fueled ethno-racial geopolitical nationalism in Europe, or as Susan Mary Grant (2013) states, "relative to many other examples in western Europe and elsewhere, both nationalism and state-formation in America happened in reverse order."

However, what is omitted in historical accounts that begin with the United States' independence from Britain, or with the colonization and wars between the various European nation-state colonizers, is the history of Indigenous genocide and slavery upon which the United States was built—pre and post-independence from Britain. The effects of this legacy are still poignantly felt in US society, and were blatantly exposed during the COVID-19 pandemic, when media coverage highlighted the higher death rates of African Americans due to racist violence and long- standing health inequities caused by historical, structural, and systemic racism—slavery's contemporary sociopolitical legacy (Centers for Disease Control, 2021; Gonzalez-Barrera & Hugo Lopez, 2020; Rothstein, 2017; Southern Poverty Law Center, 2020). To understand nativism, as well as its connection to the establishment of the United States' nation-state and the American native identity, it is necessary to examine ethno-racism and its historical, sociopolitical implications.

Nativism, Race, and Nation-State Formation

While civic nationalism was certainly implicated in the establishment of the United States, it is not possible to speak of American, ethno-racial, geopolitical nationalism at the nation's inception, as the first "Americans," by virtue of their colonizer status, lacked a historical, ethno-racial, common shared past and most importantly, lacked a claim to the territory they asserted as their own—all essential to ethno-racial, geopolitical nationalism (Grant, 2013; Guia, 2016). Indigenous peoples, or Native Americans, despite having a native claim to the colonized territory, were excluded from the new colonizers' nation-state through ethno-racial, Darwinian premises that constructed Indigenous peoples as fundamentally inferior to the Nordic European colonizers—primarily of Anglo-Saxon, Protestant descent (Fariña, 2018; Waltman & Haas, 2010). Yet, the colonizers used these same ethno-racial Darwinian premises to construct themselves as American natives to the Indigenous people's land—giving birth to American nativism and nativist ideology, "long before the word was coined" in 1840 (Higham, 1972, p. 4).

For Higham (1972), nativism is not a form of ethno-racial geopolitical nationalism that includes "every type and level of antipathy toward aliens, their intuitions, and ideas" (p. 3), but is instead best defined as an "intense opposition to an internal minority on the ground of its foreign (i.e., 'un-American') connections" (p. 4). Although Higham's definition provides some conceptual clarity, it fails to acknowledge nativism's central role in the historical demise of the Indigenous peoples in the colonized territories, and in the creation of the colonizers' nation-state. Indigenous peoples were not an ethnic minority within a nation-state, but rather an "ethnic majority" in a colonized nation-state that had been created by an "ethnic minority" on Indigenous land.

As Indigenous population records estimate, prior to European colonization, there were 5,000,000 or more Indigenous people in the United States; this number had decreased to 240,000 by 1880–1900 (Madley, 2015). There are differing explanations as to what led to the sharp population decline. Some historians attribute the mass decline to epidemiological reasons—specifically, to the Indigenous peoples' inability to survive exposure to viruses and other illnesses brought by the colonizers (Crosby, 1976; Jones, 2004). Others, while agreeing with epidemiological explanations, emphasize the violence of colonization and its effects—wars, territory appropriations, forced removals, and duplicitous treaties, enslavement, starvation, and maltreatment (Madley, 2015; Lewy, 2004). Genocide, as a reason for the demise of the Indigenous population and communities, only began to be discussed in the 1990s (Churchill, 1997; Kierman, 2007; Madley, 2015, 2017; Ostler, 2015; Stannard, 1992; Thornton, 1990). Yet, there is significant debate as to whether the term "genocide" is applicable to the fate of the Indigenous peoples in the United States (Madley, 2015, 2017).

Although twenty-first-century scholars have added further support to Indigenous genocide theories, "detailed case studies marshaling substantial evidence of both genocidal intent and specific genocidal acts to support the broad thesis of genocide in America remain few and far between" (Madley, 2015, p. 106). On the other hand, scholarship that refutes genocide and that opposes its use to name the violence perpetrated by the colonizers against Indigenous peoples remains influential. For example,

In 1992, historian James Axtell called "'genocide' . . . inaccurate as a description of the vast majority of encounters between Europeans and Indians." [In 1999] historian Robert Utley asserted that using the term "genocide" in relation to American Indians "grossly falsifies history," since "No more than a tiny portion of the white population of the United States, mainly in the West, ever advocated" the "intentional obliteration" of American Indians "by means of mass physical annihilation." [And, in] 2004, historian William Rubinstein insisted that "American policy towards the Indians . . . never actually encompassed genocide." (Madley, 2015, p. 106)

Despite scholarly disagreement, Madley's (2017) systematic account of the extermination of the Indigenous peoples in California, in *An American Genocide: The United States and the Californian Indian Catastrophe, 1846–1873*, is an undeniable record and testimony of the genocide perpetrated against Indigenous peoples in the United States, and also connects the colonizers' violence to ethno-racial, Darwinian extermination efforts. The question is not whether genocide took place, but instead the extent to which it took place.

In sum, and despite scholarly disagreement, mass epidemics brought about by the colonizers; years of Indigenous territory usurpation through wars and repeatedly violated treaties—such as the Dawes Act or General Allotment Act of 1887; as well as, Indigenous genocide, forced assimilation and marginalization, led to the almost complete eradication and erasure of the Indigenous peoples that had inhabited the colonizers' nation-state land (Dunbar-Ortiz, 2015; Fariña, 2018; Rollings, 2004; Royster et al., 2018; Royster, 1995). Ethno-racial, Darwinian premises that constructed Indigenous peoples as fundamentally inferior to the Nordic European colonizers, combined with Rousseauian principles—both central to what became American nativism—were essential to the Indigenous peoples' demise. American nativism is thereby constitutive to the creation of the United States. It legitimized the colonizers' creation of the United States based on shared, "native-colonizer" identity claims that justified their right to self-governance, thereby legitimizing the establishment of their nation-state on Indigenous land; however, nativism did not fuel the quest for independence from Britain.

Nativism, Race, and the native American Identity

Nativism, expanding on Higham's (1972) definition, is then best defined as colonizing, ethno-racial, geopolitical nationalism. First, nativism enables a colonizing ethno-racial minority group to establish itself as an ethno-racial majority within another ethnic group's territory, through force, violence, sociopolitical and economic oppression, and marginalization. Second, through national consciousness–raising, nativism enables the colonizing ethno-racial group to construct a historically, shared native identity that legitimizes their right to live together as one, in the colonized territory—as a self-governing nation-state. Third, just as ethno-racial, geopolitical nationalism did after World War I and World War II, nativism allows "native-colonizers" to occupy and gradually incorporate "foreign" land, through violence, mass migration, and resettlement—thereby increasing their mass representation and territorial dominance. Fourth, nativism relies on immigration to promote ethno-racial minority population growth to achieve ethno-racial majority representation, as well as to sustain said status. Immigration is therefore central to nativism and not antithetical to it. In fact, King George III's efforts to curtail immigration in the colonies was one of the twenty-seven usurpations and grievances held against the king, cited in the Declaration of Independence:

> He has endeavored to prevent the population of these States; for that purpose obstructing the Laws for Naturalization of Foreigners; refusing to pass others to encourage their migrations hither, and raising the conditions of new Appropriations of Lands. (*Declaration of Independence: A Transcription*, National Archives, 2023)

Although nativism is often described as an anti-immigrant political movement (see Guia, 2016; Kauffman, 2019; Mudde, 2012, 2016a, 2016b), nativism emerged in the United States due to the inextricable link between the colonizers' native identity formation process and immigration. The colonizers' initial dissimilar histories and identities did not provide them with a natural bridge to establish a sense of belonging to "a people" or the means to establish their own nation-state—according to prevailing nationalist ideals of the time (Fariña, 2018; Loewenberg, 1991, 1999; Volkan, 2013, 2018). Nativism provided the colonizers with a solution, that of a supra ethno-racial identity—*native* American. This supra ethno-racial identity, fabricated through academic *historicity*, allowed the colonizers to abandon previous European, historical, ethno-racial, cultural, linguistic identifications, to instead embrace a new identity capable of superseding identity-based particularisms; in so doing, *historicity* became as central to nativism as it was to European nationalist identity consciousness–raising processes. Madyson Grant (1916) in *The Passing of the Great Race*, best captures how historicity, through self-invention (Gellner, 2006; Leerssen, 2006), established the *native* American identity as a legitimate identity, capable of engendering large-group identification processes of sameness and belonging. For example, recognizing the colonizers' dissimilar origins—primarily from Britain, Scandinavia and the Low Countries (Fariña, 2018; Hing, 2004)—Grant (1916) invoked the supra ethno-racial dimension of the native American identity to dismiss particularisms and promote "identificatory" unity, when he argued

> The United States of America must be regarded racially as a European colony, and owing current ignorance of the physical bases of race, one often hears the statement made that native Americans of Colonial ancestry are of mixed ethnic origin. This is not true. At the time of the Revolutionary War the settlers in the thirteen colonies were not only purely Nordic, but also purely Teutonic, a very large majority being Anglo-Saxons. "New England," during Colonial times . . . was far more Teutonic than old England. (p. 74)

As Grant's writings (1916) illustrate, American scholars used the racial paradigm to create a supra ethno-racial category capable of transcending and transforming ethno-racial, European dissimilarities into shared, historical sameness—fostering a sense of "peoplehood" (Fariña, 2018; Jacobson, 1998; Tajfel, 1981, 1982; Volkan, 2013, 2018).

Grant's work was far from peripheral; his ideas were widely disseminated by mainstream newspapers, such as *The New York Times* and *The Nation* (Serwer, 2019) and accepted by prominent political figures, such as Teddy Roosevelt and Calvin Coolidge, and the "American" elites. Grant's work had far-reaching consequences not only for the United States, but also in Europe, where *The Passing of the Great Race* "went on to become Adolf Hitler's 'bible,'" providing the "justification" for Hitler's persecution and extermination of the Jewish people (Sewer, 2019, p. 3).

In the United States, Grant's work (1916) reified the Nordic colonizers as natives to "America," building on previous scholar definitions of America as a Nordic nation-state (see Schultz, 1908; Roberts, 1922). In fact, in 1908 Schultz had already argued for the *historical* Nordic origins of the native American identity and nation-state in *Race or Mongrels*, establishing a conceptual difference between pre and post-1783 immigration that altered the course of immigration policy for generations to come.

For Schultz (1908), European immigrants arriving to "America" prior to 1783 were colonizers—defined as the Nordic "men who had created law, government and civilization in America" (p. 224). Immigrants arriving to "America" after 1783 were defined as "mere immigrants," since they had arrived to an already established country and civilization. By defining colonizers and immigrants as inherently distinct, Schultz (1908) added strength to nativist thought and ideals. The colonizers and their descendants were no longer immigrants in a foreign land, they were the creators and founders of the nation; their descendants were thereby native Americans, and although Nordic, they were part of a new Nordic, native race, or as Lothrop Stoddard (1920) states in *The Rising Tide of Color Against the White World-Supremacy,* they were "Nordic native American" (p. 165). In fact, seven years earlier Grant had argued that "The native American by the middle of the nineteenth century was rapidly becoming a distinct type. Derived from the Teutonic part of the British Isle, and being almost purely Nordic" (1916, p. 19).

Nativist, ethno-racial claims ensured that post-1783 immigrant arrivals could not assert a claim to the land occupied by the colonizers, even if sharing the same Nordic supra-ethno-racial identity as the *native* Americans, as it now had a rightful owner—the Nordic *native* American. This conceptual distinction transformed post 1783 arrivals into foreign subjects, whose entry could be controlled and regulated through immigration policy—setting the stage for the 1920s nativist, immigration reform policies that were to come, such as the Immigration Act of 1924 (Fariña, 2018; Ngai, 1999, 2014).

Although immigration was initially necessary for the colonizers to become an ethno-racial majority in an occupied land, by the early 1900s the socio-political landscape, as well as the ethno-racial origins of the new immigrants had changed (Jacobson, 1998; Hing, 2004). Up to the 1840s, the Nordic race had been described as superior, including in its ability to absorb and assimilate ethno-racially congruent immigrants into the Nordic *native* American identity and "peoplehood" (Higham, 1972). By the mid 1800s, fears of miscegenation and race degeneration began to pervade the sociopolitical landscape. The new immigrant arrivals were largely ethno-racially distinct from the Nordic immigrants—most originating from Southern and Eastern Europe and religiously "other," Catholics and Jews. The immigrants' shifting ethno-racial and religious composition, together with rising migration rates, fueled support for the Know Nothing party and its nativist movement. Nativists argued with urgency for immigration control, to preserve the native American nation-state and its people, amid rising immigration rates, positing that "immigrants [were] of value to a country if the immigrants [were] of a race akin to that of the inhabitants, and if their number is not greater that can be absorbed" (Shultz, 1908, p. 225). Grant (1916), Roberts (1922), and Stoddard (1923) reflected and fueled nativist, ethno-racial identity fears through colonizing, ethno-racial, national consciousness–raising efforts. In their publications, they argued that failure to curb immigration would inevitably cause the ethno-racial transformation of the native American people, resulting in social and racial degeneration. Like Schultz in 1908, Grant (1916) directly challenged previously accepted myths that defined the "American" nation-state as an "asylum for the oppressed," stating that "Americans"

> must realize that the altruistic ideals which have controlled our social develop-ment during the past century . . . are sweeping the nation toward a racial abyss. If the melting-pot is allowed to boil without control and we continue to follow our national motto and deliberately blind ourselves to "all distinctions of race, creed, or color" the type of native American of colonial descent will become as extinct as the Athenian of the age of Pericles and the Vikings of the days of Roll. (p. 263)

Stoddard (1923) shared Grant's (1916) fears in *The Rising Tide of Color Against the White World-Supremacy*, positing that prevailing migration patterns ensured the death of the nation-state and of native Americans as a people, stating "if the White immigrant can gravely disorder the national life, it is not much to say that the colored immigrant would doom it to certain death" (p. 268). Roberts (1922) in *Why Europe Leaves Home: A True Account of the Reasons which Cause Central Europeans to Overrun America*, not only raised alarm over the inability to protect "America" and its native people from a complete ethno-racial-religious transformation but also advocated for emergency immigration reforms to halt the influx of the *foreign, ethno-racial and religious others* into "America." As Roberts (1922) argued, the American nation-state had "been confronted by an immigration emergency . . . [since] Starting [in] around 1880s, the immigrants who swarmed into the United States were of an entirely different breed from the people who discovered the country [and] colonized it" (p. 68). For Roberts (1922), immigration control provided a mechanism whereby the nation-state could return to its original Nordic, ethno-racial, religious, majority and *native* American composition, "America is confronted by a perpetual emergency as long as her laws permit millions of non-Nordic aliens to pour through her sea-gates. When this inpouring ceases to be an emergency, America will have become thoroughly mongrelized . . . inevitable ruin, corruption and stagnation [will follow] cross-breeding" (p. 97). B. L. Putnam Weale (1910) in *The Conflict of Color* best captures the nativist identity-based fears of the time. When discussing the increasing immigration rates and shifting ethno-racial, religious composition, Weale (1910) states that the United States is facing an impending invasion, that could be prevented by the *white men.* "A struggle has begun between the white man and all other men . . . to decide whether non-white men—that is yellow men, or brown men, or black men—may or may not invade the white man's countries in order to gain their livelihood" (pp. 98–99).

Although the nativist Know Nothing party had dissolved in the late 1850s, nativism had successfully infiltrated all aspects of the American nation-state by the 1920s, and most importantly the sociopolitical arena (Roediger, 2006; Higham, 1972; Fariña, 2018). By 1924, nativist thought fueled highly exclusionary immigration reforms, leading to the National Origins Quota Act or Immigration Act of 1924. The Act effectively restricted immigration from Southern and Eastern European nation-states, while barring all immigration from Asia and Africa—preserving the Nordic, *native* American ethno-racial and religious majority in the "American" nation-state (Fariña, 2018; Hing, 2004; Huntington, 2009; Johnson, 2004; Ngai, 1999, 2014). The Act sought to establish ethno-racial immigration quotas according to the 1890 population census, ethno-racial composition, where Nordic migration still predominated. However, the Quota Board faced a number of methodological challenges in trying to determine the ethno-racial origins quotas, since the 1890 census, "did not differentiate the foreign born until 1850 and did not identify the places of birth of parents of native born until 1890" (Ngai, 1999, p. 73).

To circumvent this problem, the Quota Board used the 1790 census to estimate the national origins of the population in 1890 by linking head of households' surnames listed in the 1790 census to their presumed linguistic, ethno-racial, national origin (Fariña, 2018; Ngai, 1999). The estimates led the Quota Board to conclude that "87 percent of the population" were of British descent "discounting . . . attributional errors, and . . . over-estimation produced by . . . surname Anglicization, which was not uncommon during that era" (Fariña, 2018, p. 36). Despite obvious methodological problems, "the Quota Board's findings were accepted as 'factual' and enacted into law in 1929, without further scrutiny" (Fariña, 2018, p. 36). The act accomplished its nativist goal, "successfully decreasing the influx of Southern and Eastern European immigrants, 'and struck most deeply at Jews, Italians, Slavs, and Greeks' (Hing, 2004, p. 69), while . . . barring immigration from Asian countries under the ineligibility to citizenship clause" (Fariña, 2018, p. 36).

The Immigration Act of 1924 highlights how historicity and scholarly invention were essential to American nativism, and to the preservation of the Nordic *native* American identity. At the same time, the Immigration Act of 1924 also captures nativism's complex relationship with immigration and immigration control. That is, while nativism does not completely oppose immigration, it makes use of immigration and immigration policy to select and strategically foster a desired ethno-racial and religious type of immigration. For American nativism, immigration was desired as long as it promoted and maintained the Nordic *native* American identity and its critical mass representation in their nation-state (Fariña, 2018; Higham, 1972; Huntington, 2004; Serwer, 2019).

Nativism, Defining the "People" and Its Nation-State

Congruent with its historical roots, American nativism initially used three fundamental inclusionary/exclusionary criteria based on either religious, political/anti-radicalism and/or ethno-racial claims. The criteria served two essential purposes; it first defined who the *native* American people were to then assess their degree of Americanness. As such, nativism was first divided into three distinct subtypes: religious, political/anti-radicalism, and ethno-racial nativism. Over time, their distinctions gradually faded, merging into a primarily ethno-racial nativism, where the three original criteria became essential to the *historicity* of the *native* American identity and to its colonizing, ethno-racial, national consciousness–raising enterprise.

Religious Nativism: Anti-Catholicism

As Higham (1972) states in *Strangers in the Land: Patterns of American Nativism 1800–1925*, American nativism first emerged as an anti-Catholic movement, linked to the European Protestant Reformation and the British ethno-racial origins of the original thirteen colonies. In fact, historians have often "regarded nativism and anti-Catholicism as more or less synonymous" due to the significant role that anti-Catholic sentiment played in "pre–Civil War nativist thinking" (Higham, 1972, p. 5). For nativism, to be American meant to be *native* American, which was inextricably linked to the Protestant religion. An individual's allegiance to any other religion raised questions over the individual's degree of Americanness—the capacity to "assimilate" into the *native* American identity and its traditions, without constituting a threat to the identity of the nation-state and its people.

Political Nativism: Antiradicalism

American nativism also opposed radical political movements, viewing them as un-American and incompatible with American liberal values (Duyvendak & Kesic, 2018). Although nativism embraced Rousseauian principles of *volonté générale*, consistent with civic nationalism, it regarded with suspicion political convictions that directly challenged the government and its structure. Although the American nation-state owes its existence to the Revolutionary War, unlike the French Revolution, the war for independence from Britain was fought to perfect "an existing society, not [to] build a new one on its ruins" (Higham, 1972, p. 7). Individual sympathizers of left-leaning political ideologies, such as socialism and communism, are thus regarded as un-American, and as a threat to the integrity of the nation-state and its *native* American identity—a foreign ailment that needed to be eradicated (Higham, 1972; Duyvendak & Kesic, 2018). Yet as Higham (1972) states, anti-Catholic and antiradical nativism set criteria that defined the American nation-state and the *native* American identity by what they were not, rather than by what they were—reflecting a binary logic, where the subject of inquiry is "the other," rather than the *native* group (Derrida, 1984). In other words, anti-Catholic and antiradical nativism sought to identify and "define the nation's enemies rather than its essence" (Higham, 1972, p. 9), while ethno-racial nativism defined its essence.

Ethno-Racial Nativism

Although ethno-racial nativism only emerged in the late nineteenth century, it was essential to the establishment of the American nation-state and to nativism itself. Nativism, as previously explained, was primarily concerned with the preservation of the "colonizer-native" peoples' *nationality*, which was inextricably linked to the people's identity. Ethno-racial nativism, just as ethno-racial nationalism, provided the criteria needed to demarcate who the "colonizing-native people" were, thereby delineating the *native people* who needed to be protected for the survival of the nation-state. In other words, for nativism, the viability and ongoing existence of a "colonizer-native" nation-state rested on the preservation of the peoples' *native* identity—given the nation-state's fictitious origins and the absence of a historically shared past among its people (Gellner, 2006; Leerseen, 2006; Loewenberg, 1991, 1999; Volkan, 2013). As Sister Thomas (1936) stated in *Nativism in the Old Northwest, 1850–1860*, for the Know Nothing party in the United States, and its nativist supporters, "The grand work of the American party is the principle of nationality. . . . We must do something to protect and vindicate it. If we do not, it will be destroyed. The infusion of five million foreigners into our political system every ten years will subvert it" (p. 131).

After World War I, and in large part due to the Ku Klux Klan's influence, nativism took its final and contemporary form, becoming an influential colonizing, ethno-racial, religious, and antiradical ideology by the early 1920s— each of its criteria, essential to the construction of the *native* American people and their nation-state. In this manner, the Immigration Act of 1924 became nativism's most important, national, protectionary measure. It ensured the survival of the *native* American people and that of the American nation-state, at a time when the *native* American peoples' identity was threatened by an impending ethno-racial, religious, and largely imagined political transformation (Fariña, 2018; Gordon, 2017; MacLean, 1995).

Since the 1920s, the United States has experienced similar identity driven, nativist, protectionary periods, aided often by white power movements and paramilitary groups that sought to defend the nation-state and its people. These increasing American nativist protectionary periods, just as during World War I, have historically coincided with both American international armed conflict and the rise of white power movements and paramilitary groups.

Chapter Four

Nativism, War, the Ku Klux Klan, and White Power Movements

War is an important and yet overlooked aspect in the rise of American nativism throughout the history of the United States, as well as in the rise of American white power movements, which find an ideological affinity to nativism (Belew, 2018; Johnson, 2012). While the connection between European nationalism and war is well documented, that of American nativism is most often insufficiently explored, and primarily examined in relation to the aftermath of World War I (MacLean, 2017).

Likewise, nativism's connection to the Ku Klux Klan and the segregation of African Americans is oftentimes omitted in contemporary sociopolitical discussions pertaining to nativist parties and movements, in favor of conceptual explanations that focus on its historical, xenophobic nature (see Guia, 2016; Higham, 1972; Kauffman, 2019; Mudde, 2012, 2016). Yet, it is not possible to speak about nativism as a colonizing, ethno-racial, geopolitical nationalist ideology, without discussing both slavery and the white power movements that sought to maintain control over African Americans in the American post–Civil War society, through terror and violence. Paradoxically, it was the Know Nothing party's failure to pronounce itself on the question of slavery, when tensions between the Northern and Southern states were mounting in the pre–Civil War era, that led to the party's dissolution in the early 1860s, after it split along pro-abolition and proslavery lines—the former joining the Republican party and the latter the Democratic party (Boissoneault, 2017; Higham, 1972).

Although the Know Nothing party lost its political relevance prior to the Civil War, post–Civil War nativism evolved and grew, especially after the formation of the Ku Klux Klan in 1865. While support for the Klan significantly decreased by the 1870s, the infiltration of the Ku Klux Klan's ethno-racial, white supremacist ideology into nativist literary and sociopolitical discourses in the early 1900s, along with its violent manifestations, forever changed the history of the American nation-state, its *native* people's identity, and nativism itself. In fact, early twentieth-century American nativism laid the foundation for its twenty-first-century contemporary, sociopolitical manifestations.

As in the twentieth century, in the twenty-first century, white power paramilitary and terrorist groups similar to the KKK were again instrumental in the rise of American nativism to the political sphere during the 2016 US presidential elections—although some scholars misattribute the rise of white power groups to President Trump's political platform, which shared many similarities with the 1850s Know Nothing party's nativist platform. Given this context, the insurrection at the US Capitol on January 6, 2021, where nativist, white power, and paramilitary groups united to overturn the 2020 presidential election results, both illustrates and demands a closer examination of war, white power movements, and their link to American nativism.

THE POST–CIVIL WAR ERA, THE KU KLUX KLAN, AND AMERICAN NATIVISM

The Klan was founded in 1865, in Pulaski, Tennessee, by six Confederate veterans during the Reconstruction period. By 1870, the Klan had become a large post–Civl War resistance organization that opposed Republican Reconstruction efforts seeking political and economic equality for African Americans, with membership across all Southern states. Although dominant historical accounts state that the Civil War was primarily fought either on the basis of economic interests, or to free slaves, both accounts oversimply the dynamics that fueled the Civil War, while constructing the Northern states as primarily Abolitionists and Southern states as proslavery.

As W. E. B. Du Bois (1935) states in *Black Reconstruction in America*, historicity differs from history, and the history of the Reconstruction era reflects a complex context, where the morality of slavery, the survival of the Southern plantation economy, and the Northern states' quest for industrial expansion intersected. As Du Bois (1935) argues,

> The North went to war without the slightest idea of freeing the slave. The great majority of Northerners from Lincoln down pledged themselves to protect slavery, and they hated and harried Abolitionists . . . ; business followed abolition in order to maintain the tariff, pay the bonds and defend the banks. To call this business program "the program of the North" and ignore Abolition is unhistorical. (p. 716)

After the Civil War, Southern states, which were contending "with the losses of life, property and, in their eyes, honor" opposed Republican Reconstruction efforts which included abolishing slavery—the Thirteenth Amendment (1866); granting American citizenship to freed African Americans—the Fourteenth Amendment (1868); and forbidding race-based voting discrimination—the Fifteenth Amendment (1870) (Chambers, 2013, Southern Poverty Law Center, 2011, p. 10). The loss of the Civil War and the end of slavery marked for many Southern *white natives* the end of their social and economic way of life. For plantation owners "slavery was not only a means of production but also a concrete source of capital. [Slaves were] 'the largest single investment of the Southern planter. . . worth 4 billion dollars by 1861'" and of greater value than the plantation land itself (Fariña, 2018, p. 33). With the end of slavery, Southern white plantation owners incurred a substantial and irreversible economic loss.

Further injury was brought about by the hatred and animosity harbored by Northern *white natives,* who constructed Southerners as radical *un-Americans*. For Northerners, Southern whites belonged to the lowest strata of American society, a societal class that had previously been ascribed only to Southern whites' former slaves. Southerners experienced the Republican Reconstruction efforts as a northern assault on the Southern, Nordic *native* collective identity (Fleming, 1905); this collective identity had previously enabled Southerners to assert their *legal* right to live together as a people in their own Confederate American nation-state. The feeling of Southern humiliation and exclusion from the post–Civil War *native* American society is poignantly captured by Beale (1958) in *The Critical Year: A Study of Andrew Johnson and Reconstruction* when quoting Northern Senator Chandler, "the only rights Southern whites possessed were 'the constitutional right to be hanged and the divine right to be damned.' 'Traitors North and South have no rights that [an African American] is bound to respect'" (p. 153).

The Ku Klux Klan spread throughout the South soon after its formation, capitalizing on the Southern post–Civil War sociopolitical and economic context. The Klan and its white ethno-racial, supremacist ideology not only recognized Southern whites as the legitimate *native* American citizens of the *American* nation-state, but also constructed them as superior to their Northern counterparts. Both the KKK and the new large-group identity it provided gave Southern whites a much-needed psychological mechanism to heal from the humiliations inflicted by the loss of the Civil War and of their societal standing within the nation-state (Volkan, 2017, 2018). This humiliation was most poignantly felt by Confederate veterans and their families, which became some of the strongest Klan supporters.

By the late 1860s, Ku Klux Klan membership had expanded into all aspects of Southern society. Its members were part of the Southern elites, as much as of the working class, including journalists and editors, members of the ministry, politicians and law enforcement (Braden, 1980; Chalmers, 1981;

Southern Poverty Law Center, 2011). By 1868 "the mutilations and flog-gings, lynchings and shootings, began to spread across the South" (Southern Poverty Law Center, 2011, p. 14); those who were not involved in the violence directly perpetrated against African Americans, were most often complicit through their silence and refusal to testify in court (see Chalmers, 1987). For white Southerners, the Klan was a "law and order organization" that sought to preserve the Southern, Nordic, *native* American identity and way of life (Chalmers, 1987, p. 57).

Reconstruction efforts fueled white Southerners' fears of an impending social transformation, with an inverted order and racial distribution, where the black population could ultimately outnumber whites in many Southern regions. For example, in 1860, freed and enslaved blacks in the Lower Southern states constituted 44.1 percent of the total population, whereas whites constituted 55.9 percent—2,821,944 and 3,573,199 million people respectively (San Martin, 2012). The Klan and its terror allowed white Southerners to keep Northern, black sympathizers and black Americans under *white control*, while hindering black organizing movements that sought full social integration for black Southerners. As Anne Braden (1980) describes, prior to the Klan's reign of terror and for a brief period, "free slaves were lit-erally setting up new governments in the South" (p. 56). In sum, Southerners feared not only the degradation of their identity but also the degradation of their Southern society and *native* American race.

By 1868, amid the violence and terror, Congress passed three Enforcement Acts, including the Ku Klux Klan Act. These acts granted the Federal Government jurisdiction over the Southern states to control the Klan's vio-lence, as well as the ability "to declare martial law and suspend the writ of habeas corpus." The acts also forbade "nightriding and the wearing of masks" (Southern Poverty Law Center 2011, p. 15). By the 1870s, the Klan had started to collapse, seeing its membership largely decline due to federal prosecutorial efforts and internal infighting. However, federal efforts to gain control over the white supremacist violence in the South bred contempt and resentment among white Southerners. At the time of the Klan's dissolution, Republicans had again regained "control of most Southern state govern-ments," overturning Reconstruction efforts (Southern Poverty Law Center 2011, p. 15). The Klan's dissolution occurred not because the Klan had lost its social influence, but rather because it was no longer instrumental to white Southerners—their primary goal had been successfully accomplished, render-ing the Klan largely obsolete. Southern society had successfully returned to its pre–Civil War social order, while the Klan's white supremacist ideology had infiltrated all aspects of American society, including that of Northern states. Black citizens were once again subjugated and brought under control, through an overt and covert legal and social web of oppression, resulting in their social and economic segregation (Braden, 1980; Chalmers, 1987).

WORLD WAR I, 100 PERCENT AMERICANISM, AND THE RISE OF THE KKK (1915–1924)

In the years that followed, the United States focused on industrial expansion and acquisition of manpower, making immigration needed and desirable. Southern states, especially those with a larger black population, sought to attract European immigrants, appointing "agents or boards of immigration to lure new settlers for overseas" (Higham, 1972, p. 17). Southern states' pro-immigration efforts focused on repopulating the South with desirable Nordic European white immigrants to offset the white *native* American population decline caused by the Southern whites' gradual migration to Northern states. This gradual yet incremental migration to the North had adversely affected the Southern states' labor supply, threatening their economic viability (Fleming, 1905). Nativism, along with its colonizing, ethno-racial, geopolitical nationalistic characteristics, began to reemerge during this time. Consistent with its colonizing function, nativism provided white Southerners with the needed sociopolitical and economic grounds for their pro-immigration efforts—to restore and preserve the ethno-racial demographic majority of white Southerners in their states.

By the late 1800s and early 1900s, support for pro-immigration policies began to erode as the ethno-racial and religious composition of new immigrants began to shift away from nativist, Nordic ethno-racial conceptualizations and Protestant ideals. Fears of racial miscegenation and degeneration increasingly dominated the sociopolitical landscape, fueling support for nativist movements, although these groups had a different nativist aim—to control immigration to preserve the *native* American ethno-racial and religious identity of the *native* American people. Although the 1880s immigration surge was a factor in the rise of nativism in the early 1900s, it was not its sole cause. As Hingham (1972) states "The period from about 1885–1887 was one of recurring calamities and almost unrelieved discontent, culminating in the savage depression of 1883–1897" (p. 69).

Although the 1883 depression slowly abated, by the early 1900s, nativism had successfully spread across the United States, finding in Northern states its strongest supporters (Hingham, 1972; Gordon, 2017). The early 1900s also brought the prospect of international political unrest and war in Europe, forcing the United States to turn its attention away from its internal ethno-racial divisions. World War I forever changed not only the existing European nation-states, but American nativism itself. Nativism and the 100 percent

Americanism slogan provided Southern and Northern *native* Americans with a common identity, that of *native* Americans with a duty to protect their nation-state against immigrants, radicals, Catholics, and Jews (see Chalmers, 1987; Hingham, 1972; Gordon, 2017). A rebirth of the Klan soon followed.

The second Klan, the Invisible Empire, was founded in 1915 by William J. Simmons, a veteran of the Spanish-American War. Simmons used the release of the *Birth of a Nation* (1915), the screen adaptation of Thomas Dixon's book *The Clansman* (1905), as a marketing opportunity for the revival of the Klan (see Chambers, 1981; Gordon, 2017). One week after the movie's release, Simmons ran a newspaper ad where the Klan was described as a "HIGH CLASS ORDER FOR MEN OF INTELLIGENCE AND CHARACTER" (Chalmers, 1987, p. 30). The initial marketing strategy drew some attention among middle and upper-class men, but did not produce significant results. The sociopolitical context shifted in favor of the Klan in 1915 with the publication of *The Passing of the Great Race* (Grant, 1916), the publicized case of Leo Frank—a Jewish businessman falsely accused of raping a *white* woman, later lynched (see Chamlers, 1987; Gordon, 2017), and with the release of the *Protocols of the Elders of Zion* (Ford, 1920). Grant's and Ford's publications, as well as Leo Frank's alleged rape of a white woman, all but reinforced the social fears and existing anti-Semitic, ethno-racist, nativist discourse of the era, paving the way for the Klan's successful second rise in 1920.

The ethno-racist, anti-Semitic, and anti-Catholic sociopolitical rhetoric that dominated the *white* American society, only intensified after 1917, when the United States became involved in World War I, bringing great international and internal uncertainty for the United States. At the same time, the influx of Eastern European immigrants arriving to the United States, coupled with the internal discontent of the American working class, and the labor unions' organizing efforts, raised concern over the possible social spread of communist and/or radical ideals—the first Red Scare.

Simmons saw in World War I and in the 100 percent Americanism sociopolitical discourse it produced, an opportunity to reposition the Klan as an organization that sought to defend the American nation-state against *threatening ailments* to its national and people's identity—such as the Jews, Catholics, and Eastern European immigrants, suspected of communist and revolutionary Bolshevik alliances (see Gordon, 2017; Higham, 1972). The rise of the Klan under the guise of 100 percent Americanism fueled the rise of American nativism itself in the 1920s, while *national loyalty* became inexorably linked to ethno-racism, anti-Catholicism, anti-Semitism, and anti-radicalism (Gordon, 2017; Higham, 1972). By the early 1920s, American nativism had achieved its final, contemporary form, aided by the second Klan's mass appeal; its membership had risen to "two to five million members and [counted with] the sympathy or support of millions more" (Rothman, 2016, para. 7).

The Klan, just as during the post–Civil War era, reigned through violence and chaos, however, its nativist ideals were largely accepted at all levels of the white *native American* society, including by elites and politicians alike (Braden, 1980; Gordon, 2017). As during the post–Civil War era, KKK night-riding violence, including lynchings and shootings, terrorized the African American, Jewish, and Mexican immigrant communities, among others. White *native Americans* who did not support the Klan, or who overtly disagreed with it, were also frequent targets of its violence.

During the Klan's peak in 1923, infighting began to expose the Klan's failings as an organization capable of defending and protecting American *moral principles*, while its violence became widespread. Amid the turmoil, the Klan continued to exert significant political influence due to its national membership, and its ties to both the Republican and Democratic parties. In fact, during the 1924 elections, the Klan's endorsed political candidates were largely successful. Despite these victories, the second Klan, as its first iteration in 1870, began to decline shortly thereafter, unable to capitalize on its success. The terror associated with the Klan and the internal infighting that plagued it began to dramatically weaken its social and political appeal; however, the Klan's eventual fall was in great measure due to its success. By the mid 1920s, the Klan's American nativist ideals had infiltrated all aspects of the dominant, white *native American* society. As in 1870, the Klan had once again become obsolete. The enactment of the 1924 Immigration Act, deeply tied to the Klan's political efforts, had successfully secured the demographic primacy of the white *native* American for generations to come, ensuring the identity of the American nation-state, and that of its *rightful* people. As Gordon (2017) states:

> [The Klan] declined in part because it had triumphed in several respects. State eugenics laws, providing for forcible sterilization of those of "defective stock," spread to thirty states, and those labeled defective were typically the poor and people of color. The biggest Klan victory was immigration restriction. . . . The Johnson-Reed Act of 1924, named for Washington Klansman Albert Johnson in the House and Pennsylvania's David Reed in the Senate, ensconced into law the Klan's hierarchy of . . . "races." (chapter 11)

American nativism, aided by the Ku Klux Klan, had once again achieved its colonizing, ethno-racial, geopolitical nationalistic aim.

AMERICAN NATIVISM, THE KKK,
AND WORLD WAR II (1930–1949)

By 1927, Klan membership had largely declined from its peak of about 4 to 5 million members to only 350,000 members (Gordon, 2017; MacLean, 1995). The Great Depression only served to expedite its decline (see Gordon, 2017). However, to understand the rise of American nativism and the KKK in the United States between 1920 and 1927 in its totality, the history of the United States needs to be considered within its international, global context (Steigmann-Gall, 2017).

During the post–World War I and pre–World War II period, European nationalism had evolved into a racial-ethno-cultural-linguistic nationalism that sought to homogenize existing nation-states. At its core, the European nationalism of the time aimed to subjugate and oppress ethnic minorities that resided within each nation-state. While in Europe, World War I reestablished the physical borders of nation-states, creating new ones, and separating ethnic groups between newly delineated borders, American nativism, aided by the KKK's sociopolitical efforts, enabled the reification of the nation-state as a nation, and the white *native* American identity of its people.

The rise of racial-ethno-cultural-linguistic European nationalism, which became ethno-geopolitical nationalism, bred growing tensions within and between nation-states. This sociopolitical context set the stage for the fascist movements that eventually rose to power in Italy, Germany, and Spain starting in 1922.

A discussion of fascism is beyond this chapter's scope and will be taken up later in chapter five; however, it is not possible to speak about American nativism and the first and second KKK, without recognizing how "their worldview and dynamics as social movements" were similar to those of Italian and German Fascism (Gordon, 2017; MacLean, 1995, 2017). Although contemporary analyses of American nativism and the KKK often omit these similarities, white *native* Americans of the 1920s were quick to note them (see MacLean, 1995, 2017). Further omitted, is that Italian and German fascism, and the first and second KKK, are all movements started by war veterans, in post war periods marked by defeat, "economic difficulty, class polarization, and political impasse" (Steigmann-Gall, 2017; Gordon, 2017; MacLean 1995, 2017).

Yet, as fascism began to dominate the European sociopolitical contexts of some nation-states in the 1920s, the KKK began to significantly decline in the United States during the same time period. By the time Italian and German Fascist regimes achieved their strongest sociopolitical positions, the KKK had largely been dismantled. The difference lies in that the ethno-racial inter- and intra-nation-state tensions that pervaded Europe in the post–World War I period, and that paved the way for the European Fascist regimes and World War II, were no longer present in the post-1924 US sociopolitical context. In fact, this *ethno-racial, geopolitical war* had already been fought and won by the KKK in the post–Civil War era and during its second rise— between World War I and 1927.

While in the European post–World War I era, some majority ethnic groups had found themselves separated between newly demarcated nation-state borders, suddenly living as ethnic minorities in new nation-states (such as "ethnic" Germans). In the United States, the KKK and the American nativist ideals it promulgated had successfully re-subjugated the nation-state's internal racial, ethnic, religious, and radical minorities. The integrity of the American nation-state, previously threatened by the Northern and Southern states dichotomy, had been preserved through the reestablishment of the white *native* American identity. The KKK's violence, its 100 percent Americanism, and the passing of the Johnson-Reed Act of 1924 had all secured the sociodemographic dominance of the white *native* American. By 1924, American nativism had once again regained its former sociopolitical influence and the white *native* American people's nation-state had been relegitimized. In other words, American nativism had functioned to intensely oppose "internal minorit[ies] on the ground of [their] foreign" nature (Higham, 1972, p. 4), while the KKK carried out the violence, terror and dehumanization inspired by nativist ideals that fascist movements were seeking to impose in Europe against the *demonized, devalued other*. As Hannah Arendt discusses in the *Origins of Totalitarianism* (1966), as well as Paxton (2004) in the *Anatomy of Fascism,* "Fascists need a demonized enemy against which to mobilize followers . . . American Fascists [KKK] diabolized blacks and sometimes Catholics, as well as Jews. Italian fascists diabolized their South Slav neighbors" and German fascists diabolized "the foreign, the unclean, the contagious . . . [in the] image of the Jew, Gypsies and Slavs" (Paxton, 2004).

The similarities and differences between the KKK, American nativism, and European Fascism are most readily observed when fascism is examined according to its function and to Paxton's five stages of fascism (2004). As Steigmann-Gall (2017) explains, Paxton's five-stage model of fascism identifies a progression from "the creation of fascist movements; to the successful implantation of fascism politically; to the obtaining of power; to the exercising of power; and finally, to the question of the radicalization or entropy of fascism in its final stage" (p. 98). When fascism is examined in a transnational context and as a multistage process, it becomes possible to speak of fascism as a global phenomenon, with nation-state specific manifestations and symbols—such as those particular to the United States in the post–Civil

War and post–World War I eras—and reflected in American nativism and movements such as the KKK.

What differentiates the first and second KKK movements from European fascist movements and later regimes is that the KKK did not infiltrate the political arena as a political party. Although many Republican and Democratic politicians of the time were either members of the KKK or sympathizers, the KKK did not seek to become a political party in its own right. Instead, it sought to spread its white nativist ideals through political influence and through the mass mobilization of the white *native* American people. The KKK was effective in widely disseminating American nativist ideals among the masses, mobilizing them into acts of violence and terror, and/or silent compliance; however, none of the political parties of the era, despite KKK ties and sympathies, embraced the totalitarianism that defined Italian, German, and Spanish fascism. In this manner, American nativists and nativism remained rooted in the democratic principles of the republic. Once American nativist ideals and principles became widely accepted as common sense, legitimate social and moral truths among the white *native* American people, the KKK and its reign of terror were no longer needed. Yet, the first and second KKK did embrace the violence and lawlessness that characterized European fascist movements and regimes of the time, operating outside the democratic structure of the American nation-state; the Ku Klux Klan Act of 1868, for example, illustrates congressional efforts to bring the Klan under the control of the democratic structure of the American nation-state.

The second KKK in particular, just as its contemporary European fascist movements, positioned itself as an organization that sought to reestablish and defend the moral order that the democratic and governmental structure of the American nation-state had failed to enforce. Its goal was to protect the *native* American people from those *threatening ailments* that undermined and compromised its people's identity and racial-ethnic purity. The KKK sought to accomplish this by any means necessary, whether through brutal violence or by strongly supporting efforts to pass eugenic laws across the United States, as well as immigration control.

By the end of the KKK's second rise, thirty states had passed eugenic laws to preserve the purity of the white *native* American people, and the Johnson-Reed Act of 1924 had enacted into law the KKK's hierarchy of races (see Largent, 2011; Stern, 2020). In fact, the "urge to purify the community medically [during the 1920s was] far stronger in . . . the United States and Sweden" than in Germany, until Hitler's regime (Paxton, 2004). Once in power, Hitler looked toward the United States to emulate its success at passing racial eugenic laws. Ultimately, Nazi Germany's eugenic laws and two of Hitler's Nuremberg Laws were modeled after the 1920s US black segregation and eugenic laws, and the genocide of the continent's Indigenous people. Nazi Germany's purity laws were also influenced by the transnational exchange of American eugenic scholarship, produced by Stoddard and Grant, among others (see Kühl, 1994; Whitman, 2017).

Although the transnational exchanges between the United States and Germany and the influence of the American legal racial-ethnic subjugation model on German fascism is largely understudied in the United States, it is well documented by Whitman (2017) in the United States, and by contemporary European scholars such as Kühl (1994). Nonetheless, by 1939, the transnational ties between German fascism and the United States became very explicit when some American, Northern, local KKK groups established an alliance with American Nazi groups. This connection has persisted until this day, where neo-Nazi groups coexist with contemporary iterations of the KKK and other white supremacist groups under the rubric of white power movements and paramilitary groups (Johnson, 2012; Belew, 2018).

Similarly, subsequent twentieth- and twenty-first-century uprisings of the KKK and other white power movements, as during the late nineteenth and early twentieth centuries, have coincided with American involvement with international armed conflict (Belew, 2018). For example, during the Vietnam War (1959–1975), the Gulf War (1990–1991), and the Iraq (2003–2011) and Afghanistan Wars (2001–2021), new white power movements and paramilitary groups, as well as new iterations of the KKK reappeared, achieving broad social acceptance. By invoking nativist, racial-ethno-cultural purity ideals, these new groups mobilized large segments of the white *native* American society, spreading fear of an impending demographic, racial-ethno-religious-cultural demise, that threatened both, the continuity of the white *native* American identity and its peoplehood (for a full discussion, see chapter eight and Belew, 2018). As during the 1920s, the rise of white power movements during each of these international war periods successfully strengthened and legitimized historical American nativist ideals, resulting in renewed nativist immigration restrictions and racist violence against historically subjugated racial and ethnic minority groups, including Jews and Muslims—the latter being constructed as a new contemporary threat to the safety and integrity of the American nation-state.

As Steigmann-Gall (2017) states, a historical review of the KKK and its connection to American inter- and intra-war conflict and American nativism suggests,

> the Klan [not only] fits the mold of a fascist group, but might actually constitute the world's *first* fascist movement, owing not simply to its extreme nationalism, commitment to murderous violence, and fondness for uniforms, but also to its ability to constitute an "alternative civic authority" which defended their community's "legitimate" interests in the face of a failed legal state. (p. 106)

The KKK and its more contemporary white power and paramilitary itera-tions of the late twentieth and early twenty-first centuries not only support Steigmann-Gall's assertions, but also highlight why fascism as a politi-cal phenomenon did not spread in the United States during World War II. American nativism and its historical interconnection with white power move-ments made fascism not only anti-American but also unnecessary. American nativism had successfully maintained and defended the primacy of the white *native* American people since its inception, while normalizing and legitimiz-ing the social subjugation and marginalization of the *undesirable, inferior, racial, ethnic, radical, religious other.*

Fascism was not necessary in the United States, as long as American nativ-ism could dominate the sociopolitical life of the nation-state and its *rightful* people. Only when American nativist ideals seemed to decline throughout American history did nativism need the aid of the KKK and other similar ideological iterations—which functioned as fascist movements—to ensure nativism's primacy. Over time, American nativism was able to preserve the white *native* American identity and the sense of peoplehood it created, while legitimizing the American nation-state and the oppression of its internal, minority groups. In this manner, American nativism has been essential to the *creation and historical* continuity of the white *native* American people and their nation-state (Higham, 1972).

AMERICAN NATIVISM, WHITE POWER MOVEMENTS, AND PARAMILITARY GROUPS (1990–2021)

The new white power movements and paramilitary groups that have appeared in the United States since the Vietnam War are similar and yet different from the Ku Klux Klan. Unlike the KKK's former iterations, contemporary white power movements and paramilitary groups do "not seek to defend the American nation, even when they celebrated some elements of U.S. history and identity. Instead . . . [they see] the state as their enemy . . . [and pursue] an all-white, racial nation . . . that [transcends] national borders" (Belew, 2018, p. 2). This white racial, transnational project has enabled white power movements to join efforts and coexist despite internal differences, uniting white supremacist groups such as Brotherhood of Klans, Knights of the Ku Klux Klan, and the Imperial Klan of America; neo-Nazi groups such as 14 First, the American Nazi Party, Aryan Nation, Atomwaffen Division, Folks Front, and the Nationalist Socialist Order; white nationalist groups such as the Patriot Front, the American Identity Movement, and the American Freedom Party; white paramilitary groups such as the Three Percenters,

Proud Boys, Texas Freedom Force, Oath Keepers, and the militia movement; and anti-government groups such as the Boogaloo.

White power and paramilitary groups, as during the late 1800s and early 1900s, continue to appeal to, and are tied to members of the American armed forces. In fact, Johnson (2012) in *Right-Wing Resurgence: How a Domestic Terrorist Threat Is Being Ignored* and Belew (2018) in *Bring the War Home* document this controversial connection and the recruitment tactics aimed to enlist American military members into these groups. As in the post–Civil War era, white power groups capitalize on the disappointment, discontent, and war trauma of existing American military members and veterans. White paramilitary groups focus on former or current military members to exploit their combat skills for the training of civilian members—themselves disgruntled with the federal government for its failure to protect the white *native* American people from foreign terrorism, interior minorities, and increasing immigration.

For example, the White American Resistance or White Aryan Resistance (WAR), a white supremacist organization founded in the early 1980s, by Tom Mezinger, KKK Grand Wizard, emerged in response to the post–Vietnam War period, the Civil Rights Act of 1964 and the Immigration and Nationality Act of 1965, and President Ronald Reagan's 1986 Immigration Reform and Control Act—which provided undocumented immigrants with a path to regularize their status while reinforcing border and employer sanction controls (Fariña, 2018). The White Aryan Resistance, among other groups, attributed the white *native* American people's 1980s socioeconomic, cultural, and demographic decline—particularly that of men—to the effects of the Vietnam War, and to the post-1964 expansionary civil rights and immigration policy reforms.

Since the late 1970s, white power groups have believed that the United States' government has been engaging in what they have coined as "white genocide." As Gumbel (2015) states "America's bruising experience in Vietnam radicalized the far right even further, breathing life into the so-called Patriot movement . . . [which advocated for] a return to the values of the American Revolution [to] save the country from its corrupt leaders" (p. 5). To stop this *genocide,* white power groups such as WAR saw only one way forward; white *native* Americans had to be encouraged to engage in "free thought . . . [and combine in] opposition to anti-White individuals, groups and governments," which WAR sought to foster through the *WAR* newspaper (*White Aryan Resistance,* 1985, p. 2). In a 1985 issue, for example, *WAR* made repeated calls to arms geared toward armed forces servicemen, also including brief ads that capitalized on existing *white genocide* fears among the white *native* American people. The 1985 *WAR* article "Editor at Large" is in fact an open declaration of war against the government, and a clear illustration of the 1980s White Aryan Resistance efforts to appeal to servicemen:

> Will you and I ever awake, fool? Your war as a White man and woman is not horizontal right/left, it is vertical . . . It makes no difference whether you are a P. O. W. in the bowels of the system's dungeons or a well entrenched agent of our cause in the inner workings of the system . . . It is NOW time for war . . . Some would label our struggle anarchy, but isn't that what we have now? . . . what we face . . . is a world-wide total revolution in way and means of living and surviving in the 21st Century. . . . Finally . . . we may see a light at the end of the tunnel . . . the destruction of economic determinism through racial, ethnic and cultural determinism. To that I say—viva revolution. (p. 2)

The same 1985 *WAR* issue included a fifteen-item list titled "Warning! Letter & Parcel Bomb Recognition Points" designed to instruct readers on how to mail letter and parcel bombs while avoiding governmental detection. The list warned readers to pay attention to "excessive weight; protruding wires or tinfoil; [and] excessive securing material[s] such as masking tapes, string, etc" (p. 12). The issue also included two ads, among many, designed to alarm white *native* Americans by highlighting their impending destruction and racial/ethnic demise. The first ad, titled "Equality" spoke to the Civil Rights Act era and its alleged detrimental socioeconomic effects for white *native* Americans: "Are you still working or does a non-white have your job?" (p. 17). The second sought to propagate fears of racial and sociocultural destruction "Going * going * gone. Integration destroys civilization" (p. 17).

The White Aryan Resistance continues to operate online at resist.com. This website includes a memorial to Tom Mezinger, the *WAR* newspaper's archives, and Aryan Resistance audio and video propaganda materials, including an online POW donation fund for Aryan Resistance Prisoners of War, who have acted in opposition to the government (White Aryan Resistance at resist.com). WAR is one of many white power and paramilitary groups that currently populate the internet, recruiting white civilians, as well as members of the military and law enforcement. Through their anti-government, nativist ideals, white power and paramilitary groups have encouraged domestic terrorist acts in the United States that have steadily escalated since the early 1980s; some producing large-scale devastation such as the 1995 Oklahoma Bombing. Timothy McVeigh was later charged and convicted for this terrorist attack and was executed in 2001.

McVeigh was a former member of the US military who had served during the Gulf War and became involved with the Klan during his military service; his ties to the Klan continued after his military service. Unfortunately, McVeigh is one of a number of high-profile US military and/or law enforcement members, with ties to white power movements and terrorism. For example, Louis Beam, Vietnam War veteran and author of *Essays of a Klansman*, "argued that activists needed to continue waging the war on U.S. territory using guerrilla warfare" (Jones, Doxsee, Hwang & Thompson, 2021, p. 3). Randy Duey, an Air Force veteran, was a member of the white supremacist group The Order. Randy Weaver—a former US Army member and "Christian Identity adherent who held white supremacist and anti-government views . . . [was] involved in the 1992 Ruby Ridge standoff near Naples, Idaho (Jones, Doxsee, Hwang & Thompson, 2021, p. 3). Contemporary statistics continue to support a link between the armed forces, white power movements, and domestic terrorism; in 2020, for example, 6.4 percent of all domestic terrorist acts perpetrated in the United States were "linked to active-duty and reserve personnel" (Jones, Doxsee, Hwang & Thompson, 2021, p. 1). As Gumbel (2015) states

> A 2006 report by the Southern Poverty Law Center found that the operational pressures of the wars in Iraq and Afghanistan superseded concerns about extremism. "Recruiters are knowingly allowing neo-Nazis and white supremacists to join the armed forces, and commanders don't remove them from the military even after we positively identify them," Department of Defense investigator Scott Barfield reported at the time. (p. 9)

Overall, in 2020, the Anti-Defamation League, ADL, reported seventeen domestic terrorist acts motivated by racism, islamophobia, and anti-Semitism, linked to right-wing supremacist and anti-government groups, making these groups responsible for 74 percent of the racially and/or religiously motivated acts of domestic terrorism in the United States. Between 2011 and 2020, the ADL recorded ninety-eight acts of domestic terrorism, of which 40 percent, or thirty-nine acts, were linked to individuals with ties to white supremacist organizations; 17.35 percent of them occurred in 2020 (Byman & Pitcavage, 2021, p. 2).

The incidence of racially and/or ethnically motivated hate crimes has also seen substantial increases since 2016. Between 2004 and 2021, there were 115,937 hate crimes perpetrated in the United States, according to data compiled by the Anti-Defamation League (2021); of these, 79.77 percent or 92,483 were racially, or religiously (anti-Semitic, anti-Islamic) motivated (ADL, 2021). The contemporary escalation of racially and/or ethnically motivated hate crimes and their link to white power movements is further supported by Byman and Pitcavage (2021), who found that in 2020 "white supremacists were responsible for 53 percent of the 17 domestic extremist-related murders in the United States" (p. 2) and in 2019, for "81 percent of 42 such killings"

(p. 2). During the previous ten years, "white supremacists committed 77 percent of all right-wing extremist-related murders" (p. 2).

Contemporary white power movements and paramilitary groups, while still nationalist in nature, have developed transnational ties that make these groups more difficult to dismantle at the individual national level.

TRANSNATIONAL WHITE POWER MOVEMENTS AND PARAMILITARY GROUPS (1990–2021)

The internet allows American white power groups to freely disseminate their white supremacist ideology at an international level. Through the web, these groups spread global fears of an impending "white genocide" caused by increasing immigration and ineffective governmental policies that have failed to protect the white native people of the United States and other European nation-states. Many of these websites are used to encourage individuals to act against their national governments to stop the genocide of white natives and defend their nation-state and sense of peoplehood (ADL, 2019; Hubbard, 2021; Mulhall & Khan-Ruf, 2020). American and European white power groups capitalize on the existing European governmental discontent present in many countries, along with rising xenophobia and racism, to enlist individuals into their now global networks. For example, Mulhall and Khan-Ruf's report on the "State of Hate" in Europe (2020) revealed growing governmental disapproval in France and Britain, with overall negative social "attitudes toward minorities" in all eight countries surveyed—67 percent of Italians viewed the Roma negatively, and 60 percent of Hungarians viewed immigrants in an equally negative light (p. 9). It is not surprising that France, Italy, and Hungary, as well as the United States, have seen an interrelated increase of white power movements and memberships, during that same time period.

While members of national white power groups in the United States and Europe, continue to be "primarily preoccupied with local or national issues, they invariably contextualise them continentally or even globally, [coming] together for short periods" to network and share information globally (Mulhall & Khan-Ruf, 2020). These tactics have been successfully used by the Hammerskins, an American white supremacist group founded in 1988 with international chapters across the globe in Australia, New Zealand, Spain, Germany, and the Netherlands, among many other countries. In 2018, the Hammerskins became "the largest, most organized, and most violent neo-Nazi skinhead gang in the United States" (Counter Extremism Project n.d.).

The Hammerskins network has been associated with racial and anti-governmental attacks, including arson, murders and terrorist acts in the United States and abroad, that have exposed the Hammerskins' ties to terrorist organizations. For example, in Germany, the Hammerskins have been directly linked with the National Sozialistischer Untergrund, NSU—a German domestic terrorist organization. The NSU based in Zwickau in eastern Germany was responsible for an array of murders and violent attacks, including bombings and arsons, perpetrated against Greek and Turkish nationals between 2000 and 2006. The trial of three NSU members responsible for the string of attacks revealed that the NSU cell counted on the support of over one hundred people from the right-wing scene (*Haaretz* & The Associated Press, 2018; Knight & Fürstenau, 2016).

The Hammerskins, like many other global white power groups, gather annually using music or sports to attract existing members and possible new recruits to their annual events. The Hammer Festival is one of such music festivals, where Hammerskins from various local and international chapters come together to strengthen their national and international network (see Hemmerling et al., 2021).

The global discontent with current national governments and shifting demographic changes, in part tied to transnational migrations in the United States and abroad, have united *white natives* under a racial paradigm akin to that of the late 1800s and early 1900s. While national identities still prevail and foster pronounced native cultural differences grounded on mythical historical, national constructions of peoplehood, the fear of racial degeneration and replacement continues to make white power movements essential to the maintenance of racial-ethno-cultural-linguistic European nationalism and American nativism. Moreover, the sociopolitical and economic instability of many European nation-states and the United States, coupled with international armed conflicts in the Middle East, global climate change, and forced migration, has not only increased white genocide fears but also legitimized the domestic violence perpetrated in its name—and against governments.

These conditions are approximating the first two stages of Paxton's five-stage model of fascism (2004); that is, globally, the number of, and membership in, white power movements has been steadily increasing, as well as their ties to growing ethno-geopolitical nationalist and white nativist political parties in European nation-states and the United States. Yet, these new political parties also reflect populist elements, since they construct the *true* children of the nation-state (its people) as victims of a ruling elite that has been seduced by neoliberal ideals. These characteristics are consistent with Finchelstein's (2017) conceptualization of populism as protofascism, in which populism "is defined by its contextual postwar rejection of fascist dictatorships and extreme violence, while it continues to reflect some of fascism's ideological premises" (p. 27). The uprising at the US Capitol on January 6, 2021, during President Trump's administration, is in fact, a clear example of the protofascist dynamics described by Finchelstein (2017) that underlie the contemporary, identity-driven, sociopolitical unrest experienced by many European nation-states as well.

As Federico Finchelstein (2015) states, "fascism has trans-historical characteristics; it abominates history and seeks to return to a mythical world, that is distinguished above all, by violence and murder" (p. 13). Transnational white power movements, like the KKK in the United States and the neo-Nazi Hammerskins in the United States and Europe, understood herein as contemporary fascist movements, seek exactly that; a return to a mythical, historical nation-state founded upon a national identity that never actually existed except as constructed through European nationalism and American nativism.

Chapter Five

Populism

Umberto Eco (2012), in *Inventing the Enemy: And Other Occasional Writings*, cautions "Having an enemy is important not only to define our identity but also to provide us with an obstacle against which to measure our system of values and, in seeking to overcome it, to demonstrate our own worth. . . . So when there is no enemy we have to invent it." Nationalism and American nativism are two political ideologies that have been essential to the establishment of the European nation-states and the United States. Both served to create, reinforce, and legitimize the historicized identity of a given people, thereby naturalizing their claims to live together as "natives" to their inhabited and/or occupied land and nation-state (Gellner, 2006; Leerssen, 2006). Populism is also concerned with identity, but in populism, identity is broad, and conceptualized in binary, polarizing terms—*the people* versus *the elites*. Just as in nationalism and nativism, in populism, the *people* are a mythical, historicized "'imagined community,' much like the nation of the nationalist" (Mudde, 2004, p. 546)

Yet, populism, unlike European nationalism and American nativism, does not in and of itself provide a definition by which a people can claim a shared, historicized, ethno-racial, cultural, and linguistic identity that legitimizes their right to live together as a people in their own nation-state (Mudde, 2004, p. 546). While most academics agree that populist rhetoric is marked by a simplistic, binary and polarizing conceptualization of identity, little consensus exists beyond this element as to what populism is (Arato, 2019; Finchelstein, 2017; Laclau, 2018; Mudde, 2004; Mudde & Kaltwasser, 2017; Urbinati, 2019).

WHAT IS POPULISM?

While Arato (2018, p. 18), and Wiles (1969) define populism "as a pathology of civil society" or syndrome, Laclau (2018) argues that "populism is, quite simply, a way of constructing the political" where the heterogeneous nature of a *people* is oversimplified, and vaguely conceptualized, along homogenous social, identity claims. In this populist logic, there can only be a *true people,* and a corrupt *elite* that benefits from the oppression of the *true people.* Mudde and Kaltwasser (2017) agree with Laclau in that populism separates the people of a nation-state into "two homogeneous and antagonistic groups." However, Mudde and Kaltwasser (2017) favor an ideational approach, where populism is conceptualized as a thin-centered political ideology that necessitates another established political ideology, instead of a political logic (Laclau, 2018). Mudde and Kaltwasser's (2017) ideational approach highlights what makes populism difficult to define; while in some instances, populism may manifest as a left-leaning political ideology, such as in socialist populism, it can also appear as a conservative, nationalist, or nativist political movement—hence the contemporary conflation in political discourse of nationalism, nativism, and populism.

Despite populism's ideological malleability, scholars agree that the *true people* as constructed in populist rhetoric is an empty, malleable, and vague signifier (Laclau, 2018). The *true people* of a nation-state are not defined by populism itself, other than in terms of purity and belonging, but rather by the ideology that informs the specific populist movement of the time. It is this malleability that makes populism "such a powerful political ideology and phenomenon" with a multiplicity of forms (Mudde & Kaltwasser, 2017, p. 9). Responding to this malleability, scholars such as Canovan (1981, 1999) have sought to provide some conceptual clarity by classifying populism in either socioeconomic terms (agrarian populism) or in political ones (political populism).

For Canovan (1981) agrarian populism is marked by "rural radicalism" (p. 8) and reflects historical class struggles, such as those that characterized the nineteenth-century populism of the United States, led by the People's Party, or in Russia, by the Narodniki (see Pedler, 1927; Walicki, 1980). Canovan (1981), on the other hand, defines political populism by its "political characteristics . . . [as] a political phenomenon where the tension between the elite and the grass roots loom large" (Canovan 1981, p. 9). For Canovan (1981) it is then possible to group together Peronism and reactionary populism— such as that of George Wallace (Laclau, 2018). However, defining populism along class struggles or political lines fails to explain other populist movements that present ambiguity, and decontextualizes different populist parties and movements from their historical roots, further obscuring their origins (Finchelstein, 2017).

POPULISM: THE PEOPLE, THE ELITE, AND THE PEOPLE'S GENERAL WILL

Mudde's (2004) ideational approach, although ahistorical in nature, also defines populism by its characteristics, but primarily highlights populism's "restricted core [attachment] to a narrower range of political concepts" that include the people, the elite, and the general will of the people (Mudde, 2004, p. 544; Mudde & Kaltwasser, 2017). In populism, the people are not only the *true people* of the nation-state, but are also understood as *pure* in juxtaposition to an evil and corrupt *elite*. The binary thought that characterizes populism, along with its simple and sometimes rough and offensive language—Stammtisch discourse—allows for the gradual dehumanization and objectification of the "enemy" other (Derrida, 2020). As Mudde (2004) posits, the *elite other* is "evil! [and] Consequently, compromise is impossible, as it 'corrupts' the purity" of *the people* (p. 544). Populism, therefore, positions itself as emancipatory in nature, seeking to free the *true people* of the nation-state from the subjugating elite through a process of consciousness-raising. Populism both highlights the problematic effects of the politics of the elite and constructs the values of the people as natural and imbued with common sense (Van Dijk, 2015; Wilson, 2015). As Urbinati (2019) posits "Populism expresses two things at the same time: the denunciation of exclusion [of the *true people*] . . . and the construction of a strategy of inclusion by means of exclusion (of the establishment [*the elites*]).

As Mudde and Kaltwasser argue (2017) populism mobilizes the *true people* of the nation-state under Rousseau's principle of *volonté générale*, general will. However, in populism, the general will of the people can be deployed as a mechanism to alienate those constructed as other, threatening democratic principles and governmental structures equated with the establishment. While populism can operate within the democratic process of a nation-state, it can also rise within it to undermine and erode central democratic entities that ensure the viability of a nation-state's democracy—such as attacking and limiting the power of the judiciary branch, while augmenting the executive power of the populist leader, as in the case of President Donald Trump in the United States or Viktor Mihály Orbán in Hungary (Judd & Watters, 2018; Snyder, 2019). As Urbanati (2019), and Mudde and Kaltwasser (2017) argue, populism can "legitimize authoritarianism and illiberal attacks on anyone who (allegedly) threatens the homogeneity of the people" (p. 18).

POPULISM AND AUTHORITARIANISM

Populism's malleability, simplistic, binary logic, and Stammtisch rhetoric makes populism particularly appealing for social groups harboring increasing disappointment and resentment toward the political establishment. In fact, national contexts marked by societal mistrust and disappointment provide fertile ground for the political rise of populist leaders, who strive to position themselves as the only politically viable alternative to the existing establishment. Through often-simplistic solutions to complex historical problems, populist leaders promise the long-awaited recognition and inclusion of the oppressed *true people* of the nation-state—enhancing their political mass appeal. Capitalizing on this widening social discontent, populist leaders exploit this context to mobilize *the people* against the political establishment (Mudde, 2004, 2016). In this process, the leader's characteristics and ideological platform will determine the level of authoritarianism legitimized and accepted by the now *true people* of the nation-state. In fact, right-leaning nationalist or nativist forms of populism reflect a level of authoritarianism that makes this form of populism appear as a political phenomena closely related to fascism. The shared similarities help explain the contemporary confusion in some US political media outlets that question whether former President Donald Trump was indeed fascist (Matthews, 2020).

The confusion is not unfounded, as both populism and fascism reflect a similar ideological malleability and are characterized by a simplistic, binary rhetoric and logic; but most importantly, in nationalist or nativist populism and fascism, the leader plays a central role in organizing and representing the will of the oppressed *true people* of the nation-state (Bosworth, 2021; Finchelstein, 2015, 2017; Paxton, 2004; Snyder, 2017; Urbinati, 2019). This representational, symbolic link between the people and the populist leader, who speaks for and by the people, in its most absolute incarnation leads to social dynamics in which internal differences within the people are intolerable (Finchelstein, 2017). As such, independent thought that questions the shared populist values constitutes a betrayal of one's group, and is cause for social exclusion and renewed marginalization. The social polarization in the United States during the COVID-19 pandemic, for example, clearly illustrates these dynamics—loyalty to Trump and to "we the people" required opposition to vaccines and protective measures, all equated with an infringement on the autonomy of *the people.* In European nation-states, pandemic-related restrictions fueled a similar political polarization, where supporters of right-wing, nationalist-populist parties, such as "Vox in Spain, the League in Italy, the Freedom Party in Austria, the Sweden Democrats, and the Party for Freedom in the Netherlands" expressed significant distrust toward their government's imposed restrictions, categorizing the measures as an infringement upon their constitutional freedom and rights, with the actual intent of expanding governmental control over *the people* of the nation (Leonald & Krastev, 2021).

Whether populism facilitates or hinders democratization processes, and democracy itself, is a highly contested subject. While some scholars argue that populism has the potential to either facilitate or hinder democratization processes, depending on the characteristics and ideological underpinnings of the particular nation-state's populist party or movement, others view populism as inherently counterdemocratic arguing, as Rosanvallon (2008), that populism "is a perverse inversion of the ideals and procedures of democracy" (see Finchelstein, 2017; Mudde & Kaltwasser, 2017; Rosanvallon, 2008).

Although populism and fascism share a number of characteristics, there are also significant differences; historically contextualizing both political phenomena is essential to understanding their junctures and disjunctures, as well as populism's protofascist nature.

FASCISM AND POPULISM: A HISTORICAL APPROACH

What Is Fascism?

As discussed in chapter four, fascism is conceptually difficult to define. Hannah Arendt (1966) defines fascism as a form of totalitarianism marked by total control over the people and by absolute violence. For Arendt (1966), fascism, as other forms of totalitarianism, "abuses its own ideological and political elements until the basis of factual reality . . . have all but disappeared." However, scholars such as Renzo de Felice (2017) argue that by defining fascism as a form of totalitarianism and "mass control unique to the twentieth century," fascism is reduced "to a mere technique of power" (p. 10).

Roger Griffin (2006), and Renzo de Felice (2017) argue for a different conceptualization that highlights national regeneration and rebirth, rather than violence. In *The Nature of Fascism,* Griffin (2006) argues that fascism is:

> a revolutionary form of nationalism, one which sets out to be a political, social and ethical revolution, welding the 'people' into a dynamic national community under new elites infused with new heroic values. The core myth which inspires this project is that only a populist, trans-class movement of purifying, cathartic national rebirth (palingenesis) can stem the tide of decadence.

However, Renzo de Felice, in *Fascism: An Informal Introduction to Its Theory and Practice* (2017), while initially reluctant to speak about fascism in general terms, makes an important distinction between Italian fascism and German national socialism. Felice (2017) argues that unlike Italian fascism

"Nazism . . . [seemed] to create a new society [but in actuality] . . . nazism . . . sought a restoration of values and not the creation of new values" (p. 56). Nazism sought to liberate the German man from the effects of modernism. Later, in *Fascismo*, Felice (2011) defined fascism as a revolutionary movement that aimed "to transform crowds into masses by organizing them into a political movement with characters of secular religion."

Emilio Gentile (2000) in *The Sacralization of Politics: Definitions, Interpretations and Reflections on the Question of Secular Religion and Totalitarianism*, identified four characteristics of totalitarian regimes such as fascism: the militarization of the political party, the concentration of power on the totalitarian leader, the mobilization of the masses, and the sacralization of politics (p. 20). Gentile (2000) defines the latter as the process by which "a real system of beliefs, myths, dogmas and commandments that cover all of collective existence [are institutionalized through] rituals and festivals, . . . to transform permanently the *occasional crowds* of civil events into the *liturgical masses* of the political cult" (p. 20). Like Hannah Arendt (1973), Gentile (2000) emphasizes the central role that coercion, demagoguery, totalitarian pedagogy, and discrimination against an internal *enemy other* play in totalitarianism.

Propaganda is essential to fascism, as well as to other totalitarian phenomena. In fascism, the fascist leader gradually spreads misinformation and replaces journalist inquiry and reporting with propaganda designed to alarm the *true people* of the nation-state; in other words, the totalitarian and fascist propaganda machinery seeks to spread fear among the people. The myths typically pertain to the impending demise of the people's "being" (their very existence as a people), and uses themes that forecast the end of the people's cultural, linguistic, racial, or socioeconomic way of life and existence. Ultimately, totalitarian and fascist propaganda replaces reality by myths that affectively mobilize the masses against a fictitious threat and *enemy other* (Arendt, 1973; Eco, 2012, 2020; Volkan, 2013). As Paxton (2004) argues, fascist propaganda mobilizes passions and makes explicit the emotional rather than ideological logic of fascism,

> fascism is more plausibly linked to a set of "mobilizing passions" that shape fascist action than to a consistent and fully articulated philosophy. At bottom is a passionate nationalism. Allied to it is a conspiratorial and Manichean view of history as a battle between the good and evil camps, between the pure and the corrupt, in which one's own community or nation has been the victim. In this Darwinian narrative, the chosen people have been weakened by political parties, social classes, [and] unassimilable minorities.

Paxton (2004) highlights fascism's connection with ethno-geopolitical nationalism and with the pre-interwar European period, where imagined and actual fears of ethno-racial, linguistic, cultural, and sociopolitical demise pervaded the social existence of many people and nation-states (see chapter two). In fact, it was ethno-geopolitical nationalism's precise failure to resolve the pervasive European ethno-geopolitical tensions between historicized ethno-racial, cultural, and linguistic groups and nation-states that created the necessary conditions for the rise of fascism. Consistent with this historical context, Paxton (2004) ultimately defines fascism as:

> a form of political behavior marked by obsessive preoccupation with community decline, humiliation, or victimhood and by compensatory cults of unity, energy, and purity, in which a mass-based party of committed nationalist militants, working in uneasy but effective collaboration with traditional elites, abandons democratic liberties and pursues with redemptive violence and without ethical or legal restraints goals of internal cleansing and external expansion.

In this manner, as Roger Griffin (2006, 2019) and Renzo de Felipe (2017) argue, fascism was a revolutionary political phenomenon that, capitalizing on the literal and psychological annihilatory fear of the time (Freud, 1921, 1926), exploited emotion to inflict and produce absolute violence under the guise of emancipation and regeneration for the *true people* of the nation-state. Although Italian fascism, German nazism, and Spanish falangismo are all similar and yet different totalitarian phenomena, they all aimed to either restore or achieve a new people of the nation-state (Bosworth, 2009, 2021). In this manner, they either sought to achieve a new idealized, homogenized, ethno-racial, cultural, and linguistic pure people, or a return to their former mythical and historicized nature and identity. Fascism, therefore, in its most succinct manner and as argued by Finchelstein (2017), can then be defined as an "ultraviolent dictatorship" that legitimizes the persecution and extermination of political opposition of any kind, including that of the impure other, to homogenize and regenerate the people and the nation-state.

Populism Revisited

After 1945, ethno-geopolitical nationalism could no longer maintain its European political dominance due to its ties with authoritarianism. Fascism's devastating violence and resulting death toll, and its defeat at the end of World War II forever inscribed fascism as one of the most terrifying and dehumanizing political phenomena in European history. However, as Finchelstein (2017) posits, in "the guise of post fascist forms of antiliberal democracy, fascism continued its legacy through various combinations of populism and neofascism" (p. 7).

Finchelstein's historical approach (2017), after tracing and examining fascism's and populism's historical origins, positions modern populism as a post-1945 political movement that remains connected to fascist origins, exposing its protofascist nature; however, as Finchelstein (2017) emphasizes, populism is not fascism. Although populism "reflects some of fascism's ideological premises," it rejects two of its central elements: the fascist dictatorship and absolute violence. As such, populism is best understood as a postmodern derivative of fascism—"a form of authoritarian democracy," that emerged post-1945 and that remains ambivalently positioned between its fascist origins and within and against liberal democracy (Finchelstein, 2017). While populism can revert to its fascist origins by progressing from authoritarianism to totalitarianism, in so doing, it ceases to be populism.

Further complicating the boundaries between certain forms of political populism and fascism, as previously discussed, is populism's ideological malleability and its nativist or nationalist iterations. In nationalist or nativist-populism, internal segments of the population, such as the immigrant or black other for example, are often targets of sociopolitical discursive devaluation and constructed as a threat to *the true people* of the nation-state for political gains. Anti-immigrant or anti-black rhetoric is certainly a form of aggression, but when devaluation escalates to unlawful behaviors that infringe on the rights of or oppress or intimidate the "foreign or racial other," populism as a movement begins to reflect a closer resemblance to fascism; this resemblance is best explained through Paxton's five-stage model of fascism presented earlier in this book (see chapter four).

Paxton's five-stage model, like Finchelstein's historical approach to fascism and populism, argues that fascism never fully disappeared after 1945, and continues to exist "at the level of Stage One [a movement] within all democratic countries—not excluding the United States . . . whenever lawless treatment of national 'enemies'" is tolerated. When nationalist or nativist populist movements begin to foster and promote this kind of violence, populism enters stage one of Paxton's cycle of fascism—reflecting populism's capacity to gradually revert to its fascist origins. However, it is important to note that such gradual progression should not be equated with, or labeled, fascism, and instead is conceptualized as the first stage of the fascist cycle.

For example, prior to the insurrection at the US Capitol, Robert Paxton, along with Roger Griffin, had objected to labeling Trump a fascist, favoring instead the term "illiberal democrat"—a feature of populism and populist leaders (Matthews, 2020). In fact, Sheri Berman, professor of political science at Barnard College, made this connection explicit when referring to Trump as "an illiberal populist or right-wing populist" (Matthews, 2020). However, after the insurrection at the US Capitol on January 6, 2021, Paxton stated:

> Trump's incitement of the invasion of the Capitol on January 6, 2021 removes my objection to the fascist label. His open encouragement of civic violence to overturn an election crosses a red line. The label now seems not just acceptable but necessary. It is made even more plausible by comparison with a milestone on Europe's road to fascism—an openly fascist demonstration in Paris during the night of February 6, 1934. (Paxton, 2021)

The boundaries between populism and fascism have also been shifting in European nation-states in the twenty-first century. Paxton's early stages of fascism are also palpable in the nationalist-populism that has gained political ground in a number of European nation-states since the mid 2010s. Despite some intermittent, wavering loss of support during the late 2010s and early 2020s, nationalist-populism resumed its gains across Europe in countries such as France, Austria, Germany, Italy, Spain, Belgium, and Finland, to name a few (Anderson, 2021; Green, 2016; Olsen, 2021). For example, in France, support for Marie Le Pen's Rassemblement National party—with its protofascist roots and nationalist identitarian, anti-immigrant, Eurosceptic populist rhetoric—rose from 33.9 percent in 2017 to 44 percent in 2021, trailing President Emmanuel Macron by 12 percent (Anderson, 2021). In Italy, nationalist-populist parties, with an anti-immigrant, antiestablishment, and Eurosceptic rhetoric, including the 5Stars, Lega, and Brothers of Italy (a party with post-fascist roots), obtained 50 percent of the electoral vote during the 2018 elections (Henneberger, 2022). Voting intent polls in 2021 indicated that these parties would receive 54 percent of the electoral vote if elections had been held at the end of 2021. In 2022, these predictions proved accurate, when the right-wing coalition formed by the Brothers of Italy, Lega, and Forza Italia won the Italian elections, securing "43.7 percent of votes in the Chamber of Deputies, and 44.02 percent in the Italian senate." Shortly after, Giorgia Meloni, leader of the Brothers of Italy, became "Italy's first female Prime Minister" (Statista, 2023).

In Spain, VOX, a nationalist-populist party characterized by anti-immigration, "law and order," traditional, conservative, nationalist rhetoric, initially obtained 0.2 percent of the electoral vote during the 2015 and 2016 elections (Santana et al., 2021). In 2019, VOX obtained 15 percent of the vote and became one of the third-largest parties in the country. VOX "purports to defend traditional and religious moral values against what it terms a 'progressive dictatorship' . . . fueling affective polarization" through populist discursive practices (Santana et al., 2021). VOX's political platform has attracted a diverse membership, that includes previous Falange members.

Given Spain's fascist history, the growth of a political party such as VOX, has raised concern over a possible fascist resurgence. As with the debate regarding former President Trump in the United States, there is significant dissension as to whether VOX is a fascist or a contemporary nationalist-populist party. While some refer to VOX as a radical, right-wing, extreme-right, or fascist party, scholars such as Jorge Verstrynge, political science professor at the Universidad Complutense de Madrid, Spain, strongly opposes the fascist label in favor of a nationalist-populist one, comparing VOX to Le Rassemblement National in France or Lega in Italy. VOX, as *Trumpism* prior to the insurrection at the US Capitol, operates within the Spanish democratic structure while also presenting a challenge to liberal democracy that is consistent with populism (Olivan Navarro, Reglas Escartín, Delgado Ontivero, & Jaziri Arjona, 2021).

European nationalist-populism, as well as former President Trump's nativist-populism, are examples of the early stages of Paxton's cycle of fascism, with the exception of the Greek Golden Dawn fascist party (Green, 2016; Vasilopoulou & Halikiopoulou, 2015). In 2012, the Golden Dawn Party became Greece's third-largest party, coming to prominence during the sociopolitical and economic crisis of 2008. The mass discontent with the government's policies and the austerity measures imposed to comply with the 2009 European Commission/International Monetary Fund financial assistance plan, provided the Golden Dawn Party with the ideal conditions to secure 7 percent of the popular vote and eighteen parliamentary seats (Thrilling, 2020; Vasilopoulou & Halikiopoulou, 2015). Until the 2012 elections, no other openly fascist party had secured a parliamentary presence at the national or European level; Golden Dawn was the first fascist party to do so since 1945. Golden Dawn adhered to National Socialist principles, consistent with German Fascism, and used a xenophobic rhetoric grounded on ethno-racial congruence between the people and their nation-state—ethno-racial nationalism. Under nationalist principles, Golden Dawn argued for a complete shutdown of the Greek borders during the refugee crisis that started in 2008, while advocating for the expulsion of all immigrants residing in Greece; their ideology can be summarized in two words: "blood and honor" (Trilling, 2020; Vasilopoulou & Halikiopoulou, 2015).

Violence and lawlessness were also a marker of the Golden Dawn, which was responsible for multiple attacks on immigrants, and two murders—that of a Pakistani immigrant and of a well-known rapper, Pavlos Fyssas. The murder of Pavlos Fyssas led to criminal charges and an investigation into the Golden Dawn Party, which culminated in multiple arrests that also included the Golden Dawn Party's leadership; the charges ranged from participating in a criminal organization to assault, racketeering, and murder. The investigation and trial lasted five years, ending in October 2020. The trial, heralded as the largest trial of its kind since the Nuremberg trials, led to multiple convictions and the dissolution of Golden Dawn after it was reclassified as a criminal terrorist organization (Kakissis, 2020; Vasilopoulou & Halikiopoulou, 2015).

The case of Golden Dawn is consistent with Paxton's fifth stage of fascism, characterized by either entropy or radicalization. In this case, the intervention of the courts and therefore, the democratic structure, functioned to contain and dismantle the post-1945 fascist party, preventing its further expansion and radicalization. Although some consider the collapse of the Golden Dawn Party and the incarceration of its leadership evidence of both the success of liberal democracy and eradication of fascism in Greece, others take a far more cautious approach. As Paxton (2004, 2009) and Finchelstein (2017) argue, fascism does not disappear but instead transmutes in form and expression. A year after the Golden Dawn trial, far-right groups have again gained support among certain sectors of society, including Greek youth. Some of these groups share fascist origins similar to those of the Golden Dawn, using nationalist-populist rhetoric, Nazi symbols and salutes, and violence. They include Holy Corps, Holy Body, Propatria, the Weapon, and Combat 18—the latter has been involved in numerous arson incidents (Tsoutsoumpis, 2018). Of particular concern is the ability of these neofascist groups to infiltrate Greek schools. As Konstantinos Tsitselikis, professor at the University of Macedonia in Thessaloniki, states,

> Unfortunately, there are far-right groups in many schools. . . . They are dispersed all over the country, mostly in areas which are economically deprived, where neo-Nazi groups can easily recruit teenagers. What is worse is that some teachers tolerate this recruitment or even encourage it. It's a phenomenon that needs more attention. (Bali, 2021)

Indeed, Tsoutsoumpis (2018) using a historical approach similar to that of Finchelstein (2017), argues that Greek nationalist-populist and fascist movements and parties, far from being a new phenomenon, are directly connected to Greece's post–World War II and civil war period, and to governmental efforts to control these groups through "patronage and state funds" (p. 104). Governmental control efforts included a two-prong approach by which "senior politicians publicly condemned the activities of [groups such as] 'Golden Dawn,'" while also opening "a number of political back-doors through which they tried to control [their] activities" (p. 93). As Tsoutsoumpis (2018) argues, this approach was an outgrowth of the post-1940s war period, in which the "more moderate right and the security services had [controlled] the far right through a process of co-option and patronage" (p. 93). The sociopolitical and economic crisis that unraveled by 2008 led to the collapse of this approach and exposed the populist, protofascist, and fascist movements that had always been part of Greek society. As such, sectors of the Greek society have always supported the existence of these groups and continue to enable their operations and recruitment tactics among those most vulnerable to propaganda and mind control, adolescents and young adults.

POPULISM: IN ITS HISTORICAL TOTALITY

Finchelstein's historical approach to populism provides a necessary continuity to the evolution of European nation-states, as well as the United States. While other approaches, such as Mudde and Kaltwasser's ideological approach, are helpful in identifying the characteristics of populism and its most recent iterations in the United States and Europe, they are unable to capture the protofascist nature of contemporary populist movements. By dissociating the historical context under which populism originated, it becomes difficult to understand the risk that populism can pose to liberal democracy and its raison d'être.

The collective historical and social trauma brought about by fascism and World War II is still present in the minds of people in the nation-states that took part in one of the most devastating periods of European history (Hooper & Weinwerg, 2015). The war's effects, including the mass displacement of people, were also felt in the United States. At the heart of World War II were ethno-geopolitical nationalist tensions that had sought to define the nation-state and its rightful people. However, ethno-geopolitical nationalism failed in its efforts to define and align a people's *essence and being* along territorial lines and under Rousseauian principles. The mythical nature of the historized identities developed through ethno-geopolitical nationalism to create the people of a given nation and their nation-state had proved fragile. Ethno-geopolitical nationalism, unable to withstand the complexity of human nature, fueled identity-driven sociopolitical aggression. Ultimately, it created the ideal social, economic, and political conditions for the rise of fascism.

Identity politics, far from being a contemporary phenomenon, is at its core a nationalist endeavor that was further exploited by fascism (Coulmas, 2019; Gellner, 2006; Leerssen, 2006). The human desire to belong and to demarcate the essence of belonging through a concrete signifier that gives meaning to whom one is, while reinforcing collective, group identities, has long been the subject of academic inquiry in multiple disciplines, such as individual and political psychology, philosophy, and sociology (Čapek & Loidolt, 2021; Erikson, 1968; Fariña, 2017; Freud, 1921; Tajfel, 1982; Volkan, 2017, 2018, 2020). Individual and collective identities, as briefly discussed in chapter two and explored further in chapters seven and eight, emerge from complex affective and sociocognitive identification processes that link individuals to their specific collective group(s), while also reinforcing and maintaining the collective identity of that group. In this manner, both individual and collective ethno-cultural, racial, linguistic identities, for example, mutually construct and necessitate each other.

Ideologies are most important in this process of individual and collective identity formation, as it is the society's dominant ideology that identifies the characteristics of the group and its individual members. Ideologies construct the individual and collective signifier, imbuing it with material, concrete representations that must be met to both self-identify with the group and be recognized as a group member (Fariña, 2018). Ideologies, therefore, produce particular social categories and structures that shape the individuals in that society; these sociocognitive categories are at the same time maintained through individual, early, affective attachment processes, connected to the psychological and cognitive formation of individual and collective identities (see chapter two's discussion on banal nationalism and identity formation).

European, ethno-geopolitical nationalism sought to construct the collective and individual meaning of belonging, through mythical constructions of peoplehood; individuals who identified with their specific nation-states' constructions derived a means of social belonging, and were also inextricably linked to these mythical, national identities at a psychological and affective level (Fariña, 2018; Renan, 1882; Wodak, 2017). The post–World War I intra- and inter-nation-state tensions and nationalism's failure to provide sociopolitical and economic stability created the ideal conditions for fascist movements to emerge. By preying on people's identity-based fears and emotions, fascist leaders, promising the emancipation and regeneration of *the true people*, mobilized the masses against an internal, invented enemy (Eco, 2013; Fariña, 2018; Volkan, 2013, 2018, 2020). Fascism offered simple solutions to complex socioeconomic and identity-based tensions. The cost of this mass mobilization, and of the sacralization of the political into the figure of the totalitarian, omniscient, fascist leader, produced large-scale decay and dehumanization rather than growth and regeneration; having destroyed the democratic structures that legitimized liberal democracies and the existence of the nation-state under Rousseauian principles, fascism created chaos and violence for the sake of violence.

Although the end of World War II brought fascism as a political regime to a total collapse, it did not eradicate the social and psychological dynamics ethno-geopolitical nationalism and fascism had produced. These individual and large-group identity-based processes needed to find expression by means of a new and more acceptable political and psychological phenomenon— populism. Populism provided a much-needed sociopolitical and psychological compromise; it repudiated totalitarianism and sought to operate within the democratic structures of liberal societies while also adhering to fascist tenets whereby *the true people* of the nation-state needed to be protected from a threatening internal enemy—the establishment. In other words, by drawing from fascism, and as a post-fascist answer to the ravages of World War II, populism offered a needed individual and collective psychological continuity to *the true people* of the nation-state. Populism's malleability and reliance on other established political ideologies enabled identity-based nationalism and its most extreme outgrowth of the 1900s, fascism, to continue to operate in the democratic political sphere of European nation-states without inducing the annihilatory and existential fears linked to fascism and the pre-1945 war period. As Finchelstein (2017) states and as previously discussed, European populism is therefore best defined as a post-1945 "form of authoritarian democracy" that remains ambivalently positioned between its fascist origins and within and against liberal democracy, given its protofascist nature.

In the United States, the ethno-geopolitical nationalist wars that had pervaded European nation-states and that culminated in the rise of fascism and World War II had already been fought and won by American nativism and the KKK in the post–Civil War era and between World War I and 1927. American nativism, just like its counterpart across the Atlantic, European ethno-geopolitical nationalism, constructed the identity of the *native* American. The mythical nature of this historicized identity provided a mechanism for defining who *the true people* of the United States were, while concurrently legitimizing colonization, the forced assimilation and extermination of Indigenous peoples, slavery, immigration control, and the creation of a nation-state that *native* Americans could call their own.

As discussed in chapter four, American nativism, aided by the KKK, made political fascism unnecessary in the United States—the KKK had already operated as a fascist movement long before the rise of fascism in Europe (Paxton, 2004). The post-1945 American society, just like many European societies, overtly rejected the terror inflicted by the KKK and European fascism while also equally opposing governmental efforts to expand the rights of historically subjugated racial, ethnic, and religious groups in the United States. The KKK, along with other white power movements, began to capitalize on this opposition during the Civil Rights era and thereafter, positioning themselves as the only viable alternative to liberal democracy—white *native* Americans needed to unite against a political establishment that no longer protected them, their identity, or their nation-state. The growing mistrust in the government and in its commitment to protect the interests of the *true people* of the United States, especially after the Vietnam War, created the ideal conditions for both the rise of contemporary American white power movements and nativist-populism. Post-1945 American populism, therefore, is best conceptualized as an outgrowth of both nativism and the fascist movement that ensured its supremacy, the KKK. As such, post-1945 American populism, like its European counterpart, is a protofascist political phenomenon that operates ambivalently within the democratic system it aims to overturn.

By examining Trumpism—American nativist-populism's most contemporary iteration—through this lens, Trumpism emerges as a familiar historical, sociopolitical, and identity-driven phenomenon rather than as an isolated contemporary phenomenon, spearheaded by an opportunistic leader without any ideological foundation. Like American nativism and the KKK during the post–Civil War period and between World War I and 1927, Trumpism fostered sociopolitical chaos and racially motivated lawless aggression against internal racial, ethnic, and religious groups that have historically been oppressed. As during the post–Civil War era, white power groups and movements came to the forefront to "protect" *the true people* of the United States from the corrupt political establishment, to ensure the primacy and dominance of the American nativist ideals. Consistent with populism, Donald Trump positioned himself as a Washington outsider, ready to take on the *corrupt political establishment*, to "make America great again." Most importantly, when it became clear that the democratic process would not allow President Trump to remain in power, Donald Trump, as the omniscient populist leader, rallied the masses to storm the Capitol, effectively using violence to try to overturn the election's outcome. In doing so, Donald Trump ceased to act within the democratic structure, transforming himself from an autocratic, nativist-populist leader to a fascist one (Paxton, 2021). Although President Trump's efforts ultimately failed, it is important to think of the January 6, 2021, insurrection as a warning, and not as a singular event tied to a particular leader. A large segment of the American society no longer trusts liberal democracy or the government's commitment to protect *the true people* of the United States—the white *native* American—and their nation-state.

The growing social and economic inequality caused by capitalism and neoliberalism, and their global effects, including armed conflict, poverty, and climate change, are affecting millions across the globe. The increasing sociopolitical and economic instability is forcing millions to migrate internally from rural to urban communities, and ultimately pushing many to abandon their home countries. The resulting humanitarian crisis has been a growing problem across Europe and the United States, fueling growing existential identity-based fears, internal sociopolitical instability and ultimately growing mistrust in liberal democracy and existing governments. Contemporary European nationalist-populism and American nativist-populism are seizing the opportunity provided by increasing discontent and identity-based fears to buttress their own political growth, offering simple "othering" solutions that obscure and augment the violent effects of globalization and neoliberalism (Brown, 2019). For nationalist or nativist populists, it is the "racial, ethnic, religious other" that is the problem; if this other can be controlled or expelled, *the true people* of the nation-state and their nation will be restored to their original condition, to thrive once again (Waltman, 2014; Waltman & Haas, 2011; Wodak, 2017).

PART II

Construction and Sociopolitical Mobilization of Large-Group Identities: The Integrated Sociopolitical and Psychological Analysis Model

Chapter Six

Mobilization of Large-Group Identities

The Case of the Identitarian Movement

In 2012, the French Generation of National Identity, or Génération Identitaire, incited white French youth, as well as other white European youth, to unite in armed warfare against their established governments through the YouTube video *Declaration of War* (Speit, 2018). As the video transcript illustrates, the affective evocative rhetoric deployed in the video left no doubt as to the alleged plight of the *true young French people*, or as to who could never belong to the French nation-state.

We are Génération Identitaire

We are the generation who got killed for glancing at the wrong person, for refusing someone a cigarette, or having an "attitude" that annoys someone.

We are the generation of ethnic fracture, total failure of coexistence, and forced mixing of races.

We are the generation doubly punished: condemned to pay into a social system so generous with strangers it becomes unsustainable for our own people.

Our generation are the victims of the May `68'ers who wanted to liberate themselves from tradition, from knowledge and authority in education.

We reject your history books to re-gather our memories.

We no longer believe that "Khader" could ever be our brother.

We have stopped believing in a "Global Village" and the "Family of Man."

We discovered that we have roots, ancestry and therefore a future.

Our heritage is our land, our blood, our identity. We are the heirs to our own future.

The Lambada, painted on proud Spartans' shields, is our symbol.

Don't you understand what this means? We will not back down, we will not give in.

We are sick and tired of your cowardice. You are from the years of post-war prosperity, retirement benefits, S.O.S racism and "diversity," sexual liberation and a bag of rice from Bernard Kouchner.

We are 25 percent unemployment, social debt, multicultural collapse and an explosion of anti-white racism. We are broken families, and young French soldiers dying in Afghanistan.

You won't buy us with a condescending look, a state-paid job of misery and a pat on the shoulder, We don't need your policies. Youth IS our policy.

Don't think this is simply a manifesto. It is a declaration of war.

You are yesterday, we are of tomorrow.

We are Génération Identitaire.

(Génération Identitaire, 2012)

Words matter; how they are used, their purpose, and who uses them is as central to individual and large-group identity construction processes as it is to sociopolitical large-group identity-driven mobilization processes. Words construct intentional, individual, and group representations—motivated representations (hooks, 1997). Over time, these socially constructed, motivated representations can be invoked by a leader, political party or movement to propel individuals and groups into action. The nature, direction, and effects of these motivated representations and of the mobilizations they fuel, will depend on the ideology and aim of those who invoke and incite them (Waltman & Hass, 2011).

The Génération Identitaire's "Declaration of War" leaves neither its ideology or aim ambiguous—to produce annihilating fear among white French youth and xenophobia-driven outrage resulting in armed conflict. With their manifesto, Génération Identitaire led French white youth to an inescapable conclusion: to avert the impending destruction of their identity and peoplehood, European white youth needed to unite in arms against both the national and supranational governmental establishment and their racial and ethnic, social pluralist politics (Speit, 2018).

Génération Identitaire, founded in France in 2012, is part of the larger European Identitarian Movement (IM) that started in 2002–2003 under the leadership of Fabrice Robert, Guillaume Luyt, and Philippe Vardon. The Identitarian Movement replaced the far-right group Unité Radicale after its forced dissolution following a failed assassination attempt on President Jacques Chirac that was later tied to a member of the Unité Radicale (Jacquet-Vaillant, 2021; Šima, 2021; Speit, 2018). Since the Identitarian Movement's inception, numerous organizations connected to this movement have emerged in France and across Europe, such as the Bloc Identitaire (BI) and Les Identitaires (LI), which replaced the Bloc Identitaire in 2016, as well as youth organizations such as Génération Identitaire (GI), Les Jeunesses Identitaires (JI), and Une Autre Jeunesse (UAJ) (Jacquet-Vaillant, 2021; Speit, 2018).

Since 2012, Génération Identitaire (GI) has spread across Europe, with national chapters in twelve European countries, such as in Austria—the Identitäre Bewegun Österreich (IBÖ); Germany—the Identitäre Bewegung Deutschland (IBD); Italy—Generazione Identitaria (Gi-IT); the Czech Republic—Generace Identity (GI-CZ); Hungary—Identitás Generáció (GI-HU); the United Kingdom and Ireland—Generation Identity (GI-UK); Slovenia—Generacija Identitete (GI-SL); Denmark (GI-DK); and, Russia—(GI-RU) (Jacquet-Vaillant, 2021; Nissen, 2020). As of 2016, a new chapter also emerged in the United States—Identity Evropa/American Identity Movement (IE). The Identity Evropa Movement, implicated in the 2017 Unite the Right Rally in Charlottesville, was founded by Nathan Damigo, an Iraq War veteran who argues, in a manner similar to that of the leaders of the European Generation Identitarian movement, that "America was founded as a white country—as a country for people of European heritage" (Southern Poverty Law Center, n.d.). What is most concerning is that in the United States the Identity Evropa is

> at the forefront of the racist "alt-right's" effort to recruit white, college-aged men and transform them into the fashionable new face of white nationalism. Rather than denigrating people of color, the campus-based organization focuses on raising white racial consciousness, building community based on shared racial identity and intellectualizing white supremacist ideology (Southern Poverty Law Center, n.d.).

While each Generation Identitarian chapter operates as an autonomous unit that seeks to preserve its specific, historicized, *true people*'s national identity, they are all united by a pan-European supranational identity rooted in the belief that Europe, as well as the United States in the case of Identity Evropa, belongs to *the peoples* of Europe, who share a common past and values. To this aim, the Generation Identitarian advocates for an anti-immigration politics of remigration—forced repatriation of recent and former immigrants to their birth countries—that oftentimes includes the closing of national borders and/or restrictive immigration control (Jacquet-Vaillant, 2021; Nissen, 2020; Šima, 2021; Speit, 2018). This shared trans-European Identitarian and pan-ethnic connection is reinforced through strategies common to other contemporary transnational and transcontinental, white power movements, such as "joint transnational events, including European campaigns . . . demonstrations, [and] the annual Summer University in France (with European participation since 2014)" (Nissen 2020, p. 86; see chapter four).

The Generation Identitarian formal membership, including online followers across Europe, is estimated to be in the tens of thousands. In fact, an investigation into the online presence of these chapters, including individual member and nonmember account activities, underscores the movements' wide influence and reach (Rafael, 2018). For example, according to the Global Project Against Hate and Extremism (GPAHE), in the early 2020s, Generation Identitarian had sixty-seven Twitter accounts belonging to chapters in "14 countries with nearly 140,000 followers." When individual accounts were included, such as those belonging to "GI's unofficial leader . . . of the Austrian chapter Martin Sellner (who has nearly 40,000 followers on Twitter and 69,000 subscribers on YouTube) or accounts for GI-coordinated activity, like Defend Europe, which has 27,000 followers . . . GPAHE found another 400,000 followers of 25 such accounts" (Beirich & Via n.d., p. 9). As these figures illustrate, the Generation Identitarian has been largely successful in recruiting white youth across Europe and the United States and owes much of its success to the redeployment of identity politics (Rafael, 2018; Wodak, 2021).

IDENTITY POLITICS

Identity politics, a term extensively studied since it was first used in the 1970s by Barbara Smith, a black radical feminist academic and activist, refers to "a wide range of political activity and theorizing" used by groups, historically subjugated on the basis of their social identity(ies), to dismantle structural oppression and achieve social equity and equality (see Clifford, 2000; Kaplan, 2012; Heyes, 2020; Noury & Roland, 2021). Paradoxically, and contrary to its roots, identity politics is once again at center stage but as a tool for the reassertion of dominant identities and the buttressing of their sociopolitical dominance over the subjugated groups from which identity politics originated. While chapter six will examine these identity construction processes, it is important to highlight two central dynamics, those of appropriation and recontextualization (Wodak, 2021). By first appropriating and then recontextualizing subjugated identity discourses and identity-based political strategies, groups such as the Generation Identitarian have aptly transformed their diverse, dominant, white pan-European identity into a subjugated, homogenous, oppressed, and threatened identity. By reconceptualizing this identity as "threatened," efforts undertaken to protect it from its external "enemy" other—the darker, brown, black, Muslim, Jewish, foreign, others—are not only legitimate but urgently needed for its survival.

To further strengthen their claims and large-group mobilization strategy, history also needs to be decontextualized and revised (Speit, 2018; Wodak, 2021). That is, history is used in an atemporal manner where the present and future are fused with a recontextualized, historicized, national, mythical past that is brought to life not only through public and social media discourses but also through symbolic representations, as in the Greek letter lambda—symbol of the Generation Identitarian (Wodak, 2021). As Šima states in *From Identity Politics to the Identitarian Movement* (2021), the lambda was "a symbol the Spartan army painted on its shields. [However] This image . . . does not come from historical sources, but from *300*, a popular comic book adapted into a Hollywood movie in 2006" (p. 79); the symbol now represents the Identitarian "modern-day 'Reconquista'" (Šima 2021, p. 80). Through this process of appropriation, recontextualization, and historical decontextualization and revisionism, the Generation Identitarian, under the slogan "Defend Europe," for example, has persuaded thousands of young people across Europe and the United States to rally against immigrants and their national and supranational governmental bodies, inciting violence that in some instances has led to terrorism; this violence has gradually weakened their ability to operate legally and openly (Al Jazeera, 2018)

DISCOURSE: THE RADICALIZATION OF THE SOCIAL AND THE POLITICAL

On March 3, 2021, the French government banned Génération Identitaire, declaring it a hate organization that incited violence. The ban came after members of Génération Identitaire were implicated in a number of assaults against immigrants, many of Middle Eastern descent, and also linked to the March 15, 2019, Christchurch terrorist attack in New Zealand. The perpetrator of the attack, Brenton Tarrant, a twenty-eight-year-old white Australian man, opened fire at the Christchurch Al Noor Mosque and the Linwood Islamic Center, killing fifty-one people and injuring many more. Prior to the attack, Tarrant had made donations to Génération Identitaire in France and the Austrian Identitaren Bewegung, IBÖ (Camus, 2021; Besser, 2019). The ban only affects Génération Identitaire, which is the youth wing of Les Identitaires—formerly known as the Bloc Identitaires—which continues to legally exist. In Austria, the lambda symbol and its yellow and black colors were subsequently banned in August 2021, after the Reform of Symbols Act came into effect, which was part of the anti-terror legislation passed in July 2021.

Although the French and Austrian bans aim to control and eradicate the activities of the Identitarians and other white power movements, these efforts often compound the problem by driving many of these groups and their followers underground, making it more difficult to monitor their activities and avert future potential violence. In fact, during the months following the Lambda ban in Austria, the number of new disguised social media profiles linked to IBÖ increased. For example, in Baden-Württemberg, IBÖ began to operate on Instagram, using the "kessel_revolte," "festung.ulm2.0" and "aktiv.konstanz" profiles, while also abandoning monitored and regulated platforms such as Instagram in favor of Telegram—an unregulated, encrypted online platform that enables white power groups to network without content censorship (Baden-Württemberg Landesamt für Verassungsschutz, 2021). The German government, concerned over the increasing presence of white power movements on Telegram, has recently requested a comprehensive EU approach to restrict its operations in an effort to gain control over the spread of white power groups in Germany and accross Europe.

Not surprisingly, governmental bans also have the potential to embolden white power movements and their followers. Unintentionally, efforts to restrict groups such as Génération Identitaire oftentimes only reinforce their claims of governmental persecution and subjugation; this further legitimizes their efforts to defend their pan-European identity from the pluralistic govern-ments that *protect* the *ethnic, racial, religious other* at the expense of *the true people* of the nation. For example, in July 2021, IBÖ leader Martin Sellner released a video in response to the Austrian Reform Symbols Act, titled *The Silent Death of Democracy*, in which he described the ban as "totalitarian censorship," later encouraging Identitarian members and followers to redou-ble their determination to resist *the system* (Baden-Württemberg Landesamt für Verassungsschutz, 2021).

Although much attention is paid to how white power movements mobilize large social groups into xenophobic, Islamophobic, anti-Semitic, and antigov-ernment activities and violence, less attention is paid to how they influence other aspects of civil society, such as public opinion, political platforms, and ultimately policy decisions. While white power identity constructions are often conceptualized as belonging to the radical social realm, only informing marginalized social narratives, their ability to become naturalized, common-sense facts that gradually reshape mainstream discourses is often understated (Billig, 1995; Wodak, 2021). Yet, once normalized, these white power identity constructions can reshape preexisting sociocognitive understandings of *who the true people* of a nation-state really are, shifting public opinion toward more conservative political ideologies and platforms. Ultimately, these dynamics lead to extreme sociopolitical polarization.

While traditional conservative parties gradually move further to the right, and nationalist, nativist and populist parties regain formerly lost popular support, traditional left-leaning parties either adopt a more liberal platform in an attempt to counterbalance and oppose the more extreme political right, or, without doing so, appear even more liberal in the face of more extreme right, conservative platforms. As the social and political discourses of everyday life gradually shift, the people's performance of their national identity, and its associated symbols also shifts, redefining and seeking to realign the nature of the nation-state with that of its people. These dynamics are consistent with banal nationalism and social constructivist understandings of the nation and national identity, whereas national identities are understood as both habitually performed and "discursively produced, reproduced, transformed and destructed by means of language" (Billig, 1995; Wodak, 2021, p. 98).

For example, whereas early Identitarian claims that sought to recontextual-ize European national identities as subjugated and threatened by a politics of cultural pluralism were not widely accepted in France, Germany, and Austria, they now form part of everyday discourse in more or less subtle ways. This shift began in 2008, when the number of North African and Middle Eastern undocumented immigrants, refugees, and asylum seekers arriving in Europe began to increase. By 2015, this humanitarian refugee crisis began to over-whelm the social infrastructure of various European nation-states, fueling anti-immigrant and Islamophobic sentiment within these societies (Quinn, 2016). While some of this sentiment was related to terrorist activity carried out by radical Islamic groups in Europe and the United States, the increasing influx of *foreign* others, together with the governments' failed responses to the humanitarian crisis, began to legitimize the Indetitarian rhetoric.

As concern grew among a larger segment of the French, German, and Austrian societies, Identitarian claims that constructed the pan-European citizens as a threatened and subjugated community increasingly resonated with many, becoming commonly accepted facts, difficult to disconfirm. Nationalist and populist parties that had previously struggled to appeal to the contemporary masses in these three countries, sharing similar, although sometimes less radical, political convictions to those of the Identitarian movement, seized the opportunity to capitalize on the public discontent. To this aim, and seeking to increase their electoral appeal, conservative as well as nationalist and right-wing populist parties started to integrate Identitarian discourses into their political platforms; some even formed alliances with members of the Indentitarian movement, such as the Freiheitliche Partei Österreich (FPÖ—Austria).

The connection between the Identitarian movement and established European political parties is not limited to the FPÖ; for example, Lega Nord (LN-Italy), Vlaams Belang (VB-Belgium), and Plataforma per Catalunya (PxC-Spain–now dissolved), have all been tied to the Bloc Identitaire (Jacquet-Vaillant, 2021). Likewise, investigations conducted into the Génération Identitaire by Al Jazeera's investigative unit (2021), revealed ties between the organization and the Rassemblement National party in France. Although formally denying this connection, Marine Le Pen, publicly condemned the Génération Identitaire's ban in France, along with "Conservative MEPs Nadine Morano and François-Xavier Bellamy, Frexiter MP Nicolas Dupont-Aignan, columnist and TV host Eric Zemmour and Souverainist philosopher Michel Onfray," as well as white supremacist Jared Taylor, the editor of *American Renaissance,* and Christelle Lechevalier and Sylvie Goddyn, members of the European Parliament (Camus, 2021; Al Jazeera, 2021). The ability of white power movements such as the Indentitarians to influence national and European Union political platforms, as well as the media, enables them to not only disseminate their rhetoric and identity constructions in a covert manner but also reach a far larger audience, who would otherwise reject and condemn these groups and their rhetoric.

Through this process of "common-sense" normalization and discourse radicalization, white power movements can progressively influence not only popular opinion and society at large but also the political life of the nation-state, gradually weakening and threatening liberal democracy and the nation-state they seek to protect. In fact, according to a study conducted in 2021 by the International Institute of Democratic Assistance, IDEA, "the number of countries moving in an authoritarian direction in 2020 outnumbered those going in a democratic direction" (p. 1). The United States and Poland were identified as two of the most concerning examples of this "democratic decline," where rising authoritarianism was, in large measure, popularly supported (IDEA, p. 1). Tactics such as disinformation campaigns, designed to cast doubt on mainstream journalism and on democracy itself, are often used to influence popular opinion and mobilize the masses. For example, in the United States, President Trump "promoted a general strategy termed the 'deconstruction of the administrative state,' by his chief strategist, Steven Bannon, [where] . . . problems [were] attributed to a 'deep state conspiracy promoted by the 'fake media,'" often labeled by President Trump as "the enemy of the people" (Center for Systemic Peace, 2021, p. 13). In fact, according to the 2020 POLITY scale, that "measures patterns of authority demonstrated and observed in political behaviors involving interaction events between and within state and non-state entities," the US score "dropped below the 'democracy threshold' (+6)" to that of an "anocracy (+5)" (Center for Systemic Peace, 2021). The last time the United States ranked within this range was between 1797 and 1800 (Walters, 2022).

Anocracy(ies), a term coined by Ted Robert Gurr in 1974, refers to "countries whose governments are neither fully democratic nor fully autocratic" (see Marshall & Gurr, 2005, p. 18; Walters, 2022). Barbara Walters, Rohr Professor of International Relations at the School of Global Policy and Strategy at the University of California, San Diego, and author of *How Civil Wars Start* (2022) identifies a strong correlation between anocracy and civil war, highlighting the role that social and political polarization, coupled with an erosion of democratic processes, poses to civil society and in particular to the United States. Walters (2022) attributes the polarization in the United States to identity politics, dating back to the Civil Rights Movement in the mid 1960s; polarization intensified in the 2000s, reaching new heights during the 2016 and 2020 elections.

It is important to highlight that the widening social and political polarization in the United States and Europe today breeds and reinforces existing social disappointment and mistrust in established governments. This discontent is again exploited by white power movements, nationalists, and nationalist or nativist-populist parties alike in a circular manner, creating "vicious circles of adversarial discourse," further eroding democracy itself (see chapter eight and Wachtel, 2006). To interrupt these cyclical, reinforcing, and polarizing social processes and their effects, scholars and political think tanks have identified strategies that could help "curb authoritarianism" and foster increasing trust in existing democratic governments. Some of these strategies include, recrafting social contracts that address "the gaps between what people require to meet their aspirations and what governments can currently provide," thereby realigning the Rousseauian social contract between the people and their nation-state's government; or, by rebuilding governmental, political, and media processes, to better "cope with the challenges of the century . . . [while] also . . . (re)building the mutual trust between citizens and their representatives"—all essential to liberal democracy (IDEA, 2021, p. 2).

These strategies not only seek to realign existing social contracts between the people of a nation-state and their government, but also seek to preserve the nation-state by realigning existing individual and group-identity-based sociocognitive schemas—patterned ways of thinking about oneself and the world—with those pertaining to the people of the nation, and their nation. Yet, identity and specifically national identity is not only a complex sociocognitive process, as posited by discourse-based theoretical approaches previously mentioned (see Wodak, 2021); identity formation also entails complex affective processes that link all members of a large group to each other and to the nation-state, as argued in chapter two. This process, briefly restated, begins early in life, largely out of awareness and is partially mediated in daily life, through language, cognition, and traditions—as posited in banal nationalism (Billig, 1995). However, identity formation also involves early, intense affective, psychological, developmental processes that are linked to the establishment of internal individual and large-group psychological boundaries or borders. These sociocognitive and affective processes cannot be fully explained through a solely historiographic or discursive approach, whether at the individual or large-group/collective level; instead, an integrated sociopolitical and psychological approach that incorporates and captures the centrality of affect in identity formation and large-group linking processes is needed (Fariña, 2018; Volkan, 2017).

Such an approach is essential to understanding contemporary identity-driven politics, including the rise of nationalism, nativism, populism, and white power groups in the United States and European nation-states alike. By understanding these dynamics, it becomes possible to identify new strategies that can effectively disrupt the transnational mass mobilization and radicalization of white Europeans and Americans, and its violent manifestations—particularly among youth.

THE INTEGRATED SOCIOPOLITICAL AND PSYCHOLOGICAL ANALYSIS MODEL, ISPA: IDENTITY AND COLLECTIVE MOBILIZATION

The integrated sociopolitical and psychological analysis model, ISPA, summarized here and expanded in chapters seven and eight, is a model informed by historiography, critical discourse historical analysis, and psychodynamic individual and collective identity-formation processes (Fariña, 2018; Volkan, 2018, 2020; Wodak, 2017b, 2020, 2021). The model emphasizes the centrality of identity formation processes to social problems and social policy, and seeks to identify and examine "the cognitive constructions, symbols, and affective social processes in which 'social problems' are embedded" (see Fariña, 2018, p. 2). The ISPA model begins with a sociopolitical analysis, where a historiographic and critical discourse historical approach are used to trace the historicity of a social issue. This approach exposes the discursive processes and underlying ideologies that, over time, have naturalized particular dominant social constructions.

The sociopolitical analysis first identifies the contemporary manifestations of the issue and its related, commonly accepted sociocognitive discursive schemas and master narratives; second, it links these schemas and master narratives to their historical and historicized roots; and it concludes by examining how long-standing social dynamics of dominance, oppression, and subjugation are reinforced and maintained or resisted and subverted (Wodak, Cilia, Reisigl, & Liebhart, 2009; Wodak, 2020, 2021). Ultimately, the analysis identifies the sociocognitive and discursive constructions that a society and its people use(d) to construct, maintain, and legitimize their sense of peoplehood and the nature of their nation-state—establishing individual and collective borders (Fariña, 2018; Volkan, 2013, 2017)

The sociopolitical analysis is followed by a psychological analysis, informed by psychodynamic political psychology. This second analysis examines the affective, psychological processes involved in the development of individual and large collective identities, and explains how individuals become affectively tied to their large, collective group(s) and to each other (Volkan, 2017, 2018, 2021). The psychological analysis illustrates the cyclical and reinforcing nature of individual and large, collective identity formation processes; and, makes explicit the unconscious, affective, collective processes that fuel individual and collective sociocognitive understandings of the self, whether individual and/or collective (Fariña, 2018). This conceptual framework also explains how unconscious, individual and group affective, identity formation processes produce the ideology(ies) that maintains individual and collective identities, and that also facilitate the ideology's unconscious internalization. Given this context, it becomes possible to understand identity-driven, political ideologies, not as mere products of shifting societal values and beliefs, "but rather as 'constitutive' to the dominant group's collective psyche and identity (Volkan, 2009, 2013, 2018)," and as such, they are central to the establishment of both individual and collective psychological borders and the nation-state (Fariña, 2018, p. 3).

The ISPA model concludes by integrating the central findings of the sociopolitical and psychological analyses. This integrated formulation connects contemporary, identity-driven sociopolitical dynamics to group-specific, historical, unprocessed, traumas that are related to the historical, psychological formation of individual and collective identity borders and nation-states (Fariña, 2018). This reconceptualization provides alternative mechanisms to disrupt the cyclical reproduction of long-standing sociopolitical, ideological dynamics of dominance and subjugation that, while dehumanizing both dominant and subjugated groups and perpetuating historical myths and collective traumas, hide the effects of neoliberal capitalism (Fariña, 2018; Wallerstein, Collins, Mann, Derluguian, & Calhoun, 2013; Wallerstein, 2018a, 2018b). The integrated formulation exposes and reframes contemporary, identity-driven sociopolitical platforms as both fueled and maintained by neoliberal capitalism, to ensure its ability to operate without constraints, while framing those affected by its violent effects as *the source of the problem.*

The ISPA model exposes how neoliberal capitalism has fostered global instability by increasing global inequality and poverty, which has further destabilized vulnerable economies and nation-states, augmenting political turmoil and civil unrest and weakening liberal democracies (Wallerstein, Collins, Mann, Derluguian, & Calhoun, 2013; Wallerstein, 2018a, 2018b). These national and international dynamics, which in their most extreme form have led to armed conflicts and war, coupled with the effects of global climate change due to an inability to regulate the toxic by-products of industrialization, have caused the forced mass displacement of millions arriving to the United States and Europe alike. As the demographic ethnic, racial, and religious composition of the United States and European nation-states alike changes, traditional dominant ethnic, racial, and religious groups in these nation-states fear an impending transformation of their individual and collective identity and that of their nation-state (Fariña, 2018). Nationalist, nativist, and populist parties, as well as previously marginalized white power movements, exploit these fears and discontent for their own political and ideological aims (Wodak, 2020, 2021).

Capitalizing on growing xenophobia, anti-Semitism, and Islamophobia, nationalist, nativist, and populist parties, along with white power movements, breed increasing radical, social, and political polarization that increases and legitimizes the social marginalization of internal historically marginalized ethnic, racial, and religious groups, while fostering increasingly restrictive anti-immigration policies (Barkhoff & Leerssen, 2021; Waltman & Hass, 2011; Waltman, 2014). The resulting identity-driven, sociopolitical polarization and chaos divert the dominant *people's* attention away from neoliberal capitalism and toward both the *ethnic, racial, religious other* and the people's established pluralistic governments, which are blamed for failing to control the ethnic, racial, and religious displaced other. The ISPA integrated formulation recenters global neoliberal capitalism as the problem, and reconceptualizes the *immigrant other* not as a threat to the integrity of a specific nation-state and its people but rather as a symptom of neoliberal capitalism and its violent global effects—poverty, climate change, armed conflict, and the forced, mass displacement of millions.

This reconceptualization provides a path forward by identifying new social policy remedies at the nation-state and international level that can disrupt the radicalization of identity-driven sociopolitical platforms, and the ongoing growth of transnational white power groups and movements. These new policy efforts, in line with the ISPA model (see chapters seven and eight), may for example, prioritize a politics of collective mourning, social healing and integration, while engaging in a long-needed critical analysis of neoliberal capitalism and its viability as a global hegemonic project (see chapter nine; Brown, 2019; Wallerstein, Collins, Mann, Derluguian, & Calhoun, 2013; Wallerstein, 2018a, 2018b).

Chapter Seven

Integrated Sociopolitical Analysis

Individual and Collective Identity Constructions

WHY WORDS MATTER: INTENTIONAL REPRESENTATIONS

During the 2006 elections, Geert Wilders, founder and leader of the Dutch Party for Freedom (PVV), secured seven seats in the Dutch parliament using a nationalist-populist, identity-based political platform. With his 2005 election manifesto and rhetoric such as:

> Our history compels us to fight a battle that is not an option but a necessity. After all, this is a battle for the . . . survival of the Netherlands as a recognizable nation; a country that is about to say goodbye to its ancient roots in exchange for multiculturalism, cultural relativism and a European super state, all under the leadership of a self-satisfied political elite that has long lost the plot. (Wilders, 2005)

Geert Wilders caught the attention of many and gained increasing popular support during the 2010 elections; in that year, PVV more than tripled its number of seats in the Dutch parliament, achieving a total of twenty-four seats. Although the party lost seven seats during the 2021 March elections, PVV remained as the third-largest political party in the Netherlands. Wilder's 2021 election manifesto reflects a nationalist-populist platform that also shares commonalities with the white power rhetoric of the Identitarian Movement (Muis & Immerzeel, 2017). For example, in the preface, Wilders first highlights the corruption of the national and supranational governmental elites, such as the EU, and their failed immigration-control policies, to then attribute the social problems of the Netherlands and its true people to

the immigrant *foreign* others—particularly to the North African and Middle
Eastern foreign others.

Wilders's historicized, nationalist-populist, xenophobic, and Islamophobic
political platform is clearly articulated throughout the manifesto and specifically, in the preface and Your Netherlands sections.

IT'S ABOUT YOU! ELECTION PROGRAM 2021–2025, PARTY FOR FREEDOM

PREFACE

Most political parties in this country have become interchangeable. They stand
for the same mass immigration, predilection for multiculturalism, self-loathing,
diversity bullshit, Islamization, and the EU. The different political parties may
have different names, but the taste is the same: saltless mediocrity. The PVV is
there for you. Our country has been paying a high price for this for years. Real
problems are not identified, let alone addressed. They prefer to persecute an
opposition leader and destroy our traditions. Fortunately, there is also another
Netherlands. I want to stand up for that! The Netherlands of you, of people with
a sense of reality. People who get nothing for nothing and want to work on a better future for their children and grandchildren after a heavy corona time. It takes
guts to make it all happen. People who don't want to become strangers in their
own country. But wanting to hold on to our traditions and freedoms. People who
know . . . that there is nothing more unwise than to give free rein to the Islamic
ideology that wants to take our freedom away. People with a backbone who long
for a strong, sovereign, social and proud Netherlands. (Wilders, 2021, pp. 4–5)

YOUR NETHERLANDS

The Netherlands has become an overpopulated country. Asylum seekers, family
migrants and other fortune seekers know exactly where to get residence permits,
houses and benefits. Our country has become a migrant paradise where even
illegal immigrants are still pampered.

This terrible bad . . . show is co-created by the EU, which cannot and does not
want to guard Europe's external borders. Moreover, due to the lack of internal
borders, migrants can effortlessly travel on to the Netherlands. Terrorists also
make use of these dangerous open borders. The Netherlands is paying far too
high a price for mass immigration and for political cowardice to stop it. Our welfare state and everything that our parents, grandparents, and ancestors have built
is being given away. The Netherlands has become an unrecognizable country.
Immigrant street terrorists, often Moroccans, terrorize the Dutch everywhere.

Established politics have imported masses of people who have nothing to do
with the Netherlands and even turn against our society. . . . That is the result of

bringing Islam to the Netherlands. Islam is first and foremost not a religion, but the most violent political ideology in existence.

It is unforgivable that the political elite of Europe and of the Netherlands have received this terrible Islam with open arms. All around us now the most horrific terrorist attacks are taking place; in our own country, the brutal murder of Theo van Gogh and the tram attack in Utrecht are examples of this.

It is high time to defend our freedom. To safeguard our culture, our way of life and our core values. Reversing the Islamization of our country is therefore the most important thing that must now be done in the Netherlands. It is an existential problem: the survival of a free Netherlands depends on the extent to which we manage to push back Islam.

In addition, a strong commitment to remigration is crucial. Criminals are deported (after withdrawal of their residence permit or, in the case of dual nationality, Dutch nationality). The right of residence of Syrians will also be revoked. In addition to forced remigration, voluntary remigration is promoted. Think of all those Dutch Muslims who find Islamic rules more important than Dutch laws. If you want to live according to the rules of Islam and Sharia, go to an Islamic country! The Netherlands is ours! (Wilders, 2021, pp. 7–8)

In these sections, the foreign, ethnic, racial, cultural, and religious *other* is described as a criminal, terrorist *other* who abuses and exploits the Dutch social welfare system. While corrupting and eroding the cultural traditions of the Netherlands, this *foreign other* threatens to change the demographic composition of the Dutch nation-state in an irreversible manner. Wilders leaves nothing to chance or interpretation, choosing his words carefully and in an evocative manner. As he constructs his argument, Wilders creates an intentional and motivated representation of the foreign *other* as a threat to both the people of the Netherlands and their nation-state (bell hooks, 1997). Unless the true people of the Netherlands join forces to defend their nation-state, it will be usurped by the foreign *other.*

Similar discursive, group mobilization efforts that construct the people of the nation-state as inherently good and hardworking and the foreign other as malign, criminal, and morally deviant in a polarizing and binary manner, are also found in other European and American mainstream political parties' platforms, such as in the Rassemblement National Party in France, the Freedom Party in Austria (FPÖ), the Alternative for Germany (AfD), VOX in Spain, and in former President Donald Trump's Republican party. As discussed in chapter two, in all these parties' political platforms, identity emerges as a construct that defines who the real members of a particular society are, delineating the collective territorial and sociocognitive psychological boundaries of the group. The *racial, ethnic, cultural or religious other*, whether immigrant, refugee, asylum seeker, or native born to immigrant parents, emerges as an entity that slowly establishes itself among the true people of a nation-state, eroding and eventually destroying the historized culture of the dominant group, thereby inevitably transforming the nation-state and its people (Fariña 2018). The political discourse of these identity-driven party platforms instead of constructing the *racial, ethnic, cultural, and religious other* as a minority within the nation-state depicts it as an emerging majority; if allowed to increase, the *foreign other* will gradually relegate the *true people* of the nation-state to a minority status within their own nation-state.

This anticipated and feared loss of ethno-racial-cultural-religious critical mass representation and status brings with it reverberations of the European post–World War I and pre–World War II period, where nationalism sought to achieve the ethno-racial-cultural-linguistic homogenization of nation-states through the oppression of internal ethnic minorities (Gellner, 2006; Leerssen, 2006; Zimmer, 2013). As such, these new modern-day identity-driven fears activate old, historical European collective wounds that are held largely out of conscious awareness; these wounds link a distant historical past of violent intra and inter-ethno-racial-cultural conflict that culminated in World War II, to present-day identity-driven sociopolitical dynamics and debates in many European nation-states and in the United States.

In fact, Geert Wilders's policy approach to the problem of the undesirable foreign *other* in the Netherlands supports this historical connection; for example, in the 2021 election manifesto, Wilders proposes to restore the surveillance of the Dutch border, while returning its control to the Netherlands (p. 9). He then argues for a reduction of immigration to control overpopulation, while ending migration from Islamic countries and terminating all asylum policies, including the closure of asylum resettlement centers in the Netherlands. He concludes by advocating for a politics of forced and *voluntary* remigration, and the establishment of a new Ministry of Immigration, Remigration and De-Islamization (p. 9). Wilders's politics combine nationalist-populist ideals, with an authoritarianism that closely resembles pre–World War II, European authoritarian nationalism. This shared similarity links Wilders's politics to an often forgotten and repressed protofascist past that eventually culminated with the rise of European fascism. This similarity, far from coincidental, highlights why politicians and political parties such as Geert Wilders and the PVV pose a threat to liberal democracy in the Netherlands and across Europe.

HISTORIOGRAPHY AND
CRITICAL DISCOURSE HISTORICAL ANALYSIS

Contemporary, identity-driven social dynamics and political platforms, such as the ones reflected in the Dutch Party for Freedom, PVV, have a long and complex history that is often omitted and even kept out of conscious awareness during sociopolitical discussions (Fariña, 2018; Volkan, 2020). While the past is invoked, it is often romanticized and brought into the present day through the utterance and performance of everyday, national master narratives (Billig, 1995; Seeliger & Villa Braslavsky, 2022). These narratives are particularly powerful, as they produce a set of individual and collective, organizing sociocognitive schemas that "have a long history and draw on culturally constructed, but highly influential historical myths, cultural memories and identities, [as well as on] stereotypes of national characteristics" (Barkhoff & Leerssen, 2021, p. 2).

Historiography

The ISPA, integrated sociopolitical analysis, recognizing the centrality of history "in shaping national master narratives," as well as specific internal/ external sociocognitive understandings of a people's nation and collective identity, integrates a needed historiographic and critical discourse historical analysis approach to the analysis of identity and identity-driven sociopolitical movements (Berger, 2021, p. 19). This integrated approach, as demonstrated throughout previous chapters, and in the case of Geert Wilders and the PVV party, identifies and historically contextualizes complex, contemporary identity-based master narratives to explain their internal and external psychological, social, and political effects.

It is important to highlight that identity-based master narratives can unite and strengthen a people while concurrently oppressing another—which ultimately can destroy both groups. For example, while nationalist, nativist and populist, identity-based master narratives have united various large groups as a people, creating a sense of belonging through the sociocognitive construction of national identities and nation-states, they have also fueled long-standing, inter- and intra-social divisions. These divisions are not only problematic in that they gradually fracture a nation's sociopolitical and economic way of life, but also because they foster and legitimize the oppression and subjugation of internal and external ethno-racial, cultural, linguistic, and religious minorities. At their worst, these divisions have led to violent social unrest, terrorism, war, and genocide (see chapters two, five, and six).

In fact, national, identity-based master narratives, as the integrated socio-political analyses of European nationalism and American nativism showed (see chapters two and three), are dangerous precisely because of their ability to construct and fix as real and stable specific sociocognitive, mythical large-group identities (Berger, 2021, p. 19; Gellner, 2006; Leerssen, 2006; Zimmer, 2013). Yet, history is far from objective, and neither were the historians and academics that played a central role in the creation of nationalist, nativist and populist, identity-based, master narratives between 1850 and 1950 (Berger, 2021, p. 19; Wodak, 2021). As such, their writings produced and reproduced the dominant sociopolitical ideologies and prejudices of their time, while legitimizing the identity-driven, sociopolitical master narratives they were constructing (Berger, 2021; Fariña, 2018; Wodak, 2021).

Over time, the ongoing dissemination of these historical texts led to the unquestioned acceptance of the ethno-racial, cultural, linguistic, and religious identities they promulgated, becoming social facts that didn't need to be further examined (see chapters two, three, and five). However, it is not possible to contextualize contemporary identity-driven political movements and social dynamics without first denaturalizing these historized identity constructions. Critical discourse historical analysis provides a systematic conceptual framework whereby historical national-identity master narratives can be deconstructed to expose their historicized and ideological origins, as well as the sociopolitical dynamics that led to their enthronement. Recognizing its usefulness, the integrated sociopolitical analysis incorporates a critical discourse historical analysis approach to further contextualize and denaturalize identity-driven sociopolitical parties and movements while exposing their binary and socially divisive discourses.

Critical Discourse Historical Analysis: Us Versus Them

Critical discourse historical analysis, CDHA, is a systematic, interdisciplinary, approach to critical discourse analysis that examines discursive construction processes and social power dynamics from a historical, political, sociological and psychological perspective (Fariña, 2018; Wodak, 2017a, 2017b, 2020, 2021). As such, CDHA seeks to expose the social discursive processes and power dynamics that produce, maintain, reinforce, or subvert long-standing social inequities—such as social exclusion, marginalization, dominance, and subjugation (Wodak, 2021). As Wodak (2021) states, CDHA "provides a vehicle for looking at latent power dynamics . . . because it integrates and triangulates knowledge about historical, intertextual sources and the background of the social and political fields within which discursive events are embedded" (p. 102).

Critical discourse analysis approaches, such as CDHA, define discourse as "a system of statements" that both produces and legitimizes the object it has constructed (Fariña, 2018; Parker, 1992, p. 5). For example, during the Romantic period, European nationalism used literature to create and legitimize the collective, national identities it was constructing (see chapter two). Its literary national-cultural consciousness-raising efforts ensured the dissemination of nationalist ideals as well as the intergenerational transmission of the national identities it had created; over time, the everyday performance of these identities naturalized their existence as common-sense facts that required no further examination—such as the Dutch and French national identities invoked by Geert Wilders and Marine Le Pen (Billig, 1995; Fariña, 2018; Wodak, 2017a, 2017b, 2020, 2021). These sociocognitive constructions of national identity continue to influence contemporary sociopolitical discourses in Europe and the United States, where nationalist, nativist, and populist parties, such as the Rassemblement National Party in France, the Freedom Party (FPÖ) in Austria, and the Party for Freedom (PVV) in the Netherlands, have been sponsoring a politics of national-identity preservation, immigration control and in some cases, forced remigration to gain increasing popular support. This strategy has been successful in large measure, and has increased the appeal of transnational white power groups, such as the Identitarian Movement, who accuse their local and supranational governments of engaging in a politics of multiculturalism and white genocide (see chapters four and six). This summarized integrated sociopolitical analysis highlights the relevance of a critical discourse historical approach to contemporary identity-driven, transnational social political dynamics (see chapters two, three, five, and six).

CDHA: Strategies, Assumptions, and Binary Constructions

The integrated sociopolitical analysis also incorporates some critical discourse historical analysis "discursive macro-strategies," central to the study of identity-driven sociopolitical dynamics and parties (Reisigl & Wodak, 2001, p. 43). These discursive macro-strategies are either constructive, preservative, transformative or destructive in nature and scope. Constructive strategies are used in discursive processes that develop and define a group's identity, whereas preservative strategies serve to discursively maintain a group's identity as real and fixed. On the other hand, transformative strategies are used to gradually transform a group's identity and can be accompanied by destructive discursive strategies to dismantle a group's contemporary identity (Fariña, 2018, p. 17). The integrated sociopolitical analyses of nationalism, nativism, and populism in chapters two, three, and five clearly show the power of constructive and preservative discursive macro-strategies in maintaining and mobilizing a people to defend their national identity and nation-state at any cost—whether through restrictive immigration control policies or violent armed conflict and terrorism.

The integrated sociopolitical analysis also incorporates four assumptions central to critical discourse historical analysis and individual and collective identities; these assumptions argue that:

1. Identities are always context dependent (Wodak, 2021).
2. Identity constructions are always binary. That is, they define a group by what the group is not, and in direct opposition to another group's identity. Binary identity constructions, therefore, create dichotomous, exclusionary, sociocognitive, identity patterns and borders—*us* versus *them*; *native versus foreign*; *good versus evil* (Fariña, 2018; Volkan, 1988; Wodak, 2021).
3. Identities, whether individual or collective, are produced and reproduced through discursive practices and everyday performance (see chapter two; Billig, 1995; Wodak, 2021).
4. Identity-driven contemporary political parties have been gradually influenced by the rhetoric of white power movements. Incorporating some of this rhetoric into their sociopolitical platforms, nationalist, nativist, and populist parties have progressively normalized radical, exclusionary, binary identity constructions and have gained popular support for increasingly exclusionary policy measures that would have otherwise been widely rejected due to their radical and subjugating nature. These dynamics have led to the radicalization and polarization of everyday sociopolitical discourses and political parties (see chapter six; Wodak, 2021).

The radicalization and social polarization of everyday discourse and political parties and the role of white power movements in this process became clearly visible in the integrated sociopolitical analysis of the Identitarian Movement (IM). The analysis showed that political parties such as the Freiheitliche Partei Österreich (FPÖ–Austria), Lega Nord (LN-Italy), and Le Rassemblement National party (RN-France), had not only incorporated the Identitarian Movement's white genocide rhetoric into their political platforms, but were also closely linked to the Identitarian Movement (see chapter six).

Lastly, the integrated sociopolitical analysis also incorporates two additional concepts from critical discourse historical analysis, *intertextuality and recontextualization,* to examine identity-driven sociopolitical dynamics and political movements. Intertextuality is a text linking process, where texts are linked "to other texts, both in the past and in the present" (Wodak, 2021, p. 103); whereas recontextualization refers to discursive processes where "an argument, a topic, a genre, or a discursive practice [is taken] out of context [de-contextualization] and [is restated] in a new context" acquiring a new meaning (Wodak, 2021, pp. 103–4). These two concepts were central to the integrated sociopolitical analysis of the Identitarian Movement and its white power rhetoric. Both concepts provided a mechanism to examine how the Identitarian Movement had appropriated subjugated discursive and identity politics' emancipatory processes to reconceptualize the dominant pan-European identity, as a threatened, subjugated, and oppressed identity.

Identity

While the integrated sociopolitical analysis incorporates a number of concepts derived from critical discourse historical analysis, it also differs from this approach in a fundamental manner. Whereas critical discourse historical analysis posits that identity is always discursively and habitually produced and reproduced, regarding identity as a largely sociocognitive process (Seeliger & Villa Braslavsky, 2022; Wodak, 2021); the integrated sociopolitical analysis model, accepts these core elements while arguing for a more complex, psychological-affective, conceptualization of identity (Fariña, 2018; Volkan, 2018, 2020).

From an integrated sociopolitical analysis perspective, identity is just as much a sociocognitive, discursive, habitual process as it is a deeply intrapsychic and affective one; in other words, although individuals and collective large groups do indeed "think about their identity, reproduc[ing] . . . and protect[ing] it . . . they also develop affective ties to its symbolic cultural representations" that forever link individual identities to those of their large group, in a mutually constitutive manner (see Farina, 2018, p. 40; Loewenberg, 1991, 1995; Volkan, 2013). Most importantly, as Ross (1992) states, "identity, including attachments to a group, begins to develop at the earliest stages of the life cycle and its intensity is crucial to explaining why people are willing to make great personal sacrifices in its name" (p. 22).

Recognizing the limits of a purely discursive, sociocognitive understanding of individual and collective identities, the integrated sociopolitical and psychological analysis model incorporates an integrated psychological analysis, informed by psychodynamic, political psychology to capture the complex dynamics involved in the formation of individual and collective identities (see chapter eight).

INTEGRATED SOCIOPOLITICAL ANALYSIS:
APPLICATION TO LARGE, COLLECTIVE IDENTITIES
FRANCE—LE RASSEMBLEMENT NATIONAL
(THE NATIONAL RALLY PARTY)

In 2011, Marine Le Pen took over the leadership of Le Front National (FN), replacing her father Jean-Marie Le Pen. Le Front National, founded in 1972, was spearheaded by the "revolutionary nationalism" ideology upheld by the young neofascist activists of the movement Ordre Nouveau (New Order) (Kauffman, 2016, p. 5). Much like the contemporary French Génération Identitaire, the Order Nouveau was a violent youth movement, symbolized by the Celtic cross, "hostile to the 'bourgeois order,' [and informed by] a few key ideas inspired by the German conservative revolution of the interwar period and the European fascist dictatorships: the defense of the West, a fear of mingling and of otherness, and the search for a 'third way' between communism and capitalism" (Kauffman, 2016, p. 5). Although Jean-Marie Le Pen's political convictions were more nationalist-conservative than those of the Order Nouveau, he was selected as president of Le Front National to bring political credibility to the party. Despite his more conservative political ideology, Jean-Marie Le Pen remained a controversial political figure throughout his tenure as president of Le Front National, due to his ties with former Third Reich sympathizers and collaborators such as Léon Gaultier—a member of the Milice who served in the Waffen-SS (Kauffman, 2016, p. 10).

Over the years, Le Pen's Front National party was defined by a far-right, nationalist, anti-Semitic, and xenophobic politics, as well as by a public image tarnished by some of its members' fascist pasts, such as Pierre Bousquet—treasurer and founding member of Le Front National and member of the SS-Waffen, Charlemagne Division (see Davies, 2010; Kauffmann, 2016). Since 2011, Marine Le Pen has worked to increase the party's popular appeal, trying to mainstream the party as a contemporary nationalist-populist party, rebranded as Le Rassemblement National. Marine Le Pen's efforts to distance the party from its fascist far-right roots proved successful; during the 2017 French presidential elections, Marine Le Pen and Emmanuel Macron were the two final presidential candidates. Emmanuel Macron won the French presidency, with 66 percent of the popular vote, defeating Marine Le Pen, who secured 57 percent of the votes (Politico, 2022). Emmanuel Macron and Marine Le Pen faced each other again during the 2022 presidential elections; President Emmanuel Macron obtained 27.8 percent of the popular vote during the first voting round, while Marine Le Pen obtained 23.2 percent. Ultimately, Emmanuel Macron won the 2022 elections with a significantly narrower margin than in 2017, obtaining 58.2 percent of the popular vote, while Le Pen obtained 41.5 percent—8.3 percent more votes than in 2017 (Politico, 2022).

Marine Le Pen's 2022 electoral program, Projet pour la France–Marine Le Pen, identified twenty-two policy measures designed to reshape the French nation-state according to her nationalist-populist ideals—a vision for France that was certainly compelling to many. Marine Le Pen's program begins by prioritizing immigration control, and calls for a referendum on immigration, to "ensure the protection of the French nationality and French identity" (Le Pen, 2022b, Immigration Control Project, p. 16). Her call to action is an urgent one; for Le Pen, France and the French people are at risk, and the constitution needs to be modified to better protect the nation-state and its people.

> Because the French people are the sovereigns, and the only sovereigns, the French people have the right to make the decisions they deem necessary to remain themselves. Remaining themselves requires taking energetic and unprecedented action, while immigration is out of control, and separatism is spreading in entire territories, and part of the political, media and cultural "elites" deny the French identity, the existence of a French culture and, henceforth, strive to rewrite history.

> Because the French nationality, French identity and the French heritage are being seriously threatened, they must be protected by the Constitution. Therefore, the laws that will be voted on and the decisions that will be taken by the courts will have to respect the pillars of our civilization. (Le Pen, 2022b, Immigration Control Project, p. 16)

Le Pen uses national identity, preservative discursive strategies throughout her call to action to provide the logic for the referendum and the immigration control policies she later presents; in fact, her preservative discourse both justifies and creates the need for the referendum and its policies. Le Pen refers to this referendum as the Citizens' Initiative Referendum, positioning herself as a candidate who will lead according to the people's will (see chapter five on populism). If elected, *the true people* of the French nation-state would finally have a voice, and the power to act on their own behalf and self-preservation. As the defender of the French people and nation, Le Pen pledges to protect the French identity and that of their nation-state from the forces of globalization and the multicultural elites,

> 1. Stop uncontrolled immigration by giving the say to the French people by referendum.

a. End settlement immigration and family reunification. Processing of asylum applications only while abroad.

b. Reserve social assistance for the French people, and conditional access after 5 work years in France and demonstration of solidarity.

c. Ensure national priority of access to social housing and employment. Cancel the residence permit for all foreigners who have not worked for a year in France.

d. Systematic expulsion of illegal, delinquent, and criminal foreigners.

e. Cancel the right of jus soli and limit access to nationality to naturalization based on merit and assimilation criteria. (Immigration Control Project, 2022b, p. 2)

Le Pen further supports her restrictive immigration control policies through a process of justification and legitimization based on historical, mythical, master narratives of racial degeneration and cultural national demise (see chapter two on nationalism). For example, in arguing for changes to the French constitution that oversee the naturalization process of immigrants, Le Pen states:

No condition is put on it, no love for the homeland needs to be shown. It is not acceptable to become French under these conditions. The acquisition of the French nationality is even acquired from birth for a child born in France to a foreign parent who was himself born in France. For a foreigner, acquiring French nationality must be a motivated choice. For France, giving nationality to a foreigner should only be possible if the person requesting it provides guarantees in terms of assimilation, mastery of the language, respect for our laws and our morals. (Immigration Control Project, 2022b, p. 16)

Here, Le Pen invokes Darwinian, pseudoscientific, historicized, ethno-racial, and nationalist principles to restrict French citizenship; for Le Pen, proof of French ancestry, jus sanguinis, takes primacy over birthright, jus soli, citizenship. Le Pen does provide some limited exceptions; a person may acquire French citizenship on ethno-cultural assimilation grounds, but only after meeting Le Pen's new, proposed assimilation standards—defined as tangible and objective. Consequently, Le Pen states:

The transmission of French nationality will only be . . . possible by heritage. Only people who have a French parent can be French. The acquisition of nationality through marriage will be ended. Naturalization will be governed by very strict conditions and must be the subject of a reasoned request from the interested parties. (Immigration Control Project, 2022b, pp. 16–17)

Le Pen does not explicitly articulate the *objective* criteria that would measure a person's degree of assimilation, although the ability to speak French is identified. It is only later in the Immigration Control Project that Le Pen explicitly names both language and religion as essential markers of French national identity, advocating for their protection and defense.

As Le Pen explains, "the referendum project will enable the defense of the French identity and its heritage" by modifying the French constitution (Immigration Control Project, 2022b, p. 18). These changes would assign to the Republic the responsibility of protecting the cultural-linguistic and historical integrity of the French nation-state, including its Christian religion (Immigration Control Project, 2022b, p. 18). Le Pen's rhetoric echoes Herderian linguistic, ethno-cultural principles, that emphasize the role of language in the transmission and construction of a people's national identity. Romantic nationalism's lasting influence in the shaping of contemporary, national, sociocognitive identity constructions is most palpable when Le Pen proposes banning the teaching of languages other than French. Here, Le Pen uses Romantic nationalism to legitimize her contemporary, nationalist-populist election platform and immigration control policies; in other words, Romantic nationalism provides the logic for the oppression of the *foreign other*, and for its normalization (see chapter two, Herder). As Le Pen states:

> This amendment to the Constitution will prevent the prohibition of the celebration of Christmas by installing nativity scenes or fir trees in the public places, will prevent the disfiguration of sites by installations such as wind turbines, will put an end to the teaching of native language and culture that hinders or prevents assimilation, will ensure that the 44,000 historic monuments and places of worship belonging to the communes or state will be properly maintained. (Immigration Control Project, 2022b, p. 18)

Le Pen's immigration control argumentation serves a dual function, as it also provides the justification for the Security Project, Le Pen's second policy priority, where she commits to "Eradicat[ing] the Islamist ideologies and all their networks from national territory" (Le Pen, 2022b, p. 2). By drawing on binary national-identity constructions that legitimize and normalize Islamophobia, Le Pen not only naturalizes Islamophobia but also further radicalizes and polarizes the contemporary French sociopolitical discourse. For example, when arguing for the eradication of *Islamist ideologies*, Le Pen states:

> The fight against Islamism and terrorism is not just a matter of security. . . . It is not only a fight for civilization to preserve our democratic regimes and the principles on which they are based, but also to better detect and hinder terrorist

projects by individuals or groups, present in our national territory or abroad. . . . Islamism exerts permanent pressure on mayors, school principals, principals of colleges . . . teachers, nursing staff, employers and more broadly attacks all those who oppose it. Marine Le Pen's bill will ban the practice, demonstration and public dissemination of Islamist ideology. . . . Islamism . . . [is] radical[ly] incompatib[le] with the rights, freedoms and principles recognized by the Constitution, in particular the dignity of the human person or the freedom of conscience and expression; the refusal to respect the secularism of the State, the democratic procedures, the institutions and to respect the primacy of the common law. (Security Project, 2022c, pp. 20–21).

Le Pen constructs the *true* French people as native to France, united by a Christian, ethno-racial-linguistic past, based on the principles of *volonté générale*; the Islamic other is everything that the French people are not—not Christian, anti-democratic, and ethno-racially and linguistically different. Through her preservative discourse, Le Pen reifies mythical, sociocognitive identity constructions that define what it means to be French, demarcating who belongs to the French people. These sociocognitive identity constructions and the master narratives they produce are central to the formation of individual and collective identities and provide psychological continuity for the individual and the group; as such, they can be effectively deployed to persuade a people to mobilize against a perceived or real threat. For example, in the case of France and Le Pen's electoral program, Le Pen first uses French identity-driven master narratives to remind the true people of France about their shared journey as a people—one that has expanded across time for thousands of years. She then uses the same master narratives to present her immigration control and security policies as essential to the protection of the French people and to their ability to persist as a people in the future.

Identity-driven master narratives are also directly related to the construction and maintenance of individual and collective psychological borders, and are central to contemporary identity-driven sociopolitical discourses that seek to mobilize a people, such as in the case of Marine Le Pen. Psychological borders are established through identity formation processes that are mediated by group-specific, sociocognitive constructions; these are the same constructions that produce the group's identity-driven master narratives and that in a hermeneutic manner ensure their dissemination and continuity. Over time, group-specific master narratives foster individual and collective psychological identifications and attachments that link individuals and their group to a shared, historicized past. These attachments in turn link individual identity-formation processes to those of the group, in an interdependent and mutually constitutive manner; that is, individual psychological attachments connect individuals to each other, and to their group, establishing individual and collective psychological borders that enable a people to differentiate what is *me* and *us* from what is *not me* and *them* (Fariña, 2018; Volkan, 2018). As such, psychological borders are essential to nationalist principles since they both legitimize the existence of a people as a group and provide the justification for their nation-state (see chapter two on nationalism).

Le Pen's political rhetoric and her commitment to eradicate the Islamic *other* from France are examples of the binary, collective, psychological, identity-border-construction processes just described, and of their implications—the progressive marginalization and dehumanization of the *racial, ethnic, religious other* within a society. In Le Pen's case, the immigrant *other* is not only other on ethno-racial, cultural, religious, and linguistic grounds, but is also constructed as lacking moral principles, prone to exploiting the social safety net built by *the true people* of France, violent, criminal, and a potential terrorist—a threat to the integrity of the French people. Consequently, the *true* people of the nation-state can only be imagined as moral, law-abiding, hardworking subjects, capable of controlling their violent and aggressive impulses. Le Pen's national-identity master narratives allow *the true French people* to clearly distinguish what is me and us from what is not me and them. Most importantly, binary constructions such as these allow the dominant group to achieve and maintain a sense of internal psychological coherence and historical continuity and provide the justification for the oppression of the *other*. For example, when Le Pen states, "When a foreigner residing on the national soil commits an offense or a crime, he does not show the Nation the attachment that one is entitled to expect of him." Le Pen not only emphasizes the importance of identification and attachment processes to and with the nation but also creates the legal logic for the deportation of the criminal and/ or undocumented foreign other (Security Project, 2022c, p. 18).

Marine Le Pen and the European Union: The Identity and Democracy Coalition

Marine Le Pen's 2022 presidential electoral platform is consistent with her earlier, 2019 European Union political platform, which won Le Rassemblement National twenty-three seats in the European parliament. The Renaissance Coalition, comprised of La République En Marche, the Mouvement Démocrate, Agir and the Mouvement Radical, Social et Libéral, was a close second, with twenty-two seats. Le Rassemblement National is part of the Identity and Democracy coalition, the fifth-largest political group in the European parliament, with a total of sixty-five seats. The Identity and Democracy coalition is a political group formed by ten nationalist-populist parties that include Le Rassemblement National, Lega party-Italy, and AfD-Germany, among others (see chapter two).

In *Pour une Europe des Nations*, Le Pen's 2019 European Union program, Le Pen criticized the European Union for its failure to uphold its most basic mandate, to protect the *true* people of Europe. Le Pen presented this failure as intentional, and driven by the European Union's commitment to the elites and their multicultural and capitalist sensibilities. Consistent with her nationalist-populist rhetoric, Le Pen attributes the increasing social chaos and lawlessness threatening the citizens of Europe to the gradual erosion of national, governmental sovereignty, especially in regard to border control/ enforcement and security. Le Pen uses binary, identity-driven, sociocognitive constructions to evoke and spread fear among the *true* people of France, to then position herself as the only candidate capable of protecting the French nation-state and its people from the European Union. Her identity-driven, large-group, preservative rhetoric and mobilizing strategy can be seen clearly when Le Pen constructs the European Union as Europe's enemy,

SAVE EUROPE FROM THE EUROPEAN UNION

The European Union fails in the first duty of a political entity, which is to ensure the security and even the tranquility of the citizens. Worse, every day, it increases the risks by irresponsible decisions . . . the installation in our territories of criminal gangs or Mafias from the East or the South, if not from Chechnya or Colombia, as well as the increase in attacks. . . . Violence and even ultra-violence are taking hold everywhere. . . . Even beyond crime and delinquency, never have so many increasingly oppressive threats weighed on the citizens of European countries: radical Islamism, like the chaos caused by the flooding of migrants, calls into question our ways of life, our traditions and even our values of civilization. Entire neighborhoods, towns, parts of departments are spaces "in secession," which have become not lawless zones since a law other than that of the Republic applies there, but "zones of non-France." (Rassemblement National, Pour une Europe des Nations, 2019, p. 13)

Le Pen is not the only contemporary nationalist-populist politician capitalizing on the effects of globalization and identity-driven nationalist, nativist, and populist rhetoric to reposition her party as the only solution to her nation's *impending* ethno-racial, cultural, religious and linguistic demise. Just like Marine Le Pen, Santiago Abascal Conde, leader of the Spanish nationalist-populist party VOX, has revived old nationalist attachments linked to a not-so-distant fascist past, to reposition his party as the only one capable of defending Spain and its true people from their impending demise. Under a Reconquista platform, Abascal campaigned in 2019 against the Spanish political establishment, the elites, and their politics of cultural pluralism and miscegenation. In his 2019 electoral platform, entitled La Reconquista, Abascal positioned himself as the protector of the rural working- and middle-class people, who, depicted as suffering and forgotten by the political elites, needed to take back their country (Rama, Cordero, & Zagórski, 2021; Turnbull-Dugarte, 2019; Turnbull-Dugarte, Rama, & Santana, 2020).

SPAIN—VOX

VOX was founded in 2013 as a result of an internal split within the Partido Popular (PP), the ruling conservative right-wing party between 2011 and 2018 (Rama, Zanotti, Trumbull-Dugarte, & Santana, 2021). Santiago Abascal, Jose Luis Ortega Lara, and Aleix Vidal-Quadras, all previously affiliated with the Partido Popular, formed the VOX party in response to the Spanish people's growing discontent with the Popular Party and its policies, positioning VOX as a party committed to preserving the integrity of the Spanish nation-state and its people's identity (Rama, Cordero, & Zagórski, 2021). In 2014, Santiago Abascal, the current party leader, replaced Aleix Vidal-Quadras, who led the party until September 2014. Consistent with nationalist-populist ideals, VOX describes itself as a party of and for the people that speaks for the silenced, everyday people of Spain, or Los Silenciados—VOX's 2022 slogan. VOX's nationalist-populist ideals are clearly articulated in its website, where VOX begins by defining itself as the voice of Spain, in a manner that subtly exposes its protofascist nature, and a not-so-distant Spanish fascist past (see chapter five on populism).

WHAT IS VOX?

VOX is the voice of Spain Viva. A movement of extreme necessity that was born to put the institutions at the service of the Spanish, in contrast to the current model that puts the Spanish at the service of politicians. VOX is the party of common sense, the one that gives voice to what millions of Spaniards think at home; the only one fighting against suffocating political correctness. At VOX we do not tell Spaniards how they should think, speak or feel, we tell the media and the parties to stop imposing their beliefs on society.

Our project is summed up in the defense of Spain, the family and life; in reducing the size of the State, guaranteeing equality among Spaniards and expelling the Government from your private life. We are the Spain that does not need to look at surveys or read a newspaper to know what the fashionable discourse is. Our discourse stems from our convictions, regardless of whether they are more or less popular. In short, VOX is the party of Spain alive, free and brave. (Abascal n.d., *Qué es VOX*)

As VOX states, the party positions itself as a nationalist party that will defend the Spanish nation-state, its people, and their way of life. To legitimize its nationalist ideals, VOX uses preservative discursive strategies that present a people and nation-state under siege, yet the enemy, consistent with contemporary populism rhetoric, is its own ruling government (see chapter five on populism). The Spanish people are constructed as serving, rather than being served by, a corrupt governmental elite that favors multiculturalism, globalization, and supranational economic interests and policies over a politics of national sovereignty and ethno-cultural, linguistic and religious preservation.

Vox's political website makes the party's populist political roots even more explicit when it identifies the media as complicit with the system of corruption, underscoring its role in shaping public opinion according to the needs of the political establishment, while concurrently influencing the politics of the ruling elites (see chapter five on populism). In these discursive instances, VOX recasts professional journalists and media outlets alike as tools of the state, designed, at best, to spread misinformation and political propaganda, and at worst to silence, oppress, and marginalize dissenting political voices, such as VOX (see chapter five on populism). For example, during the April 22, 2019, El Mundo interview, "Un día con Santiago Abascal (Vox) en la Granada 'reconquistada,'" Santiago Abascal depicts VOX as an oppressed party, thwarted in its ability to participate in regional political debates by the silencing power of the political establishment and its media outlets, "There is a great interest in not allowing VOX to speak, VOX's discourse is being manipulated by other political parties, and is being distorted by many media outlets, and we are even being harassed at our public events" (El Mundo, 2019).

During the same interview, Santiago Abascal uses binary constructions to further legitimize his party and its nationalist-populist ideals. For example, Abascal accuses the political establishment of betraying its own political principles by pursuing supranational policies against the common good of the Spanish nation-state and its *true* people, to then position himself and VOX as the Spanish people's only viable political alternative—a leader and party of steadfast convictions, even when these are unpopular or widely criticized. Abascal's binary and polarizing discursive strategies can be easily identified during his interview with El Mundo in 2019, when Abascal was asked why he had referred to the Partido Popular as "cowardly little right." Abascal's remarks came after the government, in compliance with the 2013 European Human Rights Court ruling, released all incarcerated ETA terrorists with extended convictions. When the interviewer noted that some of the Partido Popular's members had been victims of ETA's terrorism themselves, Santiago Abascal stated,

Because a service file is not [an excuse], I have also showed up for the Basque Country, and showing up for the Basque Country does [not excuse] betraying an electoral program, or . . . the Strasbourg sentence and release all of ETA's prisoners, [it doesn't excuse] having to eat Zapatero's legislative ideology to maintain the historical memory, to raise taxes to continue negotiations with ETA, to not give . . . a serious response to stop the Catalan, separatist coup, and that is what the 'cowardly right' of Mariano Rajoy did and we are going to continue to decry this. (El Mundo, 2019)

In fact, Santiago Abascal is not only steadfast in his convictions, he is also an omniscient populist leader (see chapter five on populism); as such, he does not need to access actual data to know what is best for the Spanish people or for the Spanish nation-state—as in the case of the humanitarian refugee and immigration crisis facing Spain. As Santiago Abascal explains to El Mundo, when asked about the data that supports his political assertions regarding illegal immigration,

I don't know it by heart, and neither do I need to. All I must do is to see the news and I don't want unregulated immigration. It doesn't matter to me if it is a 5 percent, 10 percent or 50 percent of the immigration. Unregulated immigration must be fought against. We are certain that the administrations are hiding the true immigration data. When we arrive, there will finally be a political force in Congress that will ask for the data every day, and we will make it available to the Spanish people. (El Mundo, 2019)

For Santiago Abascal there is no doubt as to the identity of the enemies of the Spanish nation-state and its people–whether internal or external; in fact, his rhetoric provides the justification for the party's national-populist ideals, and also legitimizes the party's identity-driven, nationalist, exclusionary political platform. Ultimately, Abascal's nationalist-populist argumentation sets the stage for a modern-day "Reconquista of Spain"—his 2019 electoral slogan. Abascal uses historical, mythical, master narratives related to the Spanish Reconquista, to link the present day and its complex realities to an earlier Islamic occupation—that of the Islamic Empire in the Iberian Peninsula between 700 and 1492. Abascal's discourse, and his Reconquista platform, seek to elicit and capitalize on long-standing fears of racial miscegenation and ethno-religious, linguistic cultural erosion belonging to a very different and distant past; however, this distant past and territorial occupation forever transformed the Spanish nation-state, influencing and leaving a lasting imprint on the Spanish language, architecture, and culture (see chapter two on nationalism).

In fact, Abascal's political rhetoric purposefully highlights the miscegenation that resulted from the Islamic invasion of Spain to provide the modern-day justification for a political agenda that prioritizes the expulsion of irregular immigrants and Islam from Spanish territory. For example, when asked in 2019 whether Islam brought positive things to Spain, Abascal replied:

> We have some borrowed words, . . . some . . . give us rest, like almohada, and we have remains in our historical architecture that are welcomed. But luckily we have expelled what is the worst of that civilization, that has to do with the impossibility of separating religion from the state, the impossibility of accepting the equality of women and men, and the definitive impossibility of accepting the radical freedom of man, and this is the most important, what we have to preserve, and this is why our [2019] electoral campaign begins in Covadonga and calls for a Reconquista, in many terms . . . because we have many reasons to feel proud of our history. (El Mundo, 2019)

For Santiago Abascal, a modern-day Reconquista must occur if the nation-state is to maintain its integrity and national, ethno-racial, cultural, linguistic, and religious historicized identity (Hastings, 2019; see chapter two on nationalism). To further legitimize and justify his Reconquista platform, Santiago Abascal, just like Marine Le Pen, draws on binary national-identity constructions that further radicalize and polarize the contemporary sociopolitical discourse of the Spanish nation-state (Ferreira, 2019). For example, Abascal's Islamophobic discourse depicts a Catholic, democratic, Spanish nation-state that values freedom and binary gender equality, while the Islamic other, is an ethno-racial, cultural, religious, and linguistic *other* that is threatening to transform the *true* identity of the Spanish nation-state, including its freedom and democratic structure. Spain must defend itself, and be defended, against this gradual Islamic incursion; VOX is the party that will do it, while ensuring the survival of the true people of Spain and their identity (see chapter two on nationalism; Gould, 2019; Turnbull-Dugarte, Rama, & Santana, 2020).

Abascal's Reconquista is not only limited to a Reconquista from mass, irregular migration and the Islamic enemy other; for Abascal, the time has come to rescue Spain from a corrupt, political elite, as well as from regional, separatist movements, and globalist, supranational political agendas (Rama, Zanotti, Turnbull-Dugarte, & Santana, 2021; Turnbull-Dugarte, 2019). As Javier Ortega Smith, the party's general secretary, stated in 2020, during the 528th anniversary of the *Reconquista* of Granada:

> La Reconquista has not ended in the face of the invasion of radical Islamism . . . is not over, although some believe that it is so. La Reconquista of values, freedoms, unity, brotherhood and cooperation of all Spaniards is a pending issue . . . in the face . . . of those who want to impose a totalitarian conception on Europe, that reconquest continues. (Ortega, 2020)

Yet, as Henry Kamen (2020) and Francis Ghiles (2019) state, the Victory of Covadonga, the location where VOX launched its 2019 electoral campaign, is a historicized invention attributed to "King Alfonso the Great (848–910) a century-and-a-half later" (Ghiles, 2019); and, perhaps most importantly, the term Reconquista, along with its contemporary connotation, did not emerge until "the middle of the 19th century, [when it] entered the dictionary of the Royal Spanish Academy in Madrid in 1936, the year Franco rose against the republic" (Ghiles, 2019).

Despite decontextualized, mythical, historicized identity-based political claims and arguments, Santiago Abascal's call to action resonated with the Spanish voters during the 2018 Andalusian regional elections. VOX won 11 percent of the votes, entering the regional parliament with twelve seats; not only was this VOX's first electoral win since its inception, but it was also the first time that a nationalist-populist party had achieved parliamentary representation since the end of Franco's regime in 1975 (Rama, Zanotti, Turnbull-Dugarte, & Santana, 2021). VOX and its Reconquista platform were even more successful during the 2019 Spanish general elections. In 2019, Spain held two general elections, as a coalition government couldn't be formed after the first election, in April of that year. While VOX secured twenty-four parliamentary seats during the April 2019 elections, it more than doubled its representation after the 2019 November elections, achieving fifty-two seats and becoming the third-largest party in Spain. VOX's success was celebrated in Europe and the United States by nationalist-populist political leaders, such as by Marine Le Pen in France and Geert Wilders in the Netherlands, and by David Duke, former grand wizard of the KKK in the United States. VOX's nationalist-populist Reconquista electoral platform was even more compelling in 2021, when VOX achieved another major victory in the Castilla-Leon regional elections, securing sixteen seats in parliament. The Partido Popular, with thirty-one seats, subsequently formed a coalition with VOX that gave VOX "the regional vice-presidency, three regional ministries and the speakership of the Castilla y León parliament" (Jones, 2022).

In October 2021, VOX released its 2021 electoral program, Agenda España, in opposition to the government's Agenda 2030, presenting twenty measures consistent with its nationalist-populist Reconquista sociopolitical platform. Yet, Abascal's political program, rather than prioritizing immigration control and the expulsion of Islam from Spanish territory, prioritized a different aspect of his Reconquista platform, the recentralization of government and gradual dismantlement of the existing regional, governmental autonomies. For Santiago Abascal, Spain and its future as a nation-state are primarily threatened by Spain's internal, autonomous governments, separatist movements, and by the country's Historical Memory Laws. Abascal's 2021 Agenda España reflects Abascal's nationalist concerns and urges the Spanish people to defend the Spanish nation-state and its identity by supporting VOX's political Reconquista and its policy measures, which prioritize above all "Equality between the Spanish people" and the "Unity of Spain."

To promote equality between the Spanish people, Abascal argues for the "Immediate return to the State of the competencies of Education, Health, Security and Justice, limiting regional legislative capacity as much as possible, as a preliminary step to the creation of a unitary state, administratively decentralized, that promotes equality and solidarity" among the Spanish people (Abascal, 2021, Agenda España, p. 5). In this policy measure, Santiago Abascal constructs regional, autonomous governments as a threat to social equality and to the unity of the Spanish nation-state, and concurrently legitimizes and justifies his anti-autonomic and recentralizing political measures. Through binary political constructions, Abascal transforms a people's desire to maintain and preserve their regional identity, languages, dialects, and governmental autonomy as direct affronts to the unity of Spain and to the identity of the true people of Spain. Yet Abascal's binary, nationalist, anti-autonomic rhetoric brings with it complicated fascist, historical reverberations and emotions related to Spanish fascism and to its politics of regional identity oppression—marked by intimidation, coercion, and fear (see chapters four and five).

VOX and Spanish Fascism

Santiago Abascal's political discourse, just like Franco's fascist regime, collapses the complex pluralism of the ethno-racial, cultural, linguistic, and religious identities of the people of Spain in favor of mythical, historicized, fascist master narratives wherein Spain and the people of Spain are constructed as solely Catholic, Iberian, and Spanish-speaking. The link between Spanish fascism and VOX is most explicit when VOX calls for

- Immediate suspension of the autonomy of those communities that use resources and instruments of regional self-government to attack the unity of Spain.
- Illegalization of parties, associations or NGOs that pursue the destruction of the territorial unity of the Nation and its sovereignty. As a preliminary step, any organization that seeks the destruction of national sovereignty will lose public subsidies and will be prevented from participating in the electoral processes.
- Repeal all laws that encourage confrontation and division between Spanish people, such as the so-called "democratic memory" or "historical memory" laws. (Abascal, 2021, Agenda España, p. 8)

For Abascal, as in the case of Francisco Franco, regional separatist movements seek to fragment the nation-state, and threaten the national unity achieved since 1492 by the Reconquista, when the Islamic Empire was fully expelled from the Iberian Peninsula (García-Sanjuán, 2018; La Moncloa, n.d.). Santiago Abascal's recontextualized and historicized Reconquista, and its accompanying, identity-driven master narratives seek to evoke nostalgic memories of a not-so-distant past, when Spain existed as a homogenous, unified nation-state; however, this historicized, unified nation-state never existed freely, as it was a forced creation of Spanish fascism. While some long for a return to this historicized, unified Spanish nation-state, others fear the return of a past marked by fear, coercion, and suppression of regional ethno-cultural, linguistic, and religious identities, such as the Catalan and Basque identities. Ultimately, VOX and Abascal's political rhetoric exacerbates unprocessed collective historical wounds related to the Spanish Civil War and Franco's dictatorship.

In fact, Abascal's political Reconquista is as much a direct reference and recontextualization of the Reconquista of the Iberian Peninsula from the Islamic Empire as it is to Francico Franco's own historicized Reconquista—central to the dictatorship's nationalist efforts to build a monolithic Spanish identity and nation-state (see chapter two on nationalism). As Henry Kamen well illustrates in *La invención de España: Leyendas e ilusiones que han construido la realidad española* (2020), Franco's regime, "totally bereft of ideas and cultural perspectives, was looking for ideological support in Spain's historical experience" and Menendez Pidal's historicized account of La Reconquista, in *La España del Cid (*1929) did just that. Soon after its publication, Franco's regime embraced Menendez Pidal's Reconquista, constructing and legitimizing an imaginary, Spanish nationalist, shared, medieval past—along the lines of Romantic nationalism and Herderian ethno-cultural, linguistic principles (see chapter two on nationalism; Kamen, 2020). Without Menendez Pidal's historicized and idealized Reconquista and the related scholarship produced by Franco's dictatorship, Franco would have been unable to build the unified Spanish nation-state that Abascal seeks to revive. Despite Francoist efforts to conceal Spain's internal historical diversity, the nation-state's transition to democracy enabled historians to reexamine Francoist sponsored literary and historical works, such as *La España del Cid*, exposing their internal contradictions and historical inconsistencies.

Spain's transition to democracy, La Transicion, which culminated with the ratification of the Spanish constitution in 1978, was in part aided by el Pacto del Olvido (Pact of Forgetting), and the 46/1977 Amnesty Law (Encarnacion, 2012; Lopez-Fuentes, 2022; Preston, 2020). Under El Pacto del Olvido, all political parties involved in the nation-state's democratic transition agreed to *forget* the horrors of the Spanish Civil War and of Franco's dictatorship to ensure the future social and political stability of the Spanish nation-state (Encarnacion, 2012; Lopez-Fuentes, 2022; Preston, 2020). While the pact was an informal agreement among the political elite, the Amnesty Law enacted in 1977 inscribed *forgetting* into law, as it effectively foreclosed all legal avenues for any form of transitional justice (see Encarnacion, 2012). The Amnesty Law of 1977, often described as a law accepted by a "majority of the Spanish people," stated that "acts of terrorism in opposition to the Franco dictatorship and crimes against human rights in its defence could not be subject to judicial proceedings" (Preston, 2020, p. 487); shortly after the passage of the Amnesty Law, "the archives of the Franco regime's repressive apparatus" were systematically destroyed (Preston, 2020, p. 487).

Spain's politics of forgetting, proved to be largely successful, defying prevailing reconciliation models in which acknowledgment and accountability for collective crimes were thought to be essential prerequisites to successful social transitional processes (for further discussion see Murphy, 2017; Shnabel, 2020; and López Fuentes, 2022). Despite Spain's successful democratization, it came at a price; the silence that had pervaded all aspects of society during Franco's dictatorship continued even after his death. This silence also became an intergenerational silence that fostered a disconnection between the older and new generation, augmented by an almost complete absence of content pertaining to the Civil War and Franco's regime in educational curricula (Díez Gutiérrez, 2013). Most importantly, the social and intergenerational silence also precluded many from mourning lost family members—whose bodies were sometimes never even found or recovered—during Franco's dictatorship.

In 2007, Jose Luis Zapatero, Spain's prime minister between 2004 and 2011, instituted the Law of Historical Memory or, Law 52/2007, in response to increasing social calls for remembering and accountability—often spearheaded by living relatives of many who had been killed and/or disappeared during Franco's dictatorship. The law sought to

> recognize and expand rights in favor of those who suffered persecution or violence, for political, ideological, or religious reasons, during the Civil War and the Dictatorship, promote their moral reparation and the recovery of his personal and family memory, and adopt complementary measures aimed at suppressing elements of division between citizens, all with the aim of promoting cohesion and solidarity between the different generations of Spaniards around constitutional principles, values and freedoms.

> [facilitate] knowledge of the facts and circumstances occurred during the Civil War and the Dictatorship, and ensuring the preservation of the documents related to that historical period and deposited in public archives. (Cortes Generales de España, VIII Legislatura. 2007, p. 5)

Although the Law of Historical Memory of 2007 has been widely criticized as insufficient, it signaled a societal shift away from forgetting and toward remembering. Since its inception, similar laws have been enacted in various autonomic regions such as in Rioja—Law 5/2022, Recuperación de la Memoria Democrática (Recovery of Democratic Memory) (Comunidad Autónoma de La Rioja, 2022). As the number of Spanish people who continue to push for remembering instead of forgetting rises, newly enacted historical memory laws and democratic memory laws are increasingly exposing the crimes committed during Franco's fascist regime—in part due to renewed efforts to recover the remains of victims executed by Franco's dictatorship, which has also exposed a number of mass graves (see García-Sanjuán, 2018); in fact "according to the UN, Spain is the country that has experienced the second-largest number of forced disappearances worldwide, after Cambodia" (Morris & Labonne, 2016).

As the number of exhumed bodies from mass graves continues to increase, exposing the brutality that the politics of forgetting sought to conceal about Franco's regime, the people of Spain are now being confronted by a collective, traumatic past that can no longer be silenced. However, just as during the Civil War and Franco's regime, not all segments of Spanish society are equally ready to face the past; some, especially those who supported Franco's regime, are even more invested than ever before in burying the history of the Spanish nation-state. For this segment of the Spanish nation-state, forgetting must continue and VOX and Santiago Abascal will ensure it happens. Santiago Abascal's Agenda España makes this commitment explicit, in its second policy priority, the Unity of Spain.

Abascal uses preservative, binary discursive strategies to construct democratic memory and historical memory laws as a threat to the social unity of the people of Spain, consequently arguing for their elimination, such as when he states "Repeal all laws that encourage confrontation and division between Spanish people, such as the so-called 'democratic memory' or 'historical memory' laws" (Abascal, 2021, Agenda España, p. 8). Abascal's commitment to forgetting and his preservative and legitimizing discursive strategies confuse the symptoms of the problem for the problem itself; that is, the feared social division that Abascal is trying to prevent is not caused by laws designed to recover the memory of the Spanish people, or their history, but rather by the mass collective crimes committed by Franco's dictatorship. Abascal's commitment to forgetting is not only a preservative, discursive, political strategy; it is most importantly, unequivocal evidence of VOX's protofascist political ideals. Not only does VOX and Abascal's Agenda España seek to revive a united Spanish nation-state that never existed, other than as imposed through Francoist violence, they also seek to preserve Franco's legacy and image.

The identity-driven master narratives deployed by VOX and Santiago Abascal are not only ethno-racial, cultural, linguistic, and religious in nature, they are also linked to the Spanish Civil War and to Francoism itself. As such, Abascal's identity-driven Reconquista platform evokes complex identity-driven sociocognitive and affective processes, connected to an unprocessed collective trauma, that of Francisco Franco's reign of terror. Within this context, the people of Spain are not fighting as much for the preservation of their ethno-racial, cultural, linguistic identity, as they are for the defense of their family history and memory—although with very different sociocognitive and affective attachments to Franco's regime, depending on whether they are descendants of Republican or Francoist families or both, as is the case for many.

As the case of Spain, VOX, and Francisco Franco well illustrates, territorial borders can be enforced through fear, coercion, and indoctrination, but the psychological borders of a nation-state are contingent on its people's emotional attachments to each other and to the nation itself. Collective social traumas interfere with the social bonds that scaffold and support the development of internal sociocognitive and emotional attachments to one's people and to the nation-state; sometimes, this shared collective trauma can fragment and break a people's psychological, national borders in complex and long-lasting ways, even when their territorial borders remain largely intact (Farina, 2018; Volkan 2018, 2020).

PART III

Political Psychology, Borders, and Identity Wars

Chapter Eight

Integrated Psychological Analysis

Political Psychology, Borders, and Identity Wars in Europe and the United States

In chapter seven, the integrated sociopolitical analysis approach identified the processes involved in the sociocognitive formation of national identities. It also illustrated how contemporary nationalist-populist parties use nationalist, historiographic, and discursive processes to polarize and radicalize the sociopolitical context of their nation-states while advancing increasingly exclusionary, othering policy proposals. Their strategy, as outlined in chapter seven, has been largely successful, enabling many nationalist-populist parties similar to Le Rassemblement National or VOX to increase their democratic representation—threatening liberal democracy in Europe and the United States.

Central to this strategy is an identity-driven rhetoric that uses motivated, historicized, master narratives to evoke fear among the *true* people of the nation-state. This fear can be organized according to three broad categories: 1. Fear of identity diffusion and loss—as in the case of *ethno-racial, cultural, linguistic, religious* miscegenation; 2. Fear of an impending *ethno-racial, cultural, linguistic, religious* invasion, leading to forced, identity transformation and loss—as in the case of mass migration and resettlement of *foreign others* within the nation-state; 3. Fear of national disintegration, whether as a people and/or nation-state—as in the case of internal, ethnic, nationalist-separatist movements that seek recognition as a people, with a right to their own nation-state (see chapter two on nationalism).

Regardless of how the fear manifests, it is annihilatory in nature; that is, when it emerges, it can compel a people to oppress, attack, and/or exterminate another in the name of self-protection and self-preservation (Cordell &

Wolff, 2010; Dulić, 2015; Fariña, 2018; Kaufman, 2016). Annihilatory fear, although seemingly self-explanatory, is used here in a psychoanalytic manner, consistent with Freud (1917) and Klein's death instinct (1932, 1948) and Winnicottian object relations theory (1971) (For further discussion, see De Masi, 2015; Fariña 2018; Freud, 1917; Klein 1932, 1948; Winnicott, 1971; and Volkan, 2018, 2020.). The American Psychological Association defines annihilatory anxiety and annihilation as "destruction of the self. In object relations theory, fear of annihilation (*annihilation anxiety*) is viewed as the earliest form of anxiety. Melanie Klein attributed it to the experience of the death instinct; British psychoanalyst Donald Winnicott (1896–1971) saw it as the anxiety that accompanies impingements from the environment." Although psychodynamic theories focus on individual psychological processes, it is possible to apply individual psychological processes to the understanding of large groups. In fact, such an approach is essential to the analysis of contemporary nationalist or nativist-populist parties, as they have adroitly exploited individual and large, group, national identity formation processes and annihilatory fears for their own political gains (see chapter six).

The integrated psychological analysis approach introduced herein, and informed by psychodynamic and political psychology, is designed to capture the complexity of the affective processes involved in individual and collective identity formation and in the establishment of individual and group national psychological borders (Fariña, 2018; Volkan, 2017). The integrated psychological approach complements the sociopolitical one to capture the complexity of the individual and large-group identity-formation process, mobilized by identity-driven contemporary sociopolitical movements.

POLITICAL PSYCHOLOGY

The integrated psychological analysis approach is best defined as a political psychological approach; as such, it "integrates and applies individual psychological frameworks to large, group . . . processes to explain [their] conscious and unconscious nature . . . and their sociopolitical manifestations" (Fariña, 2018, pp. 45–46). Political psychology argues that large-group processes influence and are influenced by individual, collective processes, as well as by the individual and collective, historiographical, meaning-making efforts of a people. In this manner, it is then possible to apply individual psychological theories, such as psychodynamic theories, to the understanding of large groups and their sociopolitical dynamics (see Osborne & Sibley, 2022; and Huddy, Sears, & Levy, 2013). As Volkan (2014) states,

There are echoes of individual psychology in large-group psychology shared by thousands or millions of persons, but large groups do not have one brain to think with or two eyes to cry. Thousands or millions in a large group share a psychological journey, such as going through a complicated mourning after major shared losses, or when they use the same psychological mechanism such as "externalization," making the Other a shared target. These journeys become social, cultural, political or ideological processes that are specific for the large group under study. Considering large-group psychology in its own right means making formulations as to a large groups' conscious and unconscious shared psychological experiences and motivations that initiate specific social, cultural, political or ideological processes that influence this large group's internal and external affairs. (V. Volkan, personal communication, February 22, 2014)

In a broad manner, political psychology can be most simply defined as an interdisciplinary field informed by "biopsychology, neuroscience, personality, psychopathology, evolutionary psychology, social psychology, developmental psychology, cognitive psychology, and intergroup relations" to examine political phenomena and large-group processes (Huddy, Sears, & Levy, 2013, p. 1). Despite its broad conceptual underpinning, some scholars identify three general approaches to political psychology: rational choice, biopolitics, and personality and psychodynamic approaches (see Huddy, Sears, & Levy, 2013 and Osborne & Sibley 2022). The integrated psychological analysis approach falls within the psychodynamic approach and is informed by Winnicottian Object Relations Theory, contemporary relational and intersubjective theories, specifically Cyclical Psychodynamic Theory (Wachtel, 2014; Wachtel & Gagnon, 2019) and Intersubjective Systems Theory (Stolorow, 2007, 2018), and by Volkan's psychological theory of large-group identity formation (2018, 2020).

IDENTITY: NATIONAL AND PSYCHOLOGICAL BORDERS

The integrated psychological analysis approach posits that identity formation is a lifelong process, rooted in childhood, whereby dynamics related to projection, externalization, and identification lead to the formation of individual psychological borders that delineate what is "me" and "not me." This process of individual identity formation also mediates, produces, and maintains the large, collective identity of the group to which the individual belongs—where race, ethnicity, nationality, social class, religion, etc., intersect. Individual and large-group identities are therefore, always inextricably linked to each other and are produced by efforts to delineate the individual and group-specific psychological borders, where internal sociocognitive-affective representations of self and other are integrated into a coherent self (Fariña, 2018; Stern, 2004; Volkan, 2009, 2013, 2018; Winnicott, 1965). Whereas the childhood process of identity formation produces and maintains the person's large-group identity, the large-group identity of the person shapes and maintains his/her/their individual psychological identity.

The process of childhood identity formation is a process of gradual integration, whereby split sociocognitive representations of self and other, along with their associated affective states, become integrated into whole sociocognitive-affective internal representations of self and others (for a complete discussion, see Fariña, 2013, 2018; Stern, 2004; Stolorow, 1993; Wachtel, 2014; Winnicott, 1965). Over time, this process makes it possible for the child to clearly differentiate and experience what is "me" from what is "not me," delineating the psychological borders of the self (Fariña, 2018).

Transitional objects, and the transitional space, are central to this childhood process of identity formation, differentiation, and integration (see Winnicott, 1965). Winnicott (1965) defined the transitional object as an external object that is chosen by the child and is later imbued with magical qualities—such as a two-year-old's special stuffed animal or blanket. It is both discovered and created by the child, residing within what Winnicott termed the transitional space—a third space that is both real and imagined, and where Winnicott also located the cultural life of a people (Winnicott, 1951). Transitional objects are, therefore, unique to each child, and also part of their larger, collective, shared environment and culture. Most importantly, transitional objects, due to their magical qualities, enable children to self-soothe during moments of distress, such as when separated from or frustrated by their caregiver, as they allow children to maintain the illusion of a gratifying caregiver amid disillusionment and frustration. As such, transitional objects mediate the psychological integration of the "good" and "bad" split, sociocognitive-affective representations of the caregiver and the self. This gradual integration enables children to rely less and less on their transitional objects for affect regulation, while consolidating the psychological borders of the self. The self and the other cease to exist as only "good" or "bad," and are instead replaced by sociocognitive-affective representations that reflect the complex nature of the human condition; the same person that is loving and nurturing can also hurt and disappoint, and people, including oneself, are flawed (Applegate & Bonovitz, 2004). As children achieve this sociocognitive-psychological milestone, they are increasingly able to tolerate disillusionment, while holding on to positive and negative affects related to the self and others (see Winnicott, 1951, 1965).

Psychological integration, however, is never fully achieved, as some aspects remain unintegrated throughout a person's life (Fariña, 2018, 2020; O'Neill & Fariña, 2018; Winnicott, 1965). Consequently, during the process of identity formation, children need to project onto the external world the "good" and "bad" aspects of the self, the caregiver, and the caregiver-me relationship, that could not be integrated within the individual psychological borders of the self (Fariña, 2018; O'Neill & Fariña, 2018; Volkan, 2013, 2018). In this process of projection and externalization, real external objects no longer function as mere objects, becoming instead "containers" of "good" or "bad" early childhood, preverbal, feelings and experiences (Fariña, 2013, 2018, 2019). The children and adults of any given group or society remain affectively and thus, psychologically connected to these external objects throughout life, as they function as external containers/symbols of "good" and "bad" affects related to the self and significant others (Fariña, 2018, 2019; Volkan, 2009, 2018).

The integrated psychological analysis incorporates three psychodynamic conceptual assumptions central to the understanding of individual and large-group identity formation (see Fariña, 2018, 2020). These conceptual assumptions are

1. External "good" or "bad" individual and collective group symbols function as large, collective cultural amplifiers that differentiate what is "us" from "them." As such, cultural amplifiers consolidate the large, collective group psychological borders and link individuals within the group to each other and to their large collective group identity (see Fariña, 2018; Volkan, 2009, 2013, 2018).
2. External cultural symbols are predetermined by the group's historical journey in relation to other groups (Fariña, 2013, 2018, 2019; O'Neill & Fariña, 2018; Volkan, 2013, 2018).
3. Caregivers mediate the specific large group's culture; they shape the form that the externalization process will take for all the children in that group or society (Fariña, 2018, 2020; O'Neill & Fariña, 2018; Volkan, 2009, 2013). As such, caregivers "scaffold the process by which the children in that society will come to identify the [external] objects that are understood as either 'good' or 'bad'" in that particular large group or society" (Fariña, 2019, p. 60).

For example, when caregivers attribute positive feelings to their group's language, foods and traditions, their children will eventually identify these symbols as suitable "containers" of "good" unintegrated affect related to the self, the caregiver, and the caregiving relationship (Fariña, 2013, 2019; Volkan, 2013, 2018). Likewise, a child whose caregiver harbors negative feelings toward particular external symbols, such as "the Muslim immigrant other," will eventually identify these symbols as suitable containers of negative, unintegrated affects related to "me" and the caregiving relationship (Fariña, 2013, 2018; O'Neill & Fariña, 2018; Volkan, 2013, 2018).

What is most important is that this process of projective externalization begins at the preverbal stage of development—a stage when children experience intense affects that they cannot yet reflect upon or process since they lack cognitive abstraction ability (Fariña, 2017a; Loewenberg, 1991, 1995; O'Neill & Fariña, 2018; Siegel 2012; Volkan 2013). These unprocessed, intense affects emerge later in life, and in particularly powerful ways, when a person's individual or collective group identity is under real or perceived attack (Fariña, 2018, 2020; Siegel, 2012; Stern, 2004; Stolorow, 1993; Volkan, 2013). When they emerge, and because they are associated with preverbal experiences largely held out of conscious awareness, they tend to cause internal confusion, disorganization, and anxiety in the person or large group, ultimately producing a visceral sense of fear. When this occurs, the fear induces self-preservation behaviors, characteristic of what is observed when a person is responding to a life-threatening event, regardless of whether the threat is real or only perceived as such. These self-preservation behaviors can be best understood as visceral fight-or-flight responses that also characterize psychological trauma–related responses, whether at the individual or large-group level (Fariña, 2013, 2018; 2019; Siegel, 2012; Stolorow, 1993; Volkan, 2013). In fact, these preverbal affects, whether pertaining to interpersonal and/or collective, societal interactions, are very often concurrently linked to group-specific historical traumas that, remaining largely unresolved, have been intergenerationally transmitted, as in the case of ethnic or political armed conflict—such as the Spanish Civil War. In other instances, they are linked to historical intergenerational traumas that are both transmitted intergenerationally and still experienced by a new generation—such as in the case of slavery and interpersonal and/or structural racism in the United States (Fariña, 2020; Volkan, 2015, 2021). Vamik Volkan (2021) speaks to this process when discussing large-group traumas,

> When members of an affected large group cannot mourn the group's losses or reverse its feelings of helplessness and humiliation, often they psychologically deposit their traumatized self-images, accompanied by the mental doubles of Others who played a role in the trauma, into the developing selves of children in their care. This situation is known as "transgenerational transmission. . . . A child who is a reservoir of depositing is given a psychological gene that influences his or her individual and large-group identity. Persons in the next generation—when they are not successful in dealing with the psychological tasks given to them—in turn will hand down such images with their associated tasks to a newer generation. (p. 8)

In fact, over time, intergenerational, identity-related affects that are linked to a large group's unprocessed traumas, acquire a traumatogenic dimension; when activated by a real or perceived threat, or by a threatening sociopolitical context, these identity-related affects produce and amplify individual and large group, psychological conflict, inevitably exposing the group's psychological vulnerabilities or proclivities (Atwood & Stolorow, 2014; Chu, 2011; Wachtel, 2014; Silberschatz, 2010, 2017; Stolorow, 1993; Weiss, 2005).

In other words, from an individual and large-group psychological perspective, the degree to which identity-related affects emerge at a particular point in time depends on the nature of the person's and large group's societal context, the individual and large, collective identity—whether dominant or marginalized identity—and the historical journey of the groups involved (Fariña, 2028, 2020). In instances where a large group's present context triggers historical, group, identity-related, traumatogenic affects, the group will inexplicably relive and reenact the old, unprocessed historical trauma connected to the affect, without any conscious awareness of doing so (Atwood & Stolorow, 2014; Luca, Rodomontia, & Gazzilloa, 2017; Stern, 2004; Wachtel, 2014; Safran & Kraus, 2014; Silberschatz, 2017). These instances and large, collective responses are most often connected to a group's chosen traumas.

However, whereas individual trauma tends to cause individuals to feel disconnected from others, inducing shame, that results in isolation, collective chosen traumas and their associated mental representations instead, and over time, link "all the individuals in the large group" to each other and the group (Volkan, 2021, p. 9). Through this process, the chosen trauma becomes an essential, organizing aspect of the large group's identity, as it fosters the group's identification with the trauma. Once the identity of the group becomes inextricably linked to a chosen trauma, and therefore defined by it, it becomes even more difficult for the group to mourn and process the trauma as it will threaten the integrity and coherence of their identity (see Aydin, 2017; Volkan, 2021). It is important to clarify that chosen traumas are "not an image of a relatively recent historical event," instead they are best understood as either current or dormant traumas that have and "can continue to exist for centuries" (Volkan, 2021, p. 9). Volkan (2021) best illustrates this idea when discussing his involvement in the 1990 negotiations between Estonia and Russia—designed to support Estonia as an independent nation-state. During the negotiations, the Russian delegation began to discuss the Mongol-Tatar Yoke, a Russian chosen trauma, related "to their thirteenth-century massive trauma." As Volkan (2021) explains, "through a time collapse, [the Russian delegation] linked emotions connected to this chosen trauma to problems with the Estonians after the collapse of the Soviet Union" (p. 9).

This example highlights the atemporal nature of chosen traumas and of the affects connected to them; as such, identity-related affects, when triggered by a threatening and potentially traumatogenic context, interfere with the person's and large group's ability to distinguish between the past and the present—causing a time collapse. This atemporality further intensifies the power of the identity-related affects and significantly interferes with the person's and large group's reflective abilities and capacity for cognitive abstraction. This process is a mutually reinforcing process that is best understood as a large-group vicious circle—central to Cyclical Psychodynamic Theory (Wachtel, 2006, 2014). As Wachtel (2006, 2014) explains, "divisions between contending [groups are] heightened when extreme positions in one direction elicit extreme positions in the other, and then each extreme position is experienced as 'justified' by the excesses of the other side."

These large-group, identity-related vicious circles not only legitimize polarizing sociopolitical discourses but also fuel and legitimize acts of inter- or intragroup aggression and violence; that is, regardless as to whether a real threat to the group(s) exists, such as in instances of propaganda and manufactured threats, the violence is understood as essential to the protection of the individual and large-group self. These large-scale, vicious cyclical patterns of interaction further polarize the large groups involved, while reinvigorating the groups' chosen traumas and their individual/large-group linking processes as a people. As large, group vicious circles become more entrenched, sociopolitical discourses become further polarized and breed further social and political polarization. These sociopolitical dynamics induce, maintain, and augment individual and large-group identity-related fears that are both fueled and exploited by contemporary nationalist and/or nativist-populist parties. By positioning themselves as the protectors and defenders of the *true* people of their nation-states, these parties have been successful at mobilizing the *true* people of their nation-states against mythical and historicized internal and external enemies, while increasing their political power. The consequences have been felt across Europe and the United States alike, causing the gradual weakening of liberal democracy and its structures; the growth of white power and paramilitary groups; and the mainstreaming of highly exclusionary ethno-racial, cultural, linguistic, and religious policies.

INTEGRATED PSYCHOLOGICAL ANALYSIS: APPLICATION TO LARGE COLLECTIVE IDENTITIES FRANCE—LE RASSEMBLEMENT NATIONAL (THE NATIONAL RALLY PARTY)

Marine Le Pen and Le Rassemblement National party have been largely successful in mobilizing the *true* people of the nation-state through their identity-driven, nationalist-populist sociopolitical platform. Despite losing the presidential elections in 2022, Marine Le Pen won 3 million more votes than in 2017, and her party is now the second-largest party in parliament, with eighty-nine parliamentary seats. Chapter seven examined Le Pen's identity-driven sociopolitical platform and its success from a socio-cognitive perspective. However, Marine Le Pen's success is due to more than discursive, historiographic, ethno-racial, nationalist-populist identity constructions and master narratives. The induction of annihilatory fear among the *true* French people is central to Marine Le Pen's increasing political gains and to her sociopolitical platform. This fear is intimately related to the preservation of the psychological borders and identity of the French people and their nation-state.

For Le Pen, and Le Rassemblement National party, to be French means to be white European and specifically a direct descendent of a French, Christian native. Within this context, the French culture is deeply tied with ethno-racial, linguistic, Herderian, and Darwinian nationalist principles, and it must be protected from anything that may threaten its purity. Le Pen's rhetoric taps into fears of identity-diffusion and loss, related to miscegenation, that foreshadow a gradual, cultural and identity demise. For Le Pen, this demise can be averted if *the ethno-racial, cultural, linguistic, and religious other* is expelled from the nation-state and if France can be freed from globalist and multicultural, supranational governmental agendas—France needs to be returned to the French people. Le Pen's rhetoric also reveals fears related to a *foreign, ethno-racial, linguistic, cultural, and religious* invasion; that is, the increasing mass representation of the foreign other in the French nation-state will ultimately transform the essence of the French true identity and nation-state. By tapping into fears of identity transformation, loss, and ultimately annihilation, Le Pen has successfully mobilized the *true* historicized, mythical, French people into action for her own political gains.

The fear that Marine Le Pen has induced, however, is not only a product of nationalist-populist rhetoric (socio-cognitive), but rather a very real affective experience, connected to the psychological formation of the mythical, historicized, nationalist French identity. From an integrated psychological perspective, the French ethno-linguistic cultural traditions, including the Christian religion, are external containers (symbols) in which the dominant French society, over many generations, has projected its unintegrated loving feelings related to the self and the caregiving relationship. These adults, as well as their children, are psychologically connected to these external symbols that function as French cultural amplifiers; the threat of their transformation threatens a part of the individual and large-group self that is deeply linked and identified with these external symbols (Fariña, 2018, Volkan, 2020, 2021); most importantly, these symbols are shared by all members of the dominant, large French adult group and by their descendents and foster a sense of belonging and shared "weness" that enables them to psychologically differentiate *what is me* from *what is not me*. The gradual transformation of these external cultural amplifiers not only threatens these identity markers but also and most importantly threatens the psychological internal structure and continuity of the individual and group dominant French self (Fariña, 2018; Volkan, 2013, 2020, 2021).

Within this context of identity transformation and loss, the *Islamic other* constitutes a threat to the mythical, nationalist, French identity. Whether the dominant French nationalist identity is real or a product of romantic nationalism is of little psychological consequence for those who, throughout generations, have developed a psychological investment in the existence of a true French identity—they are inextricably psychologically connected to it. The complexity of the annihilatory fears evoked by Le Pen's identity-driven nationalist-populist rhetoric is compounded by a history of war and terrorism in which the Middle Eastern and North African Islamic other was the enemy combatant or terrorist other. As Volkan (2018, 2020, 2021) states, chosen traumas are atemporal and induce traumatogenic affects that produce a time collapse. The activation of these traumatogenic, identity-driven affects in turn prevents introspection and cognitive abstraction, which initiates a fight-or-flight response to protect the individual and group self. In the case of France, the Islamist terrorist attacks perpetrated since the early 2000s are deeply ingrained in the collective psyche of the French people, such as the July 14, 2016 terrorist attack in Nice, where more than eighty people were killed during Bastille Day. Marine Le Pen has aptly exploited the trauma inflicted by Islamist terrorism for her own nationalist-populist ambitions.

Reasons for the rise of Islamist terrorism in Europe, and particularly in France, are beyond the scope of this book; nonetheless, it is important to mention that scholars identify multiple contributing factors to this escalation, including France's history of occupation and intervention in the Middle East and North African regions (MENA)—including the occupation of Algeria and ongoing military intervention in Iraq, Afghanistan and Syria and a largely inadequate policy approach to immigrant integration—resulting in the exclusion and marginalization of many immigrant arrivals, especially those from MENA regions (for further discussion see Kepel, 2020; Mihalache, 2016; Shapiro & Benedicte, 2003; and Rahal, 2022).

The history of armed military occupation and ongoing intervention in the Middle East and North Africa has made the Islamic other into a perfect external container of negative, unintegrated affects related to the dominant, French self and identity. While the Islamic other is violent, a terrorist, a religious other, and culturally and linguistically unassimilable, the French native is Christian, law-abiding, democratic and a symbol of the cherished French ethno-racial, linguistic and cultural identity—over centuries, significant love has been deposited into this identity. This binary, external, socio-cognitive construction reinforces internal psychological splits within the individual and large-group psyche; that is, internal working models or schemas of the French self are connected to positive psychological representations and affects, while internal schemas of the Islamic other are connected to negative representations and affects that are unidimensional, without an opportunity to become complex, multidimensional representations of the self and other—that is, a self formed by positive and negative aspects. These internal socio-cognitive and affective split schemas prevent psychological contamination while interfering with psychological integration; as such, French individuals and the dominant society as a whole need to repress while unconsciously *forgetting* (dissociate) the events and experiences that contradict the split psychological representations of the French self and the Islamic other.

For example, rather than reflecting on the effects of French military and political intervention in Middle Eastern and North African countries, which could evoke complex feelings of guilt and shame, the focus is on the violence perpetrated by the Islamic other (Demmers, 2012). Unable to *remember* the violence inflicted by French military and political intervention in the MENA regions, and unable to acknowledge the marginalization experienced by MENA immigrants on French soil, Islamist violence legitimizes and fuels French political retaliation and self-protection (Comas-Díaz, 2021). Consistent with large-group vicious circles of interaction (Wachtel, 2014), French sociopolitical retaliatory measures breed further oppression that invariably results in an escalation of renewed violence perpetrated by Islamist terrorist groups—the image of the Islamic other as a perpetrator of violence and terror is therefore psychologically reified and legitimized.

These identity-driven, violent, sociopolitical dynamics also embolden and naturalize white power and paramilitary groups, which, capitalizing on the French society's annihilatory fear, intensify their recruitment efforts while infiltrating the French sociopolitical arena through Marine Le Pen's nationalist-populist party. The white power group ideals, normalized by the dominant French society's annihilatory fear, further strengthen the identity-driven, large-group vicious circle of interaction; consequently, the subjugation and marginalization of the Islamic *enemy other* is thereby consolidated, while the French nationalist, historized identity is once again enthroned as real and fixed. The psychological borders of the nation-state are in this manner ultimately preserved.

SPAIN—VOX

While the case of Santiago Abascal and VOX is similar to that of Marine Le Pen and Le Rassemblement National, it differs in regard to the nature of the annihilatory fear elicited by VOX's nationalist-populist, sociopolitical platform. The VOX slogan, La Reconquista, highlights fears of an impending *ethno-racial, cultural, linguistic, religious* invasion, leading to a forced identity transformation and loss, that coexists with fears of a national disintegration brought about by internal, ethnic, nationalist-separatist movements that seek recognition as a people, with a right to their own nation-state. However, both of these fears are part of a chosen trauma that has remained unprocessed within the individual and large collective psyche of the Spanish people, that of the Spanish Civil War and Franco's dictatorship. As chapter seven discussed, VOX's nationalist-populist sociopolitical platform, while arguing for the expulsion of Islam from the Spanish nation-state, also invokes homogeneous ethno-cultural, linguistic, and religious nationalist sociocognitive constructions that were mythically and historiographically produced by Franco's regime. Consequently, the identity-related affects evoked by Santiago Abascal's political platform are deeply embedded within unprocessed large-group trauma that could not be *acknowledged or remembered* until now.

Certainly, Spain's history, like that of France, is marked by armed conflict, occupation and political intervention in the Middle East and North Africa. While the Islamic Empire occupied and forever changed the ethno-racial, cultural and linguistic nature of the identity of the *true* people of Spain, the Islamic *other* was expelled from the Iberian Peninsula as of 1492 (see chapter seven). However, armed conflict and political intervention in the MENA regions has persisted up to the present day. In fact, Spain continues to occupy Ceuta and Melilla, in North Africa, despite ongoing Moroccan governmental demands of a return of these territories, which were previously under Moroccan control. In 2021, the political tensions between Morocco and Spain escalated when Spain repatriated unregulated Moroccan immigrants who had entered the Spanish nation-state in large numbers. The conflict culminated with the military deployment of the Spanish armed forces to Ceuta and Melilla (Abdelhadi, 2021). However, in the collective psyche of the Spanish people, the Islamic other is most vividly remembered in terms of the March 11, 2004, Madrid terrorist attack—the worst terrorist attack ever perpetrated on Spanish soil, or in any European nation-state since World War II (see Kamedo, 2007). In the attack, ten bombs exploded simultaneously in four different Spanish trains, killing 191 people and injuring about 2,000 more;

the bombing seemed to be retaliatory and in response to the deployment of Spanish military forces to Iraq during the Iraq War (2003–2011).

As in the case of Marine Le Pen and France, the influx of undocumented MENA immigrants and the trauma of Islamist terrorism make the Islamic other an ideal external psychological container for the negative affects of the Spanish society. As such, the *true* people of Spain can psychologically deposit into the Islamic other the negative and unintegrated affects connected to their individual and collective mythical, Spanish, Franco-nationalist, identity and self. This psychological process enables the individual and collective psyche of the *true* Spanish people to create and maintain split, working models or symbolic representations of the individual and group self and of the Islamic other. Whereas the internal representations pertaining to the *true* Spanish individual and group self are largely positive and linked to positive feelings, such as the Spanish as law-abiding, democratic, of Iberian descent, Catholic, and Spanish-speaking; those pertaining to the Islamic *other* are largely negative and connected to disturbing violent and threatening images and affects. However, unlike the cherished, French ethno-racial, linguistic, and cultural identity, the Spanish identity is fraught with internal psychological conflict related to the Spanish Civil War and to the ethno-cultural, linguistic oppression of Spain's internal ethnic minority groups.

As Santiago Abascal points out in his Reconquista sociopolitical platform, the Reconquista is not only about preventing a second Islamic invasion but also about protecting the integrity of the Spanish nation-state as such. The unprocessed wounds of the Spanish Civil War and the terror inflicted by Franco's dictatorship are all part of a dormant chosen trauma that has been transmitted for decades from one generation to another. El Pacto del Olvido and later the 46/1977 Amnesty Law, made *forgetting* a prerequisite for the Spanish nation-state's peaceful transition to democracy (see chapter seven; RTVE, 1995). *Remembering, validation* and *acknowledgment,* all essential components in the treatment of trauma, whether at the individual or collective level, were considered too threatening for the individual and large collective psyche of the Spanish people and the nation-state (see Nicolas, Wheatley, & Guillaume, 2015; Saul, 2022; Volkan, 2018). At the time of the Spanish Transicion, the depth of the very real physical (death toll) and psychological wounds of Franco's dictatorship were too raw and open to have enabled any overt transitional justice process, such as those facilitated by Truth and Reconciliation Commission structures (see Encarnacion, 2012 and Saul, 2022). In fact, those most affected by the violence of Franco's dictatorship, the political left, were the strongest supporters of El Pacto del Olvido and the 1977 Amnesty Law; as Omar Encarnacion (2012) states,

Paradoxically, this view was popularized by the left, which bore the brunt of the violence of the Civil War and the repression of the Franco dictatorship, as reflected in this statement from Communist leader Carrillo from May 1977, "In our country, there is but one way to reach democracy, which is to throw out anyone who promotes the memory of the civil war, which should never return, ever. We do not want more wars, we have had enough of them already." (p. 186)

In this quote, Encarnacion (2012) refers to Santiago Carrillo, General Secretary of the Spanish Communist Party between 1960 and 1982. Santiago Carrillo spoke for many, who in 1977, did not want to recall the horrors they had survived; his words, although not psychological in nature, implicitly speak to the raw and intense trauma related affects that can emerge when events connected to a large-group trauma are prematurely brought to conscious awareness by remembering (Chu, 2011). In fact, psychological research on trauma has long underscored the negative effects of encouraging trauma survivors to remember trauma related material prematurely, without having first strengthened and developed affect regulation and distress tolerance skills. Some of the most dangerous consequences include potential retraumatization caused by the intense affects, largely connected to unbearable feelings of shame and guilt, and to vivid recollections that, overwhelming the self, can fuel suicidal impulses (Aydin, 2017; Chu, 2011; Herman, 2015; Stolorow, 2007; Volkan, 2021); in such instances, remembering is not only counterproductive but also damaging. At the large-group, collective level, when the trauma has involved mass killings, for example, premature efforts to engage in collective healing can ultimately reignite new violence and aggression, fueled by intense feelings of hate, blame, shame, and guilt. Through time collapse, efforts to engage in dialogue quickly revert to intractable conflict, where historical identity-driven conflict and injuries reemerge in a psychic equivalent manner that interferes with the individual and large group's reflective and cognitive abstraction capacities, otherwise known as mentalization (Demmers, 2012; Duschinsky & Foster, 2021; Volkan, 2021).

Whereas in mentalization "Thoughts and feelings are used to account for and explain observable behaviour and perceptual experience," during periods of psychic equivalence sense perception, including feelings, are "mistaken for reality," eventually interfering with the capacity to distinguish between past and present (Duschinsky & Foster, 2021). What is most important to identity-driven, large-group violent traumas is that "high arousal/emotionality" both triggers and sustains "psychic equivalence by hindering access to . . . mentalizing" processes; as psychological time collapse sets in, cognitive abstraction and perspective-taking abilities are lost, triggering a trauma related fight-or-flight response that unleashes the violence of the past (Duschinsky & Foster, 2021). These trauma related psychological dynamics help explain

Spain's 1977 Pacto del Olvido, and why even those most affected by Franco's violence advocated for a politics of *forgetting* to prevent further armed conflict, death, and loss.

However, repression, denial, and dissociation—understood herein as a "defense mechanism in which conflicting impulses are kept apart or threatening ideas and feelings are separated from the rest of the psyche" (APA, n.d.)—come at a price. Under these circumstances, neither the victims/survivors nor the perpetrators can process the trauma, remaining psychologically involved with it; unable to mourn, the trauma is always close to the surface and easy to reignite. While those who inflicted dehumanizing violence (perpetrators) are partially aided by these psychological defenses in their efforts to fend off the intense shame and guilt that remembering could induce; those who suffered the dehumanizing effects of the violence (victims/survivors) are often unable to engage in a necessary mourning and collective healing process, while contending with intense feelings of shame, anger, and loss that cannot find an outlet. Because they are unable to fully mourn, the unresolved trauma is deposited into the next generation, even when, as in the case of the Spanish Civil War and Franco's dictatorship, caregivers may have remained silent about the past (Volkan, 2021). As Saul (2022) states when discussing the transmission of intergenerational collective traumas,

> Whether their parents spoke or were silent about their . . . past, children often felt that their parents' past had somehow penetrated them as if by "osmosis." Adult children of survivors spoke about not being able to remember actual moments when their parents told them about their past, yet somehow they could recall images, phrases, and incomplete memories related to what their parents had experienced during the war. (p. 24)

However, large groups, as individuals, eventually seek psychological resolution to their difficulties. In the case of the Spanish people, time and *forgetting* provided the psychological distance needed to deactivate intense trauma related psychic equivalence processes, and the consequent time collapse that would have activated past violence. At the same time, recent generations have been gradually learning about the Spanish Civil War and Franco's regime, both through history textbooks that are progressively including this omitted content, and through Historical Memory and Democratic Memory laws that are uncovering an increasing number of mass graves (Capellà i Roig, 2021). This gradual process has allowed some families, who had long fought for acknowledgment and closure, to have some renewed hope; in a process that is both painful and long overdue, some have finally recovered the remains of their disappeared loved ones.

While Spain is gradually beginning to reckon with its violent past, some would like to continue to bury it—particularly those who actively participated in, and supported, Franco during the Spanish Civil War and once he was in power. For these families and their descendants, uncovering the truth of Franco's regime entails having to take responsibility for the terror inflicted on many while contending with feelings of blame, shame, and guilt. Given this latent context, it is not surprising that Santiago Abascal and VOX's political Reconquista platform has gained momentum within the Spanish nation-state, as it protects the internal psychological stability and identity of those who supported the Franco dictatorship and that of their descendants. Santiago Abascal's political platform, and in particular his opposition to Historical Memory Laws and Democratic Laws, is comforting to those who are either unwilling and/or psychologically unable to confront the horrors of Franco's dictatorship. For this segment of Spanish society, Santiago Abascal and VOX are politically and psychologically necessary. Abascal's political agenda not only protects them from having to embark on a long-avoided mourning process but also forestalls a resisted, psychological, identity transformation (Dalton & Huang, 2014; Hanke, Liu, Hilton, Bilewicz, Garber, Huang et al., 2013).

From a psychological perspective, mourning is a gradual process whereby an individual or collective group works through the feelings (affects) connected not only to physical losses but also to more abstract and symbolic losses, such as the loss of a previously idealized, individual and collective identity (Freud, 1917). What is most important about psychological mourning processes related to a group's chosen traumas is that in mourning, the collective group gradually develops the capacity to tolerate previously painful and threatening affects that, due to their intensity and/or to the group's psychological inability to tolerate them, were split off and deposited on to an external other—the enemy (Volkan, 2021, 2020, 2018). As the large group develops greater psychological capacity to tolerate previously distressing, traumatogenic affects, it is increasingly able to mentalize about, rather than to affectively react to, its psychological distress (Saul, 2022). This gradual mourning process leads to the progressive integration of previously split-off affects and parts of the collective self, which ultimately allows the group to achieve a more complex understanding of its collective self. This trauma related mourning process ultimately leads to the development of a new, complex, and three-dimensional identity that is no longer defined by the group's collective trauma (Fariña, 2018; Hirschberger, 2018). While this psychological resolution liberates both the collective group and its *enemy other* from their historical trauma and its related intergenerational reenactments and transmission, it also leads to the transformation of the group's collective identity (Saul, 2022).

Although this identity transformation is necessary to promote psychological healing and growth, it is initially collectively and psychologically resisted since it interferes with and threatens the psychological linking processes that have historically connected individual group members to each other and to the group itself—processes central to the development of a sense of belonging to the group (Bilali & Vollhardt, 2019). As such, it is impossible to separate individual identities from the historical contexts and large, group, collective identities, in which they emerged. As Erikson (1968) argues, each historical period limits the "number of socially meaningful models for workable combinations of identity fragments" and, individual identity and socio-historical crises "define each other" in a mutually reinforcing manner (E. Erikson, 1968, p. 28 and pp. 53–54).

Consequently, the psychological linking processes that are initially threatened by a group's trauma related mourning process are both connected to the group's symbolic cultural amplifiers and to the group's identity-driven, chosen trauma (Chu, 2011; E. Erikson, 1956; E. Erikson, 1985; K. Erikson, 1976; Fariña, 2018; Volkan, 2021). This psychological context also explains the collective annihilatory fear that initially appears when a group engages in a long-avoided trauma related mourning process, as this process inevitably entails a psychological loss—the loss of the idealized and historiographically constructed, collective group identity.

As the psychological idealization that had supported the group's collective identity begins to falter, exposing the flaws and splits of the collective identity, the group's collective sense of internal psychological continuity and coherence is temporarily destabilized, producing significant annihilatory fears. If the group can tolerate and reflect on these intense effects, while mourning its idealized identity, it will ultimately achieve a different, more adaptive identity, that will provide renewed psychological stabilization and growth. Alternatively, the failure to persist and complete the mourning process, will keep the collective group in its familiar and historical traumatogenic state of psychological agitation, and annihilatory fear. This fear, along with other complex affects, will be once again deposited onto the *enemy other*, reinforcing old maladaptive and traumatogenic vicious cyclical patterns of interaction (Wachtel & Gagnon, 2019; Wachtel, 2014; Volkan, 1988, 2021). Eventually, the projected annihilatory fear and its accompanying vicious, traumatogenic cyclical patterns may lead to renewed external aggression, fueling further psychic equivalency processes, affective reactivity, and societal polarization (Fariña, 2013, 2018; Freud, 1917; Wachtel & Gagnon, 2019; Wachtel 2014; Volkan, 2021).

In the case of Spain, Santiago Abascal's efforts to protect the integrity of the Spanish nation-state and its historicized, Francoist, national identity, are not only fueling societal dissension and polarization, but also reigniting old traumatogenic wounds and patterns of interaction. For example, Abascal is determined to curtail ethnic separatist movements to preserve and maintain the homogeneous Spanish nation-state and identity—both products of Franco's dictatorship, and imposed through coercion and violence. In fact, Abascal's sociopolitical Reconquista seeks to revive policies similar to those enacted under Franco's dictatorship and with the same aim—to subjugate the nation-state's internal ethnic minorities. Abascal and VOX's commitment to overturning Historical Memory Laws not only makes Abascal's connection to Francoism clearly explicit, but also reopens unprocessed societal traumatogenic wounds pertaining to a past that has long been suppressed and denied. For Abascal, as in Franco's case, the unity of the Spanish nation-state must be preserved at all costs, even when this nation-state and identity never existed, other than as enforced through terror and repression (Preston, 2021).

Given this context, Abascal's platform, far from promoting greater national cohesiveness, is maintaining the Spanish society in an ongoing state of collective traumatogenic agitation, that is further complicating a much-needed and unavoidable collective mourning process. What is most important about this state of collective psychological agitation, is its overreliance on manic defenses (see Klein, 1940). These defenses require "the denial of psychic reality" to reduce and cope with difficult feelings of "loss, guilt, helplessness, [and] dependency," and are used by a group, without conscious awareness, when the group's capacity to tolerate the psychological "pain associated with loss" has significantly decreased (Rudan, Jakovljevic, & Marcinko, 2016, p. 335). The Spanish society is at such a juncture. As the terror inflicted by Franco's dictatorship continues to be unearthed, some are recovering the remains of their long- lost loved ones—achieving a degree of closure; others are being confronted with the dehumanizing actions they either inflicted or supported—a reality that they have long repressed and defended against. However, repression, and its sociopolitical manifestations, such as El Pacto del Olvido and later the 46/1977 Amnesty Law, eventually become maladaptive and begin to falter.

For example, over time manic defenses interfere with a person's or large group's ability to maintain or achieve a complex, multidimensional psychological perspective of reality, as it involves the use of projection and identification processes. Projection—understood as a psychological process whereby a dominant large group and/or individual deposits onto an external other unwanted aspects and affects that belong to the large group and/or individual self (Volkan, 2021)—enables a dominant group to turn a subjugated *other* into a psychological container of the dominant group's unwanted and unintegrated negative affects and traits, etc. In the case of Spain, after the Civil War and during Franco's dictatorship, Republicans and those suspected of being Republicans, as well as those adhering to their minority ethnic identities and languages, such as Euskera, Catalan, etc., became the external containers of the Spanish dictatorship's aggression, which led to their systematic persecution and murder (Preston, 2021). Their efforts to protect themselves from arrest and execution, rather than being perceived as legitimate, were instead used to reinscribe them as enemies of the Spanish nation-state and Franco's dictatorship.

Projection initially frees a dominant group from psychological distress and internal disorganization, as it allows the group to avoid the projected threatening and unwanted affects that are inconsistent with the group's psychological representation of the self, and therefore difficult to reconcile as part of the self (Fariña, 2013, 2018). Yet projection unwittingly links the dominant group's psychological stability to the subjugated *enemy other* in two different ways. First, the *other* is needed to preserve the dominant group's idealized self-image—necessary to maintain intact their self-image and psychological stability. Second, projection keeps the dominant group psychologically preoccupied with the actions of the subjugated *enemy other*, as this enemy symbolically represents in a concrete manner, the unwanted threatening affects and traits of the dominant group (Volkan, 1988, 1998, 2013).

Manic defenses, in this context of projective identification, interfere with perspective taking and mentalization, eventually giving way to psychic equivalence processes and intense affects. These affects, as stated earlier, are no longer related to the present-day conflict but rather to the chosen collective trauma of the people involved. Ultimately, these large-group, identity-based psychological processes reinforce the old, historical, trauma related sociopolitical vicious circles of interaction, leading to gradual distrust, conflict, and polarization; in their most extreme form, these dynamics culminate in the dehumanization and extermination of the "other." In the case of the Spanish nation-state, Santiago Abascal and VOX are exploiting the people's manic state of agitation, while mobilizing old identity, trauma related, vicious circles of interaction, that are becoming increasingly similar to those that existed in 1936—prior to Franco's coup d'état. In fact, during VOX's Viva22 rally held in October 2022, fifteen thousand people applauded as the musical group Los Meconios sang lyrics that called for a return to 1936. This call for a return to 1936 is far from accidental; a few days earlier, the Spanish Senate had passed a new memory law, the Democratic Memory Law of 2022, that rectifies some of the shortcomings of the 2007 Historical Memory Law (Basu, 2022; Llach, 2022).

The new Democratic Memory Law requires secondary schools to include in their curricula content pertaining to the Civil War, shifts the responsibility of exhuming and identifying "the dead in mass graves" to the government, and mandates reparations for the families of victims of Franco's dictatorship (Basu, 2022; Llach, 2022). Although these changes are important, what is even more relevant to the Spanish society's collective mourning process and to the transformation of its Francoist, historicized, national identity, are three additional provisions included in the 2022 law. The first, transforms *El Valle de los Caídos*—an external, national Francoist identity symbol and cultural amplifier—into a national cemetery that will honor the victims of the Civil War; the second, imposes fines on those who continue to display Francoist symbols—effectively forbidding these identity-related cultural amplifiers; and the third, "bans the Francisco Franco National Foundation" (Basu, 2022). These provisions, not only change and forbid the most relevant symbols of Francoism, but most importantly, they threaten and destabilize the psychological linking mechanism that had united Francoist families and their descendants to each other; as such, the 2022 Law, and in particular these three provisions, threaten the continuity of the identity of a significant segment of the Spanish society, as well as their psychological stability.

VOX's call for a return to 1936, a few days after the Democratic Memory bill was voted into law, instead of unexpected, is a dangerous sign of the intense annihilatory fear that the new law has unleashed within a substantial segment of the Spanish society. In response, another segment of the Spanish society called for a legal investigation, characterizing the lyrics as a hate crime (Llach, 2022). The historical vicious circles of interaction connected to the trauma of the Spanish Civil War and of Franco's dictatorship are once again clearly palpable; while some would like to return to a historiographical Francoist homogeneous Spanish nation-state and identity, others continue to resist a return to 1936.

The Democratic Memory Law of 2022 provides a legal mechanism for Spanish society to increasingly acknowledge and mourn a painful past in a manner that may lead to societal reconciliation and eventually to a new identity as a people (Fariña, 2018). This process will inevitably transform the psychological identity borders of the various groups involved, thereby redefining and transforming the psychological, and perhaps also, physical borders of the Spanish nation-state. However, before Spanish society can engage in this process, large, identity-driven affects, inducing psychic equivalence processes and activating manic defenses, need to be contained and worked through (see chapter nine). Contrary to this, Santiago Abascal and VOX's political strategy is designed to increase the manic agitation of Spanish society by capitalizing on historical, traumatogenic, identity-driven, annihilatory fears that could ensure the party's ongoing electoral success and eventual rise to power.

INTEGRATED SOCIOPOLITICAL AND
PSYCHOLOGICAL ANALYSIS FORMULATION

Nationalist and nativist-populist parties and leaders, such as Santiago Abascal and VOX in Spain, or Marine Le Pen and Le Rassemblement National in France, are capitalizing on their societies' collective, identity-based, psychological chosen traumas. In the case of the Spanish nation-state, Santiago Abascal and Vox, are mobilizing the masses by exploiting historical traumas and collective, psychological processes linked to the Civil War and to Franco's dictatorship, that are also responsible for the historical oppression of the nation-state's internal ethnic minority groups. In the case of France, Marine Le Pen and Le Rassemblement National are mobilizing the masses by exploiting traumatogenic identity-driven affects related to both the Islamic other, and the corrupt, ruling elites—with their multicultural, supranational, global agendas.

Despite differences, Marine Le Pen and Le Rassemblement National, and Santiago Abascal and VOX, are only two contemporary examples of how European nationalist-populist leaders are exploiting traumatogenic, affective, historical vicious circles of interaction for their own political gains; in fact, this psychological-political strategy characterizes and links present-day nationalist and nativist-populist movements in Europe and the United States to each other (see chapter nine). This intercontinental alliance enables local nationalist and nativist-populist parties to spread the manic societal agitation they foster in their own nation-states to the international arena, while amplifying its local effects. This strategy, along with the collective, psychological annihilatory fear it induces, further legitimizes local, historiographic, identity-driven master narratives, that are then sociopolitically manipulated to mobilize the true people of these nation-states against the local and global *enemy others*. In this context, nationalist and nativist-populist parties are not fighting to maintain their nation-states' physical borders, but rather their historicized, psychological, identity borders. VOX's Viva22 rally, widely supported by other European nationalist-populist and American nativist-populist leaders, illustrates clearly these complex dynamics and their international scope. The rally featured videos from European and American nationalist and nativist-populist leaders, where fear inducing, identity driven national/ nativist-populist slogans were applauded by the people, and widely accepted,

from Donald Trump ("Spain must protect her borders . . ."), Italy's Giorgia Meloni ("We must save the European civilisation from catastrophe") and Hungary's Victor Orban ("Our weakness is our enemy's strength"). The Polish Prime Minister Mateusz Morawiecki was present in person, and he claimed

national sovereignty was under attack everywhere from meddlesome interna-
tionalists. (Basu, 2022)

VOX is now the third largest political party in Spain, while other
nationalist-populist parties are gaining increasing political prominence, rising
to power during national elections, such as Giorgia Meloni and the Brothers
of Italy, in October 2022 and the Sweden Democrats party, which became
the second-largest party in the country after the September 2022 elections.
Far from losing popular support, nationalist and nativist-populist parties in
Europe and the United States continue to garner increasing momentum and
power (MacDougall, 2022; Silver, 2022).

PART IV

An Integrated Sociopolitical and Psychological Approach to Contemporary Identity-Driven Conflict and Historical Collective Traumas

Chapter Nine

An Integrated Sociopolitical and Psychological Approach (ISPA) to Identity-Driven Conflict and Historical Collective Traumas

Identity, as discussed throughout this book, has been a European nationalist and American nativist enterprise, exploited by fascism, and now by its most recent political iteration, nationalist and nativist-populism (see chapter five; Coulmas, 2019; Gellner, 2006; Leerssen, 2006). Whereas national identity, from an integrated sociopolitical and psychological perspective, links individuals to each other, and ultimately to their group and nation-state, some national identities alienate and oppress particular segments of their societies, by declaring them *other*—legitimizing *their* marginalization and subjugation. Nationalist and nativist-populism has further amplified these dynamics, by declaring these *others* enemies of the true people of the nation-state (Fariña, 2018, p. 65; Renan, 1882; Stern, 1995; Ross, 1997; Tajfel, 1982; Volkan, 2013, 2017).

The rise of European nationalist and American nativist-populism has fueled societal conflict, sociopolitical polarization, and violence across both continents, gradually dismantling the societies they claim to protect and defend—as previously done by fascism. Their success is in large measure due to a sociopolitical, discursive, and psychological-affective strategy that is designed to induce and exploit annihilatory fear among the true people of the nation-state (see chapters seven and eight). This fear is related to an uncertain future that threatens the psychological borders, and therefore continuity, of the *true people* of the various nation-states—defined according to prevailing nationalist and nativist, historiographical, sociocognitive, and affective identity constructions (Lake & Rothschild, 2020). However, this sociopolitical, identity-driven, mass mobilization strategy is deeply tied to European fascism, American nativism, and to the KKK and its most contemporary iterations—white power and paramilitary groups (see chapters three, four, and five).

Identity-driven conflict management and resolution approaches to collective traumas, such as the integrated sociopolitical and psychological analysis model (ISPA), are particularly well positioned to thwart the contemporary spread of European and American nationalist and nativist-populism, and of the white power movements that have become part of these societies' mainstream. As such, the integrated sociopolitical and psychological approach to identity-driven conflict and collective traumas offers a needed, contemporary mechanism to denaturalize othering, identity-driven sociopolitical discourses, while creating a possible path toward collective mourning and healing.

VIOLENCE, CONFLICT MANAGEMENT, AND RESOLUTION APPROACHES

Although violence is often conceptualized as manifest violence, identity-driven conflicts culminate in manifest violence when two other forms of violence, structural and cultural, operate in a society without being acknowledged and addressed (Carment & Fisher, 2010; Demmers, 2012; Lund, 2009; Snyder, 2017). Whereas manifest violence is overt and easy to recognize, structural and cultural violence are latent forms that, although invisible, are just as destructive. Demmers (2012) and Galtung (1996) define structural violence as violence caused by "systems of exploitation and repression that are harmful and damaging [to those oppressed by them], hence—physical—hurtful and violent," such as the deprivation caused by poverty in capitalist societies (Demmers, 2012, p. 59). Cultural violence, on the other hand, is defined as violence that stems from "the symbolic sphere of our existence–exemplified by religion and ideology, language and art, empirical science and formal science (logic, mathematics)—that can be used to justify or legitimize direct or structural violence" (Galtung, 1996, p. 196). Identity-driven, conflict management, and resolution approaches, such as the ISPA approach, focus on cultural violence and its overt manifestations to delegitimize the sociopolitical discourses that activate identity-driven psychological affects—central to contemporary social conflicts.

Although some make a distinction between conflict management and conflict resolution approaches, with the former focusing on containment and the latter on resolution, conflict resolution first necessitates the containment of violence (Siniver, 2017). The ISPA approach to identity-driven, trauma related conflict first seeks to contain intergroup conflict–understood herein as derived from historical, intergroup specific, psychic equivalence processes and patterns of interaction—to then, gradually increase the collective capacity to tolerate dissociated, identity-related affects (see chapter eight). The ISPA approach accomplishes this by providing an integrated sociopolitical and psychological framework to individual and large-group identity formation that is easily combined with other theories, such as relational psychodynamic and/or trauma theories, to effectively mediate and address intra- or intergroup, identity-driven conflict (see Aaron, Grand, & Slochower, 2018; Atwood & Stolorow, 2014; Benjamin, 2018; Chu, 2011; Courtois & Ford, 2016; Fonagy & Allison, 2014; Silberschatz, 2010, 2017). The flexibility of the ISPA approach allows mediators to select and incorporate within the ISPA framework the psychological and/or social conflict theory that is most pertinent to a specific inter- or intragroup conflict, to then work toward social reconciliation.

This versatility allows the ISPA framework to serve two distinct and complementary functions; first, as a stand-alone, integrated sociopolitical and psychological analysis model for identity-driven conflict; second, it can be expanded and used as a conflict management and resolution approach to guide social/collective stabilization and reconciliation efforts. In the latter, mediators first complete an ISPA analysis of the conflict to understand its sociopolitical and psychological nature and history, to then identify the best psychological and/or social theory to promote intra- or intergroup psychological containment and stabilization. This theory is then incorporated into the ISPA group-specific analysis framework to create a mediation map that can be followed as mediators engage with each side. The road map to conflict management and resolution is specific to each group and seeks to achieve, at a minimum, social stabilization and greater individual and collective conscientization; most importantly, mediators also share the mediation map with each side, using it as a tool to promote increasing self-reflection and conscientization that, if achieved, could ultimately create a path for intra- or intergroup reconciliation.

STEPS OF THE ISPA APPROACH TO CONFLICT MANAGEMENT AND RESOLUTION

Although the complete application of the ISPA approach to conflict management and resolution is beyond the scope of this book, its relevance to contemporary identity-driven conflict in European nation-states and the United States warrants its brief inclusion herein, to highlight its overarching principles and processes.

The ISPA approach begins with the ISPA, integrated sociopolitical analysis. During this step, mediators examine the historiographic, sociocognitive constructions linked to the identity-driven affects at the heart of the intra- or intergroup conflict (Chu, 2011; Volkan, 2021; Wachtel, 2014; Wachtel & Gagnon, 2019). Mediators meet with each group separately, and initially only with selected political and community representatives on each side, to gather information that will gradually identify the group specific sociocognitive constructions about the self, the other and the conflict itself. This emphasis reflects the instrumentalist and constructivist underpinnings of the ISPA approach (Lake & Rothschild, 2020).

Whereas instrumentalist approaches to ethnic conflict posit that identity is merely a "tool used by individuals, groups, or elites to obtain some larger . . . end," constructivist approaches argue that "conflict is caused by . . . pathological systems, which individuals do not control" (Lake & Rothchild, 2020). The ISPA approach departs from this binary conceptualization, instead arguing for an instrumentalist-constructivist approach to identity-driven conflict. For example, in the case of contemporary nationalist/nativist-populism and white power and paramilitary groups, the ISPA approach posits that the rise of these movements in Europe and the United States, is as much a symptom of the pathology of the current capitalist neoliberal global economic system as it is a direct result of the political elites and white power movements' efforts to capitalize on this system's violent effects (Reisigl, 2017; Wodak, 2021).

Once the sociopolitical analysis is completed, mediators move to the second step, the integrated psychological analysis of large-group identity formation of each group. Mediators continue to meet with political and community leaders on each side, and using the ISPA psychological framework, they examine how each group has established their psychologically group borders, focusing on identifying the nature of the identity-driven affects tied to the collective identity and its borders.

The integration of the sociopolitical and psychological analyses into an integrated, ISPA formulation allow mediators to develop a conflict intervention plan, that is informed not only by the ISPA framework and its conclusions, but also by the psychological and social theory that is best positioned to foster psychological containment and gradual, collective stabilization for each group. This conflict intervention plan is shared with the political and community members identified on both sides of the intra- or intergroup conflict for further revision and modification. Once the plan is finalized with each group, a strategy for its gradual implementation is developed, which also includes testing the conflict intervention plan with small ad hoc groups. Once it has been tested and modified, the final integrated plan identifies the key social players on each side, that together with the mediators and original group representatives, will implement the conflict mediation plan. The first goal for each side of the conflict is to achieve affective, psychological containment, while gradually engaging different societal groups in a conscientization process informed by the ISPA mediation plan. The conscientization process ultimately seeks to assist each group in mourning their specific collective trauma, while assessing the collective intragroup capacity and desire for intergroup reconciliation.

If the ISPA, group-specific mediation plan succeeds in gradually decreasing the societal, intragroup manic agitation on each side, it becomes possible for each side to begin to mentalize or reflect upon their experience; as this occurs, the collective emotional reactivity that had marked the conflict also begins to lessen. This process enables each group to articulate, often for the first time, repressed, group specific, sociocognitive-affective experiences that had been previously kept out of conscious awareness due to their affective intensity (Chu, 2011; Duschinsky & Foster, 2021; Van Dijck, 2018). This process of consciousness raising (conscientization) and containment slowly decreases the unconscious, psychological power that the group-specific, early identity-driven affects had held over the groups' behavior, opening the possibility for change within the groups' historical pattern of interaction (Freire, 1970). What is most important to highlight is that the ISPA sociopolitical-psychological framework seeks to explore the "image formation" of the groups involved, to make explicit the underlying sociopolitical and psychological dynamics of the intra- or intergroup conflict, as well as its traumatogenic history (Siniver, 2017, p. 190).

The ISPA process of social conscientization ultimately builds the foundation for social reconciliation, as it promotes internal liberation from symptomatic dominant and in-group norm conformity. In this manner, it also opens the possibility to achieve a new and different sociocognitive-affective understanding of the collective self and identity, and that of the *enemy other* (Freire, 1970; hooks, 2010; Wachtel, 2014; Wachtel & Gagnon, 2019; Stolorow, 1993; Silberschatz, 2017). While a discussion of social reconciliation is beyond the scope of this book (see Bloomfield, 2003; Kohen, 2009; Tutu, 1999; Vollhardt, Jeong, & Bilali, 2022; Zehr, 2015), for the purpose of the ISPA approach to conflict resolution, social reconciliation is understood as

> a way to live that permits a vision of the future; the rebuilding of relationships; coming to terms with past acts and enemies; a society-wide, long-term process of deep change; a process of acknowledging, remembering, and learning from the past; and, voluntary. (Bloomfield, 2003, p. 14)

As such, reconciliation is a process that requires the mourning of a painful traumatic past, and of the collective identities that were tied to it (Freud, 1917). This is a difficult process that is often resisted (see chapter eight) not only by the groups involved in the conflict, but also by the system and the political elites that have benefited from it. The ISPA approach, recognizing the role of resistance and the vested interest that different stakeholders may

have in maintaining the status quo, emphasizes the importance of commitment to the ISPA conflict intervention plan, and is designed to continuously
assess the commitment level of central key stakeholders to the process.
Mediators and group-specific stakeholders reconvene to revisit the plan
should the assessment indicate that some stakeholders may resist the gradual
collective psychological and behavioral changes achieved by the ISPA intervention plan.

This process uses the principles of the ISPA framework to aid stakeholders in reflecting on the sociopolitical and psychological dynamics fueling
the emerging resistance. Only when these central stakeholders have recom-
mitted to the process can the ISPA conflict intervention plan resume; efforts
to proceed without recommitment can lead to historical re-traumatizing
vicious circles of interaction, fueled by stakeholders with a vested interest in
maintaining the sociopolitical and psychological chaos they have historically
exploited and benefited from. Consequently, the ISPA approach incorporates
strategies designed to examine each group's sociopolitical context, to expose
its collective effects and promote sociopolitical change. Only when each
group is conscious of how their traumatogenic wounds are being exploited,
can they unite to mourn their collective trauma, allowing for the gradual
transformation of an identity that no longer serves their psychological growth
as a people and society. Historical memory laws, among other political measures, are essential tools incorporated as part of the ISPA approach, to develop
the social and political structures that will over time support a peoples' conflict resolution and reconciliation efforts (Mohamed, 2015; Vollhardt, Jeong,
& Bilali, 2022).

Despite conflict management efforts, people may continue to psychologically resist the transformation of their historical identity, reinforcing their
psychological attachment to it. Previous chapters examined these dynamics
through the application of the ISPA analysis model to the cases of Spain,
France, and the United States, but with a primary focus on the rise of nationalist and nativist-populism, rather than on the plight of immigrants, refugees,
and asylum seekers. However, such an analysis is essential to fully illustrate
how contemporary immigration policy, and particularly American immigration policy, functions as a legal tool that enables a people to resist the transformation of their identity, while forestalling the mourning of the collective
traumas associated with it.

Chapter Ten

Historical Collective Traumas and Resistance to Identity Transformation and Mourning

American Immigration Policy

According to the UN, an "estimated 45 million people across 37 countries risk starvation in 2023 . . . while more than 100 million people are now displaced worldwide as a result of climate events, the war in Ukraine and Covid-19" (Roush, 2022). Nowhere has this crisis been more felt in North America, than at the US-Mexico border, where surrounding states either refused to respond, or tried—only to find themselves ill equipped to do so—ultimately fueling anger and resentment toward the federal government's inadequate approach to the crisis. This failure reflects both the fragmented federal immigration system of the United States and the country's historically fraught relationship with immigration from Latin American countries—both deeply intertwined with American nativism.

Contemporary American nativist-populists, predictably, responded to the border crisis through restrictive immigration reforms designed to protect the nation-state and its identity. Such an account, although compelling and simple, inadvertently hides and colludes with powerful collective psychological identity-driven processes. When understood as such, contemporary American immigration reforms are as much a political tool as they are a psychological tool, designed to resist the transformation of the collective, *native* American identity, as well as the collective mourning of its unresolved historical trauma. The integrated sociopolitical and psychological analysis included herein seeks to expose these dynamics, as well as their devastating consequences for the American society and those displaced by forced migration.

INTEGRATED SOCIOPOLITICAL AND
PSYCHOLOGICAL ANALYSIS OF
AMERICAN IMMIGRATION POLICY
AND NATIVIST-POPULISM

American immigration policy has historically oscillated between exclusion-ary and inclusionary periods, consistent with the prevailing immigration sociopolitical rhetoric of the time (see chapters three and four; Fariña, 2018). While the period between 1882 and 1940 was highly restrictive, the 1960s, and specifically the Immigration and Nationality Act of 1965, marked the beginning of an expansionary period that, lasting until the late 1980s, per-manently changed the demographic composition of the United States (see Cuison Villazor & Chin, 2015; Chacon, Johnson, & Hing, 2021; Massey & Pren, 2012; Ngai, 2014).

The Act of 1965 abolished the restrictions of the Quota Act of 1924, reopening immigration from Africa, Asia, and Southern and Eastern Europe, while seeking to reverse the effects of the Quota Act on Southern and Eastern European families through a family reunification provision. The provision was central to the passage of the act, as it exempted family members of American citizens from immigration quotas that had previously separated family members for generations, making the act particularly appealing to many white Americans. The provision was also welcomed by nativists, who based on the demographic composition of the United States at the time, had falsely assumed that most of the family migration would come from Southern and Eastern European countries.

However, the Act of 1965 also erected new immigration barriers for certain groups. Mexican immigrants, for example, quickly became part of an unregulated and undocumented, de facto American labor force market, when the Bracero Program was ended and replaced by the 1965 H-2 guest worker program. The H-2 program limited the number of guest worker visas available for Mexican immigrants, and also created additional barriers for employers, who found the program cumbersome to navigate and costly. The surplus of undocumented workers created by the Act of 1965, together with the growing demand for manual labor and the lack of employer sanc-tions, disincentivized employers from using the guest worker program, while covertly enabling them to benefit from the unprotected, undocumented labor market that the Immigration and Nationality Act of 1965 had created (see Fariña, 2018; Massey & Pren, 2012). The problem was further compounded in 1976, when the Immigration and Naturalization Act was amended to include country-specific immigration quota caps. For many Latin American and Asian immigrants, the family reunification provision quickly became the only legal path left to join their family members and enter the United States (Fariña, 2018; Massey & Pren, 2012).

Ultimately, the family reunification provision, contrary to nativist expectations, mostly benefited the groups that the Immigration and Naturalization Act of 1976 had attempted to control through its country specific-quota caps. Together, the Act of 1965 and the Act of 1976 inadvertently set the stage for what many in the mid-1990s and early 2000s—including American white power groups—called an impending Hispanization of the United States, or Hispanic challenge (Figueras & Bazan-Gonzalez, 2017; Huntington, 2009; Knight, 1995)

By 1986, the increasing visibility of the de facto, largely Latino and primarily Mexican, undocumented labor force in the United States led to further immigration reforms, and to the Immigration Reform Control Act of 1987, IRCA. The act focused on border control enforcement, and instated employer criminal and civil sanctions for "knowingly hiring illegal immigrants" (Fariña, 2018, p. 93). IRCA also provided undocumented immigrants with a path to regularize their status, if they were long-term residents who had entered the United States prior to January 1, 1982, or agricultural workers who had entered prior to May 1, 1986 (Massey, Durand, & Malone, 2003). Although three million immigrants regularized their status in the United State through IRCA, the ongoing "agricultural labor needs . . . and the prospect of . . . better wages" continued to drive immigration from Latin America, and particularly from Mexico (Fariña, 2018, p. 94). By the late 1980s, the American sociopolitical discourse, just as it did between 1915 and 1924, began to refer to immigration as a Mexican *immigration crisis* that was threatening the *integrity* of the United States and its *national security* (see chapters three and four; Massey, Durand, & Pren, 2016).

Nativism, and its anti-immigrant discourse, as between 1915 and 1924, was once again on the rise, and with it a new period of immigration control and retrenchment; however, unlike previous immigration reform periods that had focused on border control, the 1990s brought with it a different kind of nativist discourse that advocated for the expulsion of the Hispanic immigrant other from the United States.

In 1994, amid growing fears of a Hispanic invasion fueled by white power movements that were increasingly infiltrating the United States' mainstream sociopolitical discourse, coupled with the rise of domestic terrorism, President Bill Clinton adopted a new approach to immigration control, control through deterrence (see Belew, 2018; Fariña, 2018; Massey & Pren, 2012). The new approach proved insufficient to deter immigrants from crossing, although the treacherous conditions of the new migration paths led to a sharp increase of immigrant deaths (Argueta, 2016). By 1996, amid increasing anti-immigrant, nativist rhetoric and protests, President Clinton passed into law the Illegal

Immigration Reform and Immigrant Responsibility Act (IIRIRA) and the
Antiterrorism and Effective Death Penalty Act (AEDPA), marking the beginning of a new politics of immigration interior enforcement and deportations
(see Fariña, 2018; Jaret 1999).

A full review of IIRIRA and AEDPA, as well as of subsequent programs
instituted through these two acts to foster cooperation between state and local
law enforcement and ICE, such as the 287(g) or the Secure Communities
Programs, is beyond the scope of this book (for a review see American
Immigration Council, 2021a; ACLU, 2022; and TRAC, 2017). However,
it is important to underscore their human toll, which has been well documented. For example, since the inception of IIRIRA, 7,007,193 immigrants
have been deported from the United States—between 1996 and 2021
(Homeland Security, 2022); 44 percent, or 3,066,457, of these deportations
occurred under President Obama's administration, whereas only 17 percent
or 1,201,945 took place under President Trump (Homeland Security, 2022;
Nowrasteh, 2019). Since 1996, these deportations have primarily targeted the
Latino/x community, particularly Mexican and Central American immigrants,
often silently separating American and immigrant children alike from their
parents. In fact, 231,000 parents of American citizen children were deported
from the United States between 2013 and 2018; in 2019, this trend continued,
with a total 27,980 parental deportations of American citizen children, living
in mixed-status families (American Immigration Council, 2021b). Between
January 1, 2020, and December 31, 2020, ICE pursued 11,925 removal orders
of parents of American citizen children, secured 5,018 final removal orders
of immigrant parents with at least one American citizen parent, and removed
15,325 immigrant parents of American citizen children (Department of
Homeland Security, 2021a; Department of Homeland Security, 2021b).

It is important to highlight that these parental deportations were interior
deportations, and different from those that occurred at the border under the
Trump administration due to the inception of the Zero Tolerance Policy and
the invocation of the 1997 Florence Settlement—which mandates the release
of children from DHS custody to an appropriate adult or licensed program
within three to five days, or within twenty days under extenuating circumstances (see Human Rights First, 2020; Southern Poverty Law Center, 2022).
Through the Zero Tolerance Policy and the Florence Settlement, the Trump
administration separated five thousand immigrant children from their parents between 2017 and 2019, without keeping adequate records for parental
reunification; as a result, in 2020, 545 immigrant children remained in state
custody, unable to be reunified with their parent(s) due to lack of parental
information (Gross, 2022; Southern Poverty Law Center, 2022).

Although President Biden pledged to reform immigration and stop the
separation of immigrant children from their parents, separations have

continued, although on a smaller scale—372 interior family separations occurred between 2021 and 2022 (Department of Health and Human Services, 2022a; Department of Health and Human Services, 2022b; Washington & Brigida, 2022). These general and parental deportation statistics clearly illustrate that the deportation of the Latino/a/x other, as well as that of their American-born children, is far from a Trumpist, nativist-populist phenomenon. Instead, these statistics make explicit the hypocrisy that has characterized American immigration policy since its inception, as well as that of the different administrations that have presided over the United States in modern times. While President Trump reinstated and expanded some of the programs phased out by President Obama's administration, such as the 287(g) or Secure Communities Programs, and President Biden reversed these expansions, he also continued some of President Trump's policies, with significant consequences for mixed-status families and asylum seekers.

Children in Mixed-Status Families and the Rise of American Nativism

As of 2018, reports estimate that 6.1 million American children live with at least one undocumented family member; 4.4 million have at least one undocumented parent (American Immigration Council, 2021b). Despite these statistics, the parental deportation of American children and its effects, are seldom openly discussed by the media and are largely unacknowledged by the mainstream of American society, which mainly regards deportation as a problem that affects undocumented adults and children alike. The toll of parental deportation on children is well documented, including short- and long-term educational, behavioral, and mental health problems; higher rates of poverty; and food and housing insecurity, as well as difficulty conceptualizing themselves as members of the American society. This interferes with their sense of belonging and integration. (See American Immigration Council, 2021b; Capps, Koball, Campetella, Pereira, Hooker, & Pedroza, 2015; Dreby, 2015; Fariña, 2018.)

What is often missed in discussions pertaining to parental deportations is the number of American children that have left the United States to avoid a permanent separation from one or both parents—referred to by many scholars as de facto deportees (Caldwell, 2019; Fariña, 2018; Masferrer, Hamilton, & Denier, 2019; Hamilton, Masferrer, & Langer, 2022). Whereas in 2005, the number of American-born children of Mexican parents living in Mexico, for example, was 240,000, by 2018 this number had doubled to 550,000 (Fariña, 2018; Hamilton, Masferrer, & Langer, 2022). While some argue that these de facto deportees are an unintended consequence of immigration interior enforcement and control, some argue that the IIRIRA and AEDPA acts were covertly designed to remove not only undocumented immigrants, but also a new growing threat—the American-born children of Hispanic immigrants (Fariña, 2018). For white power groups and nativists alike, these new Americans, both Hispanic and American, were only exacerbating the transformation of the ethno-racial, cultural, and linguistic landscape of the American society. That is, white power movements and nativists argued that the impending Hispanization of the United States was not only a direct result of rising Hispanic undocumented immigration, but also directly related to the growing number of American-born children of Hispanic immigrants—this threat could not be curtailed through existing immigration policy.

For nativists and white power groups, the reforms included in the IIRIRA and the AEDPA acts represented renewed hope; both acts included provisions to facilitate the deportation of undocumented and documented immigrants, and together, they created a legal context that turned American-born children of immigrant parents into potential de facto deportees (Hamilton, Masferrer, & Langer, 2022). In other words, first, the AEDPA act, "expanded the types of crimes that . . . [constituted] an aggravated felony and included crimes of moral turpitude as criminal grounds for deportation," of both undocumented and legal immigrants (Fariña, 2018, 100); second, the IIRIRA act included provisions that facilitated and expedited the deportation of the Hispanic, criminal other; and, third, whereas prior to 1996 an alien could petition the cancellation of removal due to the hardship that dependent family members could experience as a result of the person's deportation, IIRIRA narrowed this hardship clause. Under IIRIRA, the hardship standard [required caregivers to] "'provide evidence of harm to his spouse, parent or child substantially beyond that which ordinarily would be expected to result from the alien's deportation' (Conference Report to accompany H.R. 2202, as cited in Fix & Zimmermann, 1999, 'Dividing Families,' para. 5)." (Farina, 2018, p. 101).

During the years preceding the passage of IIRIRA and AEDPA, white power movements, such as the Aryan Nations, the White Aryan Resistance, and the Skinheads, had started to aggressively recruit young white adults across the nation, including in high schools and college campuses, through identity-driven, anti-government master narratives that capitalized on growing fears related to an impending Hispanization and demographic shift in the United States (Belew, 2019; Johnson, 2012; Southern Poverty Law Center, 2011). Their rhetoric blamed the government for the current immigrant invasion, decrying its inability to protect the border and the white *native* American citizens from an impending white genocide. The rise in domestic terrorism, coupled with the Gulf War in 1990, only amplified the prevailing annihilatory fear that was fast spreading among the mainstream of society; as the United States entered into a recession during the war, white *native* workers also faced increasing uncertainty due to the socioeconomic downturn (Eberly et al.,

2001). By 1992, politicians such as Patrick Buchanan, a paleoconservative, began to capitalize on the rising identity-driven and socioeconomic fears of the white *native* American population to gain popular support for their own political aspirations. For example, in 1992, during a speech in Smuggler's Canyon, Patrick Buchanan argued for the closing of the American border, while blaming the government for what many perceived as an undocumented immigration invasion, stating "I am calling attention to a national disgrace . . . the failure of the national government of the United States to protect the borders of the United States from an illegal invasion that involves at least a million aliens a year" (Hemmer, 2022). Buchanan, consistent with paleoconservative ideals, argued that unregulated immigration posed a threat to the cultural homogeneity of the United States, and specifically, to the white *native* American culture. Sara Diamond's 1996 article "Right-Wing Politics and the Anti-Immigration Cause" explains well the sociopolitical discourse of the time, as well as the paleoconservative, right-wing political platform of the 1990s,

> paleoconservatives ignored the question of whether "illegal" immigrants take jobs away from U.S. citizens and instead focused on the threat to cultural homogeneity posed by the influx of nonwhite immigrant groups. In a decade's worth of articles, the paleoconservatives argued that ethnicity, not a shared belief in core American values, was what gave the nation its identity. Some . . . [claimed] that liberal elites sought to use large numbers of immigrants from Third World countries to increase the power of the state, by creating a new "underclass" and increased social problems—crime, illiteracy, and interethnic conflict that only a New Class of elite bureaucrats would then be able to solve (Francis, 1995). The focus on cultural homogeneity was central to early anti-immigrant activity. (p. 157)

As the white power and nativist rhetoric progressively entered the sociopolitical mainstream of the United States, identity-driven master narratives of an impending white genocide due to a Hispanic immigrant invasion became widely accepted, fueling increasing political polarization. The common-sense normalization of white power and nativist rhetoric not only fueled increasing support for immigration reforms that included interior mass deportations, but also led various groups to demand a revision of the Fourteenth Amendment of the American Constitution—which grants American citizenship to anyone born in the United States.

Ultimately, white power groups and nativism itself, as throughout the history of the United States, were again able to ensure the temporary preservation of the historiographic, mythical, white *native* identity, when in 1996, President Clinton signed into law the IIRIRA and AEDPA acts. Since then, subsequent administrations have deported millions of Hispanic/Latino/x immigrants from the interior of the United States, while permanently separating mixed-status families and forcing thousands of American children to leave their home country.

Nativist-Populism, White Power and Paramilitary Groups, and Immigration Policy

While a connection between white power groups, political parties, and immigration policy has always been part of American history, President Trump was the first contemporary president to openly embrace and integrate white power ideals in an electoral, nativist-populist political platform since the early 1990s. His strategy proved successful, when in 2016, he secured the presidency of the United States. While some argue that President Trump enabled white power and paramilitary groups to emerge from the shadows during his presidency, the brief integrated sociopolitical analysis of contemporary immigration policy just outlined herein supports a different conclusion. White power groups, and nativism itself, had been progressively infiltrating the mainstream of American society since the early 1990s. President Bill Clinton's immigration reform policies, rather than being liberal in nature, reflected instead the sociopolitical influence that nativists and white power groups had achieved by 1996. President Trump, recognizing the long-standing rise of white power and nativist ideals within the mainstream of American society and the increasing popular mistrust of the political establishment and the elites adroitly capitalized on this context when running on a nativist-populist sociopolitical platform in 2016. Consistent with this strategy, once in office, President Trump signed into law the 2017 Border Security and Immigration Enforcement Improvements Executive Order and the Enhancing Public Safety in the Interior of the United States, Executive Order (see Executive Order, 2017a; Executive Order, 2017b). These two orders, far from introducing new immigration reforms, only reinforced the IIRIRA and AEDPA acts, expanding some of the programs that the Obama administration had gradually curtailed and terminated by 2016—such as the 287(g) and Secure Communities Programs.

President Trump's executive orders, while decried by many, ensured the loyalty of his most influential supporters—contemporary white power and paramilitary groups. Indeed, on January 6, 2021, when President Trump lost the Presidential elections, white power and paramilitary groups such as the Oath Keepers, Proud Boys, and the Three Percenters stormed the US Capitol to overturn the elections in support of their president, Donald Trump. Since then, leaders of the Proud Boys and the Oath Keepers, among others, have been charged with seditious conspiracy; some, such as Stewart Rhodes, founder of the Oath Keepers, and Kelly Meggs, leader of the Florida chapter, have been successfully convicted of sedition (Al Jazeera, 2022).

Asylum Policy, Nativist-Populism, White Power, and Paramilitary Groups

The influx of asylum seekers arriving to the United States border due to sociopolitical unrest, violence and climate change has been steadily increasing since the early 2000s. In 2016, the United States received 115,399 asylum applications, "39 percent more than the year before and more than 100 percent increase since 2014. This [was] the seventh consecutive annual increase and the highest level since 1995, when applications reached close to 144,000" (Mossaad & Baugh, 2018, p. 7). This trend continued until 2017, with a total of 139,777 asylum applications, before shifting downward as of 2018, when the number of applications decreased to 105,472 (Mossaad, 2019). In 2020, the total number of applications decreased further, to a total of 93,224—a 4.1 percent decrease from 2019.

During this same time period, and beginning in 2014, the number of affirmative asylum applications "from Central America's Northern Triangle Countries (El Salvador, Guatemala, and Honduras)" sharply increased; this trend continued until 2017, when the number of asylum applications from the Northern Triangle Countries reached a total of 31,100 (Mossaad, 2018, p. 6). By 2020, asylum applications from the Northern Triangle Countries had dropped to 19,763 (Baugh, 2022). In fact, whereas most asylum seekers between 2005 and 2010 came from Haiti, Colombia, Indonesia, Mauritania, Venezuela, and Iraq, between 2011 and 2016, most came from Mexico, Honduras, Eritrea, Nepal, Somalia, El Salvador, and Guatemala (TRAC, 2016). Coinciding with this new trend, asylum denial rates, which had steadily decreased from 80 percent in 1996 to about 45 percent in 2012, began to climb, reaching a total of 57 percent in 2016—when asylum applications from Central American countries, and specifically from the Northern Triangle, had sharply increased (TRAC, 2016). This connection is clearly illustrated by the country-specific denial rates between 2011 and 2016, which were highest for claims from Mexico, 40 percent, followed by El Salvador, 30.8 percent, Guatemala, 25.1 percent, and Honduras, at 35.6 percent (TRAC, 2016).

By 2014, as the number of Central American unaccompanied minors and migrant caravans arriving to the US-Mexico border continued to rise, media outlets turned public attention to the humanitarian crisis unfolding at the border (Villiers Negroponte, 2014); nativist, white power, and paramilitary groups manipulated the media coverage, to increase mainstream fears of an impending Hispanic invasion—blaming the government for failing to secure the border. Consequently, nativist, white power, and paramilitary groups, renewed their anti-government and anti-immigration efforts through a rhetoric that constructed Hispanic/Latino/x asylum seekers as a security and health risk to the American society—criminals, drug traffickers, gang members belonging to MS-13, rapists, and disease infested. Soon after, conservative media outlets, such as Fox News, embraced this rhetoric, enabling nativist, white power, and paramilitary groups to covertly reach a larger mainstream audience. For example, in October 2018,

> Laura Ingraham argued on her Fox News show, "The Ingraham Angle," that the people in the caravan are creating a health issue, [asserting] "We don't know what people have coming in here. We have diseases in this country we haven't had for decades." She also called the people in the caravan an "invading horde." [While on the *Lou Dobbs Tonight* show] Florida Congressman Matt Gaetz . . . told Dobbs, "This [caravan] is not just a group of desperate migrants. We have people who are criminals and thugs." (*Mainstreaming Hate: The Anti-Immigrant Movement in the U.S.*, 2018)

By 2014, the United States had also been at war in Afghanistan for thirteen years; what had initially started as an act of retaliation in response to the September 11, 2001, terrorist attack, had become a violent, protracted armed conflict, with a significant human toll and no end in sight (Grandin, 2020). Many resented the ongoing US involvement in Afghanistan and blamed the government and the political elites for the lives lost, as well as for the ongoing terrorist attacks in the United States and Europe. Nativist, white power, and paramilitary groups capitalized on the growing social discontent, as well as rising fear of Islamist terrorism, to further polarize and radicalize mainstream sociopolitical debates about immigration. To this aim, nativist, white power, and paramilitary groups deployed a coordinated misinformation campaign; as part of this strategy, they alleged that Islamist terrorists were entering the United States, passing as Central American migrants in the caravans arriving to the border. Although no evidence was ever found to support these claims, white power and paramilitary groups successfully turned their allegations into facts that were increasingly accepted by some in the mainstream of society—including President Donald Trump (Allen, 2019; *Mainstreaming Hate: The Anti-Immigrant Movement in the U.S.*, 2018; Meyer & Pachico, 2018). By 2019, nativist, white power, and paramilitary groups had further radicalized mainstream debates about asylum and immigration while positioning themselves as the true defenders of the white *native* American people of the nation-state—further legitimizing their increasing vigilante activities at the border.

White power and paramilitary vigilante activity along the US-Mexico border, however, has a long and violent history that predates the surge that took place in the 2000s. As Grandin (2020) states, confrontations between white power and paramilitary groups and migrants along the border had been marked by violence, death, and intimidation since the 1970s, and particularly in California:

> As San Diego's sprawl began to push against agricultural fields, racist attacks on migrants increased. Vigilantes drove around the back roads of the greater San Diego area, shooting at Mexicans from the flatbeds of their pickups; dozens of bodies were found in shallow graves. Anti-migrant violence was fuelled by angry veterans returning from Vietnam, who carried out what they called "beaner raids" to break up migrant camps. Snipers took aim at Mexicans coming over the border. Led by a 27-year-old David Duke, the KKK set up a "border watch" in 1977 at California's San Ysidro point of entry, finding much support among border patrol agents. Other KKK groups set up similar patrols in south Texas, placing leaflets with a printed skull and crossbones on the doorsteps of Latino residents, warning "aliens" and the federal government to fear the klan.

White power and paramilitary vigilante violence, as Grandin (2020) argues, was not only openly tolerated in the 1970s, but also involved members of the border patrol, "local and state law enforcement," and veterans from the armed forces (Belew, 2019; Grandin, 2020). This context continued into the 1980s and 1990s, turning the US-Mexico border into

> a zone of lawless violence and impunity over a century in the making. For the most part, the borderlands, with all their seething racism and militarised and paramilitarised cruelty, remained apart—a world away from the American heartland. News from the border, no matter how bloody, stayed beyond the nation's consciousness, even as Ronald Reagan once again launched the US beyond the frontier and Bill Clinton made his pitch that no line separated US interests from the world's interests. (Grandin, 2020)

Despite Bill Clinton's sociopolitical rhetoric, in 1996, during the fourth year of his presidency, asylum denial rates were at an all-time high—80 percent. Although denial rates gradually decreased to 62 percent toward the end of Bill Clinton's presidency, interior enforcement deportations had been rising sharply. While President Clinton deported a total of 869,646 between 1993 and 2001, most deportations (730,506) took place between 1996 and 2000, and disproportionately affected Hispanic/Latino immigrants (Golash-Boza, 2012). By 2000, annual deportations had reached their highest level since 1996—188,467 (TRAC, 2016).

By 2006, nativist, white power, and paramilitary groups had already gained significant strength and influence over the sociopolitical discourse of the United States. Groups such as the Minuteman Project, for example, had quickly spread across the country; central to their recruitment efforts and ability to influence mainstream sociopolitical debates was an anti-government rhetoric that exploited the human toll of the Iraq and Afghanistan Wars and the ongoing influx of Latino immigrants and asylum seekers. Their anti-government and anti-immigration rhetoric and recruiting strategy, as during the 1970s, 1980s, and 1990s, were most successful among the armed forces, including "returning veterans," law enforcement, and border patrol agents (Grandin, 2020). As the mainstream of American society continued to embrace covert and overt nativist, white power, and paramilitary rhetoric and ideals, political efforts aimed at comprehensive immigration reform to address the unfolding humanitarian crisis were consistently opposed.

Despite the very public rise of nativist and white power and paramilitary groups during the 2000s, President Obama's electoral win in 2009 allowed a large segment of the American society to argue that the United States was a post-racial society; unfortunately, this couldn't have been further from the truth (Dawson & Lawrence, 2009). In April 11, 2009, a confidential DHS report entitled *Rightwing Extremism: Current Economic and Political Climate Fueling Resurgence in Radicalization and Recruitment*, was leaked to the media (Johnson, 2012). The report, in sharp contrast to the 2009 liberal and conservative post-racial society narrative, warned government officials about the danger that the rise of nativist, white power and paramilitary groups could pose for civil society (Johnson, 2012). Upon the leak of the report, white power and paramilitary groups, such as the Oath Keepers, appropriated and recontextualized historically subjugated, identity-based discourses to reposition themselves as victims of the liberal and cultural government elites (see chapter six). The website post published by the Oath Keepers on April 11, 2009, provides a good example of this appropriation and recontextualization,

Subject: "SHOCKING New DHS Report!! Concerned Americans and activists are now Dangerous Right Wing Extremists!" "Hello brothers, this just came in here in San Diego, California. It looks like Washington has heard of the Oath Keepers, more lies coming from the anti American left wing communist . . . [it is a] brand new confidential report from FBI and DHS dated April 7th and leaked by a DHS insider to Roger Hedgecock. YOU are now a dangerous terrorist according to the Obama Administration. Read this shocking report. . . . FORWARD THIS TO EVERY AMERICAN!" (As cited by Johnson, 2012)

The report became highly controversial in mainstream sociopolitical media outlets, and was largely underplayed by DHS. Despite efforts to undermine the threat, on April 19, 2009, the Oath Keepers emerged for the first time as a public organization, during an opening ceremony in Lexington, Massachusetts—a location connected to the American Revolutionary War and to other white power and paramilitary groups, such as the Minuteman Project. In this ceremony, the Oath Keepers positioned themselves as "the guardians of the Republic." (Johnson, 2012)

As nativist, white power, and paramilitary groups continued to radicalize the sociopolitical discourse of the American nation-state, media outlets and political parties alike were also reflecting similar polarization and radicalization themselves. In fact, between 2008 and 2018 political parties such as the Republican Party developed close ties with these groups, while media outlets such as Fox News continued to provide nativist and white power groups with a mainstream forum, where their propaganda could reach a large national audience (*Mainstreaming Hate: The Anti-Immigrant Movement in the U.S.*, 2018). The increasing polarization and radicalization of mainstream American political platforms and media outlets alike, interfered with any other substantial analysis of the Central American humanitarian crisis at the border (Massey, 2020).

As political parties and mainstream nativist, white power, and paramilitary groups focused on how to control the influx of asylum seekers arriving to the border, historiographic, identity-driven claims that constructed the American nation-state as either a nation of immigrants or of white *native* Americans pervaded mainstream sociopolitical debates; yet, the history of American governmental intervention in Central America and its connection to the humanitarian crisis at the border was largely absent from these debates. However, as Noam Chomsky (2015) aptly describes in *Turning the Tide: U.S. Intervention in Central America and the Struggle for Peace*, the displacement of millions from the Northern Triangle countries, rather than a Latin American problem, is largely the result of American foreign intervention in Central America. As Speckhard (2018) states:

> The fact is that the nations in . . . the Northern Triangle of Central America—El Salvador, Guatemala and Honduras—are grappling with a set of economic and social problems that the U.S. played a role in making, and we have a huge stake in their future. The civil wars that gripped El Salvador and Guatemala during the 1980s, fought with varying degrees of U.S. military support, have given way to criminal activity by gangs and criminal organizations that have forced many families to flee. . . . The resulting organized crime and extreme violence that has bedeviled these countries has been a key driver in migration to the United States. In the case of El Salvador, these gangs, such as Mara Salvatrucha 13 (MS-13), were formed in the United States and exported *back* to Central America by deported Salvadoran members.

By the end of President Obama's administration, and in the year leading to the 2016 presidential elections, the rise of nativism and of white power and paramilitary groups and their ties with the Republican party could no longer be denied. Nativist and white power and paramilitary rhetoric and ideals had found a home within the Republican party and its front-runner, Donald Trump (Rowley, 2018). Once Trump was in office, nativist, white power, and paramilitary groups, came out into the open, organizing rallies while engaging in hate crimes and lawless violence with the support of President Trump, such as during the 2017 Unite the Right Rally in Charlottesville. During this rally, nativist, white power, and paramilitary groups engaged in ethno-racial protectionary chants, such as "You will not replace us, you will not replace us," echoing identity-driven fears of an impending white genocide at the hands of globalist, multicultural, and corrupt governmental elites—a fear that was uniting international white power groups across Europe and the United States, such as the Identitarian Movement and the Identity Evropa Movement (see chapter six; Rowley, 2018).

As nativist and white power and paramilitary groups gained increasing political influence through President Donald Trump and his nativist-populist administration, the violence and economic crisis forcing millions of Central American children and families into exile continued to escalate (Meyer & Pachico, 2018). However, President Trump had already aligned with white power and paramilitary groups, as had a large segment of American society. While President Trump had often served as a powerful amplifier of white power and paramilitary ethno-racial, cultural, and linguistic exclusionary rhetoric, his remarks in February 2018, as the Central American humanitarian crisis continued unabated, were unequivocal

> As we speak, . . . "large, organized caravans are on the march to the United States. We have just heard that Mexican cities, in order to remove the illegal immigrants from their communities, are getting trucks and buses to bring them up to our country in areas where there is little border protection." Should these invaders succeed, he cautioned, working-class Americans would "pay the price" with "reduced jobs, lower wages, overburdened schools, hospitals that are so crowded you can't get in, increased crime, and a depleted social safety net." (Allen, 2019)

Soon after, on December 20, 2018, the Trump administration directed the Department of Homeland Security to implement the Migrant Protection Protocols, MPP. Section 235 (b) (2) (c) of the Immigration and Nationality Act (INA), 8 U.S. C & 1225 (b) (2) (c) allows the United States to return to Mexico or Canada noncitizens arriving on land from these contiguous countries. The 2018 Migrant Protection Protocols expanded DHS authority to also return non-Mexican arrivals to Mexico, while their application was under review in the United States (Mayorkas, 2021). Under this policy, the Trump administration returned seventy thousand migrants to Mexico (*The*

"Migrant Protection Protocols," American Immigration Council, 2022); however, MMP was only the first step toward a greater goal—the closing of the US-Mexico border for Central American asylum seekers.

As American society continued to be highly polarized on the issue of immigration and the humanitarian crisis at the border, the sociopolitical land-scape of the United States, as well as the mainstream of society was in chaos. Acts of domestic terrorism, largely associated with nativist and white power and paramilitary groups, which had been on the rise since the beginning of Trump's presidency, had continued to increase (Jones, Doxsee, & Harrington, 2020). In fact the number of right-wing terrorist attacks in 2016, 2017, and 2019, "matched or even exceeded" the number perpetrated in 1995—one of the highest years for right-wing terrorism (Jones, Doxsee, & Harrington, 2020, p. 3).

Amid this chaos, in March 2020, the United States, like the rest of the world, was unexpectedly confronted with a fast-spreading health crisis—COVID-19, which prompted many countries to close their borders while enforcing public health lockdowns. The Trump administration responded by halting all MMP application hearings until July 17, 2020, when they were indefinitely suspended (*The "Migrant Protection Protocols," American Immigration Council,* 2022). Title 42 quickly followed on March 20, 2020, and eventually replaced MMP, permanently closing the border for migrants and asylum seekers alike.

Title 42 of the Public and Health Act of 1944, which had remained largely inactive and forgotten until it was invoked by President Trump during the COVID-19 pandemic, "permits the Director of the CDC to" bar any individual from entering the United States if they could pose a serious public health risk. As such, Title 42 confers border patrol agents, as well as other customs and border protection officers, the authority to turn away anyone who they suspect could threaten the public health of the American people (*A Guide to Title 42 Expulsions at the Border,* 2022). On March 20, 2020, President Trump invoked Title 42 to permanently close the border, barring all Central American asylum seekers and migrants alike from entering the United States, on grounds of a national health emergency. After reaching an agreement with the Mexican government, "the Border Patrol began sending to Mexico most Mexican, Guatemalan, Honduran, and Salvadoran families and single adults encountered at the southern border" (*A Guide to Title 42 Expulsions at the Border,* 2022). Between March 2020 and December 2022, border patrol agents invoked Title 42 more than 2.4 million times to deny entry into the United States to Central American migrants and asylum seekers—although this number does not correlate with the number of returned asylum seekers or migrants, since the rate of recidivism (multiple crossings) rose to 27 percent during Title 42 (García & Schumacher, 2022).

After decades of trying to bar Hispanics/Latinos/x from entering the United States, nativist, white power, and paramilitary groups had finally found in Title 42 the legal mechanism to accomplish their goal—as well as the president who would implement their nativist and white power ideals. The Hispanic other had now been permanently inscribed as a disease- infested other, and as such, permanently barred from entering the United States. Most importantly, by sealing the border and stopping the Hispanic *invasion*, the white native identity had once again been preserved from its impending transformation and Hispanization; having successfully defended their psychological borders, white *native* Americans could now persist as a people into the future.

However, the 2020 presidential elections brought an unexpected turn of events for American nativist-populism and white power and paramilitary groups alike; their candidate, Donald Trump, was unable to secure the presidency for a second term. Instead of facing defeat, President Trump, aided by nativist, white power, and paramilitary groups, tried to overturn the election, urging the true people of the American nation-state to engage in sedition; chaos erupted and violence quickly followed (see chapters four and five). Ultimately, their attempt failed, and President Biden took office on January 20, 2021. While many human rights and immigrant advocacy organizations looked to the Biden administration with renewed hope, nativist, white power, and paramilitary groups, as well as some conservative political leaders, continued to resist any comprehensive immigration policy reforms that could alter the status of Central American migrants and asylum seekers.

Although President Biden did implement a number of immigration reforms during the first year of his administration, Title 42 continued unabated. In December 2022, after the US District Court in Washington, DC, ordered the Biden administration to terminate the policy by December 20, 2022, many began to look again toward the US-Mexico border; quickly after, on December 27, the Supreme Court temporarily halted its termination until it could hear arguments on the case. Prior to this ruling, the Biden administration had tried and failed to end Title 42, after being challenged in court by Republican states (García, 2022). This is, however, an incomplete account, as during that same time span, President Biden had also been quietly expanding Title 42 to include other previously exempted groups, such as Venezuelan asylum seekers. The contradictory stance of the Biden administration became even more visible when it authorized the return of 24,000 Venezuelan asylum seekers, while acknowledging that Venezuelans, Cubans, and Nicaraguans were forced into exile by their countries' failing communist regimes—despite this acknowledgment, the administration did not change its final decision (Beitsch & Bernal, 2022). The ambivalent stance of the Biden administration toward Hispanic/Latino immigrants and asylum seekers is, unfortunately, consistent with the history of American immigration and asylum policy.

In February 2023, as the Supreme Court was preparing to hear arguments on Title 42, the Biden administration announced its decision to terminate Title 42 in May 2023. On April 27, the Biden adminisstration released its plans to return to Title 8. Under Title 8, "individuals who unlawfully cross the U.S. Southwest border" will face expedited removals—becoming ineligible for asylum under the "proposed Circumvention of Lawful Pathways regulation"—as well as a minimum five-year reentry ban (Homeland Security, 2023). To prevent these outcomes, asylum seekers are instead being directed to apply for asylum through the CBPOne app and then report to a US port of entry, instead of entering between ports (Homeland Security, 2023).

To facilitate access to US ports, the Biden administration reached an agreement with several countries, including Colombia and Guatemala, to establish US Regional Processing Centers (RPCs), where asylum seekers could be interviewed, "and if eligible, . . . processed for lawful pathways to the United States, Canada and Spain" (Homeland Security, 2023).

Overall Title 8, as well as some of its expanded measures, significantly restricts and thwarts the ability of many vulnerable children and families to seek asylum in the United States, in violation of American domestic and international law that states "any non-citizen arriving in the US or already there—regardless of immigration status or how they entered—has a right to seek asylum" (Villarreal, 2023). The US Citizenship and Immigration Services union, concerned about legal human right violations, has "urged Biden to rescind [Title 8], so that officers do not become 'complicit in violation of U.S. and International law'" (Villareal, 2023). Other organizations, including the United Nations High Commissioner for Refugees, have also spoken against President Biden's new border policies. Whether Title 8 will stand legal challenges remains unclear; however, what is certain is that white power and paramilitary groups will resume and increase their vigilante activity across the border, now that it has reopened without needed comprehensive immigration reforms.

IMMIGRATION AND ASYLUM POLICY: RESISTANCE TO IDENTITY TRANSFORMATION

Contemporary nativist, white power, and paramilitary groups in the United States have sought to capitalize on the influx of Central American immigrants and asylum seekers arriving to the US-Mexico border for their own political and ideological aims. By positioning themselves as the protectors of the white *native* American people and nation-state, nativist, white power, and paramilitary groups have polarized and radicalized American society, as well as the political platforms of mainstream parties; ultimately, their strategy has been weakening liberal democracy, undermining the society and nation-state that they proclaim to protect and defend. Unlike previous nativist periods, the 2000s marked the rise of a nativism that capitalized on growing anti-government sentiment—nativist-populism. Likewise, white power movements had also been changing during this time; instead of working to protect the nation-state, as during previous uprisings, white power groups joined paramilitary groups, and their anti-government rhetoric. Together, they sought to overthrow a government that had become the primary enemy of the true American people. That is, white natives could only be protected if the American nation-state was returned to its true owners, and, to accomplish this, liberal democracy and its neoliberal multicultural elites needed to be destroyed.

As Hispanic/Latino immigration increased in the late 1990s and early 2000s, nativist, white power, and paramilitary groups began to influence mainstream sociopolitical discourse by framing immigration as an invasion that would permanently change the identity of the American nation-state and of its true people. Their strategy induced identity-related fears of impending annihilation, supported by media coverage that consistently broadcasted images of thousands of migrants approaching and crossing the border. As nativist, white power, and paramilitary groups had intended, mainstream sociopolitical discourse began to look toward the government and its ruling elites for a solution to the immigration crisis. Despite mainstream pressure, multiple administrations tried and failed to pass any meaningful comprehensive immigration reforms in response to the humanitarian crisis unfolding in Latin America; their failure only legitimized the prevailing and now mainstream, nativist and white power anti-government sociopolitical discourse. Consequently, they argued that while the white *native* people of the nation-state had to contend with dangerous undocumented Hispanic immigrants, who were also taking jobs away from the hardworking white *natives*, the corrupt ruling elites paid little attention to their plight, focusing instead on their neoliberal, multicultural sociopolitical goals. Nativist-populist media added further credibility to such discourses, often showcasing news of undocumented or documented Hispanic immigrants engaging in *criminal activity*.

As the identity-driven, annihilatory fear spread among the mainstream of society, negative, racist interactions between white *natives* and Hispanic/Latinos also became more ingrained, reinforcing identity-related vicious circles of interaction (see chapter eight). As anti-immigrant and anti-government rhetoric escalated, societal and ethno-racial, cultural, and linguistic divisions increased, creating binary dynamics of *us versus them*—white natives versus the Hispanic, immigration/asylum seeker other. This increasingly divisive context fueled a collective state of psychological agitation (manic) among white *natives* that interfered with their capacity to manage and inhibit complex identity-related affects, including fear and aggression.

As previously discussed, collective processes of manic agitation interfere with mentalization and abstraction, which leads individual and group members to experience intergroup conflict on a visceral, life-or-death level (see chapter eight). This is the social and psychological context that nativist, white power, and paramilitary groups wanted to induce through their binary, and polarizing, identity-driven rhetoric—the white native identity, and the American nation-state was under attack, and the enemy Hispanic immigrant/ asylum seeker other needed to be stopped at all costs. Once a society has been fractured in such a manner, and especially due to identity-driven conflict, loyalty to the group becomes essential for the survival of each group, while also making group members more vulnerable to compelling rhetoric, propaganda, and manipulation. This was the actual context that nativist, white power, and paramilitary groups exploited for their own goals and aspirations; it made their identity-driven and anti-governmental rhetoric increasingly more compelling to a larger segment of the American society, as well as to many conservative political elites, eventually radicalizing conservative sociopolitical platforms.

These collective psychological processes ultimately lead to the gradual dehumanization of the enemy *other*, such as the Hispanic or asylum seeker other, creating fertile ground for aggression and violence—such as the nativist, white power, and paramilitary vigilante activity at the US-Mexico border. However, this aggression can also take other forms, manifesting under the guise of laws or policies that have an annihilatory or destructive aim. The IIRIRA and AEDPA acts of 1996, are two such examples, and their effects on thousands of children and mixed-status families have been extensively documented; however, despite the harm that these children and families have and continue to endure, the IIRIRA and AEDPA acts continue to be in effect. Title 42, as well as the Migrant Protection Protocols, are similar examples, affecting thousands fleeing violence, poverty, social unrest, and climate change.

Ultimately, the rise of nativist, white power, and paramilitary groups in the United States, culminated in the uprising at the US Capitol, on January 6, 2021—a moment that tested liberal democracy in the United States. Although many of the nativist, white power, and paramilitary groups are facing judicial prosecution, it would be dangerous to assume that a similar act of sedition could not repeat itself in the years to come. Donald Trump may no longer be president, but nativist-populism will continue, as it has been embraced by the Republican party. Most importantly, contemporary nativist-populism is unequivocally protofascist in nature, and clearly connected to nativist, white power, and paramilitary groups. As long as these conditions remain in place, American liberal democracy will continue to be vulnerable and subject to further erosion; as such, the question is not whether liberal democracy will be tested again, but rather how and when it will happen.

In the interim, the humanitarian crisis in the US-Mexico border remains unabated, and without a clear future solution. Historical identity-driven conflict between the United States and Latin America and fears of an impending Hispanic invasion mobilized a large segment of the American society and political elites against immigrants and asylum seekers alike. However, immigrants and asylum seekers are not the problem; they are a symptom of neoliberal capitalism and US foreign intervention in Latin America. While nativist-populism, as well as white power and paramilitary groups, have largely turned the humanitarian crisis into an identity-driven conflict, as long as the conditions that gave rise to the humanitarian crisis remain unaddressed, migrants and asylum seekers will continue to flee their countries and communities in desperation and to survive. Efforts to prevent the impending transformation of the white *native* identity, independent of how the humanitarian crisis is resolved, only delay its inevitable transformation, while keeping the American society in a perennial state of manic agitation and thwarted mourning—unable to heal from the collective trauma incurred in the formation of the white native identity and the American nation-state (Fariña, 2018). Although white *natives*, and some segments of the American society continue to resist this change, the impending demographic change of the United States cannot be stopped—even if all Hispanic immigrants were to be deported (Fariña, 2018). A politics of forgiveness and reconciliation will be necessary at some point, if all groups are to coexist as part of a nation-state that they can call their own.

Chapter Eleven

Russia and Ukraine

The Development of a New Identity and Thwarted Mourning

Resistance to mourning, as related to identity-based chosen traumas and identity transformation, is not unique to societies facing the rise of nationalist or nativist-populism. Multiple nation-states are facing similar conflicts; some even more dehumanizing and violent than others, as in the case of the war between Russia and Ukraine. The complex dynamics that led to this most recent war cannot be thoroughly explored in this final chapter; however, a brief integrated sociopolitical and psychological analysis of this war could not be omitted, given the central role that identity and nationalism have played to legitimize this devastating war.

NATIONALISM, IDENTITY, AND HISTORICAL MEMORY: RUSSIA AND UKRAINE

Khazanov (2008) in *Whom to Mourn and Whom to Forget? (Re)constructing Collective Memory in Contemporary Russia, Totalitarian Movements and Political Religions*, makes an important distinction between remembering and a people's public commitment to remembering and mourning,

> The ways post-totalitarian and post-authoritarian countries deal with their disturbing pasts tells much about their contemporary political order as well as about the national identities they are seeking in the present. The issue is not whether horrors and crimes are remembered and commemorated, but whether society at large—outside the circle of survivors—makes the task of memory a public commitment. Dealing with the past remains a painful problem in virtually all former communist countries. (Khazanov, 2008)

161

Since the 1980s, European nation-states such as Germany, Austria, Spain, Poland, Ukraine, and Russia have passed historical memory laws (Koposov, 2020). Initially, memory laws, such as those in Germany, sought to criminalize historical negationism, specifically Holocaust denial; subsequent laws broadened historical negationism to include crimes against humanity, such as those committed by Franco's dictatorship. However, in recent years memory laws have been used for what some scholars call a "nationalization of the past" (Kurrilla, 2020). Ukraine's decommunization laws (2015), as well as Russia's memory laws (2014), are two such examples, albeit with profound differences. While Ukraine's laws criminalize the denial "including in the media, [of] the criminal character of the communist totalitarian regime of 1917–1991 in Ukraine," Russia's memory law forbids "any public attempt to equate the aims and actions of the Soviet Union and Nazi Germany during World War II, as well as to deny the decisive role of the Soviet people in the victory over fascism" (see chapter eight; *Duma Adopts in First Reading Ban on Putting Soviet Union, Nazi Germany on Same Footing*, 2021; Koposov, 2020; Marples, 2020, 2018). Memory laws are now at the center of national identity politics and reflect and reinforce the nationalist historical master narratives involved in the production of group-specific national identities. The character of these historical master narratives not only shapes the people's collective identity, but also deeply influences the sacrifices that a people will make to defend who they and their nation-state are. However, identity-related master narratives are also used by political leaders to mobilize a people; as such, master narratives linked to historical negationism have the capacity to become common sense, accepted truths that eventually function as state-driven propaganda—when this occurs, myths become facts that don't need to be questioned, or in extreme cases, cannot be questioned, such as during German fascism (see chapter five; Iliyasov & Gutbrod, 2022). Russia and Ukraine share a long and complex past that involves control, subjugation, and intergroup conflict; ultimately, Ukraine broke away from Russian control, establishing itself as an independent nation-state in 1991—this independence is now being tested under the guise of ethno-racial, cultural, religious, and linguistic identity politics and protectionism.

Prior to Ukraine's independence, Ukraine had been part of the former Soviet Union, and held an important position within the union. In fact, in 1954, Nikita Krushchev transferred Crimea, a primarily Russian-populated territory, to Ukraine, to strengthen their ties. Although Ukraine achieved its independence from Russia in 1991, a significant percentage of ethnic Russians remained in Ukraine. According to Ukraine's most recent (2001) population census, eight million ethnic Russians lived at that point in the south and east regions of Ukraine, mostly, "in the regions of Donetsk and Luhansk, making up 40 percent of the population, [as well as in] the regions of Zaporizhzhia and Kherson," accounting for 25 percent and 15 percent of the total population (Goncharenko, 2022). While the Soviet Union collapsed a few weeks after Ukraine held its referendum on independence, Russia experienced the separation of Ukraine as a significant loss and narcissistic injury. This injury never truly subsided, and only deepened, since Ukraine gradually developed closer ties with Western European organizations such as the EU and, most recently, NATO (Masters, 2022).

During this time Russia was also undergoing significant change and transformation. With the collapse of the Soviet Union, and under president Boris Yeltsin, Russia had started to confront its past, and the crimes committed by the Soviet Union (see Iliyasov & Gutbrod, 2022). However, the collective and political efforts to engage with a complicated, traumatic, and violent past were short lived. Although some of the historical content was included in Russia's school curriculum during the 1980s and 1990s, by the late 1990s the majority of the Russian population had begun to direct its attention away from the past, and its dehumanizing effects (Khazanov, 2008; Miller, 2017). As Khazanov (2008) states, "Today, the Soviet crimes occupy an insignificant place in the collective memory in Russia, if they exist at all. In any case, they remain diverse, fragmented, compartamentalised and localised" (p. 294).

This collective dissociation and denial increased in 1999, when Vladimir Putin rose to power. In fact, Putin focused on building a new Russian identity emphasizing nationalist ideals; rather than looking at the past, acknowledging its violence and the complex feelings associated with it, such as shame, loss, and humiliation, Putin sought to restore Russia to its former glory.

Gradually, collective repression, denial, and dissociation became pervasive, and with it the use of historical recontextualization. History books were rewritten according to master narratives that emphasized the strength and glory of the former Soviet Union, and its people (Kurilla, 2018); at the same time, and to foster internal unity among the Russian people, Russia was often presented as a misunderstood country that needed to defend and protect itself from foreign manipulation and interference. By idealizing the past and maintaining a needed state of repression and denial, it became possible to induce a collective state of nostalgia and longing for what had been. As Khazanov (2008) states, "Many Russians . . . became nostalgic about the times when, in a way, life was easier and simpler because the state prescribed for them what to do and what to think but, in turn, provided them with employment, a social security net and the pride of living in a superpower" (p. 299). As nostalgia set in among the mainstream of society, Putin positioned himself as a powerful and determined leader, capable of restoring the nation-state to its former glory. His actions were about to demonstrate it. As his rhetoric became increasingly more authoritarian, so did his actions, beginning to exert more political control over the country and undermining the democratic process.

At the same time, Ukraine had been strengthening its position in Europe and deepening its ties with the European Union, until President Yanukovych reversed course amid increasing political pressure from Russia (Masters, 2022). However, by 2014, Putin had created the conditions that would ensure mainstream support for Russia's expansion—Russia would recover some of its lost territories and power. Ukraine's defiance and increasing relationship with the European Union created the ideal conditions for the invasion of Crimea. Putin legitimized the annexation through nationalist identity claims of ethnic reunification and preservation—since the ethnic Russian population in Crimea had become an ethnic minority after its transfer to Ukraine in 1954. Ultimately the annexation of Crimea was part of a larger goal—to restore Russia to its former glory. The annexation of Crimea, however, was more than a mere victory for Putin and the Russia people; it also provided an opportunity to heal from the narcissistic injuries incurred during the collapse of the Soviet Union and the economic decline that followed (Iliyasov & Gutbrod, 2022; Toal, 2017). Putin's strategy proved successful in Russia, where he strengthened his position as a determined and powerful leader.

Ukraine, on the other hand, had been reckoning with its past. Rather than seeking to maintain an alliance with Russia, Ukraine wanted to distance itself from Russia while repudiating its communist past; the 2014 decommunization laws were a central step in this process. For Ukraine, the period between 1917 and 1991 needed to be understood as criminal in nature—a crime committed for seventy-four years against Ukraine and by the communist, Soviet totalitarian regime. However, Ukraine's views were incompatible with both Putin's ethno-racial, cultural, religious, and linguistic nationalist master narratives, as well as with his goals of Russian expansion and glory. As Putin stated in July 2021, in his article "On the Historical Unity of Russians and Ukranians,"

> To have a better understanding of the present and look into the future, we need to turn to history. Certainly, it is impossible to cover in this article all the developments that have taken place over more than a thousand years. But I will focus on the key, pivotal moments that are important for us to remember, both in Russia and Ukraine. Russians, Ukrainians, and Belarusians are all descendants of Ancient Rus, which was the largest state in Europe. Slavic and other tribes across the vast territory—from Ladoga, Novgorod, and Pskov to Kiev and Chernigov—were bound together by one language (which we now refer to as Old Russian), economic ties, the rule of the princes of the Rurik dynasty, and—after the baptism of Rus—the Orthodox faith. The spiritual choice made by St. Vladimir, who was both Prince of Novgorod and Grand Prince of Kiev, still largely determines our affinity today. (Putin, 2021)

Putin's words reflect an ethno-racial, cultural, religious, and linguistic nationalism similar to the one that existed during the years between World War I and World War II (see chapter two). During that time, ethno-racial, cultural, religiousm and linguistic nationalism created and defined the people of the nation-state, and legitimized their right to live together as one. As such, new nation-states were created, while the physical boundaries of some existing nation-states were redrawn—sometimes transforming ethnic majority groups into ethnic minorities. However, it was this ethno-geopolitical nationalism that created the conditions that culminated in World War II and the rise of fascism. Given this context, it is not surprising that when the war between Russia and Ukraine erupted, fear of a third World War quickly spread across the European continent.

Complicated historical dynamics related to collective identity formation, loss, and transformation are central to the war between Russia and Ukraine. These dynamics are also deeply linked to the collective violence, coercion, and repression inflicted and endured in the name of, and/or to preserve, these identities. The collective inability to both acknowledge and process these large-group traumas ultimately fuels manic agitation and psychic equivalence processes that amplify identity and trauma related affects. Aggression emerges that, if unabated, leads to the dehumanization of the other. Ultimately, as in the case of Russia and Ukraine, these conflicts become intractable and violent, with a high human toll.

CLOSING THOUGHTS: THE POWER OF A STORY

Stories have power, and the history of nationalism, nativism, and populism shows the very real consequences of these stories. Some have the capacity to dehumanize and kill, while others have the capacity to heal and regenerate a people. It all depends on who is telling the story and on why they are choosing to tell it at that particular moment. Yet, it is also possible to resist the power of these stories and of their storyteller. This requires listening carefully to identify and examine the discontinuities that exist in the stories. When this happens, a small space opens up in which other previously silenced and subjugated stories can enter the social consciousness of a people. If the affects attached to the dominant stories are slowly contained to support further conscientization efforts, the dominant stories and storytellers gradually begin to lose their power. It is at this point when a people can begin to see a glimpse of a different and long-forgotten story and past. If they can hold on to this glimpse long enough, they will have a unique opportunity to rediscover who they have been, who they are, and who they could become—freed from the ghosts of a past that had been haunting them, even if largely out of conscious awareness.

References

Abascal, S. (n.d). Qué es VOX. VOX. https://www.voxespana.es/espana/que-es-vox.

Abascal, S. (2021, October 8). AGENDA ESPAÑA. VOX. https://xn--agendaespaa -beb.eswp-content/uploads/2021/10/AgendaEspana_VOX.pdf.

Abdelhadi, M. (2021). Ceuta and Melilla: Spain's enclaves in North Africa. BBC. https://www.bbc.com/news/world-africa-57305882.

ACLU. (2022). *License to Abuse: How ICE's 287(g) Program Empowers Racist Sheriffs.* ACLU. https://www.aclu.org/report/license-abuse-how-ices-287g -program-empowers-racist-sheriffs.

Al Jazeera. (2018, December 10). *What Is Generation Identity?* https://www.aljazeera .com/news/2018/12/10/what-is-generation-identity.

Al Jazeera. (2022, December 12). *Oath Keepers plotted to use force on January 6: US prosecutor.* https://www.aljazeera.com/news/2022/12/12/oath-keepers-plotted -to-use-force-on-january-6-us-prosecutor.

Allen, I. (2019, February 8). Trump's 'Caravan' Is a Made-up Monster Fabricated by the Far Right. *The Nation.* https://www.thenation.com/article/archive/caravan -white-supremacist-campaign-trump/.

American Immigration Council. (2021b, June 24). *U.S. Citizen Children Impacted by Immigration Enforcement.* https://www.americanimmigrationcouncil.org/research /us-citizen-children-impacted-immigration-enforcement.

American Immigration Council. (2021a, July 8). *The 287(g) Program: An Overview* https://www.americanimmigrationcouncil.org/research/287g-program -immigration.

American Immigration Council. (2022, May 25) *A Guide to Title 42: Expulsions at the Border.* https://www.americanimmigrationcouncil.org/research/ guide-title-42-expulsions-border.

American Psychological Association. (n.d.). Annihilation. APA Dictionary of Psychology. https://dictionary.apa.org/annihilation.

American Psychological Association. (n.d.). Dissociation. APA Dictionary of Psychology. https://dictionary.apa.org/dissociation.

Anderson, E. (2021, January 4). European elections to watch in 2021. Politico. https: //www.politico.eu/article/2021-elections-to-watch-europe/.

Anti-Defamation League, ADL. (2019, August 8). *White Supremacist's Anti-Immigrant Rhetoric Echoes Comments from Public Figures.* https://www.adl.org/resources /blog/white-supremacists-anti-immigrant-rhetoric-echoes-comments-public -figures.

Anti-Defamation League, ADL. (2021). HEAT Map™. https://www.adl.org/resources/tools-to-track-hate/heat-map.

Antiterrorism and Effective Death Penalty Act of 1996. Pub. L. No. 104–32, 110 Stat. 1214. (1996). www.uscis.gov/sites/default/files/ocomm/ilink/ 0-0-0-8598.html.

Arato, A. (2019). Populism, Constitutional Courts, and Civil Society. In C. Landfried (Ed.), *Judicial Power: How Constitutional Courts Affect Political Transformations* (318–41). Cambridge University Press. doi:10.1017/9781108348669.016.

Arendt, H. (1966). *The origins of totalitarianism*. Harcourt, Brace & World, Inc.

Argueta, C. N. (2016, April 19). *Border Security: Immigration Enforcement Between Ports of Entry*. FAS Project on Government Secrecy. https://sgp.fas.org/crs/homesec/R42138.pdf.

Aron, L., Grand, S., & Slochower, J. (Eds.). (2018). *De-idealizing Relational Theory: A Critique from Within*. Routledge.

Atwood, E., & Stolorow, R. (2014). *Structures of subjectivity: Explorations in psychoanalytic phenomenology and contextualism*. Routledge.

Aydin, C. (2017). How to Forget the Unforgettable? On Collective Trauma, Cultural Identity, and Mnemotechnologies, *Identity, 17*(3), 125–37, DOI: 10.1080/15283488.2017.1340160.

Baden-Württemberg Landesamt für Verfassungsschutz. (2021, August 12). *IBÖ demonstriert gegen Lambda-Verbot*. Verfassungsschutz BW. https://www.verfassungsschutz-bw.de/,Lde/IBOe+demonstriert+gegen+Lambda-Verbot.

Bali, K. (2021, October 17). Golden Dawn is down, but Greek far right rises. DW. https://www.dw.com/en/golden-dawn-is-down-but-far-right-rises-again-in-greece/a-59528529.

Ball, T., Dagger, R., & O'Neill, D.I. (2019). *Ideals and Ideologies: A Reader* (R. Dagger, & D.I. O'Neill, Eds.) (11th ed.). Routledge. https://doi.org/10.4324/9780429286827.

Barkhoff, J., & Leerssen, J. (Eds.). (2021). *National Stereotyping, Identity Politics, European Crises*. Brill. http://www.jstor.org/stable/10.1163/j.ctv1v7zbzt.

Basu, A. (2022, October 22). Spain Is One Step Closer to Exorcising Francisco Franco. The Wire. https://thewire.in/history/spain-is-one-step-closer-to-exorcising-francisco-franco.

Baugh, R. (2022, March 8). *Annual Flow Report March 2022—Refugees and Asylees: 2020*. Homeland Security. https://www.dhs.gov/sites/default/files/2022-03/22_0308_plcy_refugees_and_asylees_fy2020_1.pdf.

BBC. (2019, November 13). Europe and right-wing nationalism: A country-by-country guide. BBC News. https://www.bbc.com/news/world-europe-36130006.

Beale, H. K. (1958). *The Critical Year: A Study of Andrew Johnson and Reconstruction*. F. Ungar Publishing Company.

Beirich, H., & Via, W. (n.d). *Generation Identity*. Global Project Against Hate and Extremism. https://globalextremism.org/reports/generation-identity/.

Beitsch, R., & Bernal, R. (2022, October 18). Biden embraces Trump's Title 42 with expansion to Venezuela. The Hill. https://thehill.com/latino/3693444-biden-embraces-trumps-title-42-with-expansion-to-venezuela/.

Belew, K. (2019). *Bring the War Home: The White Power Movement and Paramilitary America*. Harvard University Press.

Belew, K. (2018, April 18). The History of White Power. *New York Times*. https://www.nytimes.com/2018/04/18/opinion/history-white-power.html.

Benjamin, J. (2018). *Beyond doer and done to: Recognition theory, intersubjectivity and the third*. Routledge.

Benner, E. (2016). Nationalism: Intellectual Origins. In J. Breuilly (Ed.), *The Oxford Handbook of the History of Nationalism* (36–55). Oxford University Press. https://doi.org/10.1093/oxfordhb/9780199209194.001.0001.

Berger, S. (2021). Confronting the Other/Perceiving the Self: National Historiographies and National Stereotypes in Twentieth-Century Europe. In J. Leerssen & J. Barkhoff (Eds.), *National Stereotyping, Identity Politics, European Crises* (15–30). Brill.

Bergman, J. (1998). Was the Soviet Union Totalitarian? The View of Soviet Dissidents and the Reformers of the Gorbachev Era. *Studies in East European Thought, 50*(4), 247–81. http://www.jstor.org/stable/20099686.

Besser, L. (2019, March 27). Austrian far-right group faces ban after donation from alleged Christchurch shooter. ABC. https://www.abc.net.au/news/2019-03-28/austrian-far-right-group-faces-ban-brenton-tarrant-donation/10947002.

Bilali, R., and Vollhardt, J. R. (2019), Victim and Perpetrator Groups' Divergent Perspectives on Collective Violence: Implications for Intergroup Relations. *Political Psychology*, 40: 75–108. https://doi.org/10.1111/pops.12570.

Billig, M. (1995). *Banal nationalism*. Sage.

Biswas, K. (2020, February 4). How the Far Right Became Europe's New Normal (Published 2020). *New York Times*. https://www.nytimes.com/2020/02/04/opinion/far-right-europe-austria.html.

Bloomfield, V. (2003). Reconciliation: An introduction. In D. Bloomfield, T. Barnes, & L. Huyse (Eds.), *Reconciliation after violent conflict: A handbook* (10–28). Stockholm, Sweden: International Institute for Democracy and Electoral Assistance, IDEA.

Boissoneault, L. (2017, January 26). How the 19th-Century Know Nothing Party Reshaped American Politics. *Smithsonian Magazine*. https://www.smithsonianmag.com/history/immigrants-conspiracies-and-secret-society-launched-american-nativism-180961915/.

Bonikowski, B., Halikiopoulou, D., Kaufmann, E., and Rooduijn, M. (2019). Populism and Nationalism in a Comparative Perspective: A Scholarly Exchange. *Nations and Nationalism 25*(1), 58–81.

Bosworth, R. J. B. (Ed.). (2009). *The Oxford Handbook of Fascism*. Oxford University Press.

Bosworth, R. J. B. (2021). *Mussolini and the Eclipse of Italian Fascism: From Dictatorship to Populism*. Yale University Press.

Braden, A. (1980, Summer). Lessons from a History of Struggle. *Southern Exposure, VIII*(2), 56–57.

Branton, R., Dillingham, G., & Miller, B. (2007, September). Anglo Voting on Nativist Ballot Initiatives: The Partisan Impact of Spatial Proximity to the

U.S.-Mexico Border. *Social Science Quarterly, 88*(3), 882–97. https://doi.org/10.1111/j.1540-6237.2007.00488.x.

Breuilly, J. (2006). Introduction: nations and nationalism. In E. Gellner, *Nations and Nationalism* (1st ed., xiii–llll). Blackwell.

Breuilly, J. (Ed.). (2013). *The Oxford Handbook of the History of Nationalism.* Oxford University Press.

Brounéus, K. (2019). *Truth and Reconciliation Commission processes: learning from the Solomon Islands.* Rowman & Littlefield.

Brown, G. (2019, January 9). *Globalization at a Crossroads by Gordon Brown.* Project Syndicate. https://www.project-syndicate.org/magazine/globalization-at-a-crossroads-by-gordon-brown-2019-01.

Brubaker, R. (1996). *Nationalism Reframed: Nationhood and the National Question in the New Europe.* Cambridge University Press.

Byman, D. L., & Pitcavage, M. (2021, April). *Identifying and exploiting the weaknesses of the white supremacist movement.* Brookings Institution. https://www.brookings.edu/research/identifying-and-exploiting-the-weaknesses-of-the-white-supremacist-movement/.

Caldwell, B. C. (2019). *Deported Americans: Life after Deportation to Mexico.* Duke University Press. https://doi.org/10.2307/j.ctv11cw5qf.

Canovan, M. (1981). *Populism.* Junction Books.

Canovan, M. (1999). Trust the People! Populism and the Two Faces of Democracy. *Political studies.* 47(1), 2–16.

Camus, J. (2021, March 11). *Génération Identitaire ban could rally supporters of the radical right in France.* openDemocracy. https://www.opendemocracy.net/en/countering-radical-right/g%C3%A9n%C3%A9ration-identitaire-ban-could-rally-supporters-of-the-radical-right-in-france/.

Čapek, J., & Loidolt, S. (2021). Phenomenological approaches to personal identity. *Phenom Cogn Sci 20,* 217–34. https://doi.org/10.1007/s11097-020-09716-9.

Capellà i Roig, M. (2021). El derecho a interponer recursos y a obtener reparación de los familiares de personas desaparecidas durante la guerra civil española. *Eunomía. Revista en Cultura de la Legalidad, 20,* 104–40. DOI. 10.20318/eunomia.2021.6065.

Capps, R., Koball, H., Campetella, A., Pereira, K., Hooker, S., & Pedroza, J. M. (2015). Implications of Immigration Enforcement Activities for the Well-Being of Children in Immigrant Families. Urban Institute. https://www.urban.org/sites/default/files/alfresco/publication-exhibits/2000405/2000405-Implications-of-Immigration-Enforceme-activities-for-the-Well-Being-of-Children-in-Immigrant-Families.pdf.

Carment, D., & Fischer, M. (2010). Conflict prevention. In Karl Cordell and Stefan Wolff (Eds.), *Routledge Handbook of Ethnic Conflict.* Routledge.

Centers for Disease Control. (2021, November 24). Racism and Health | Minority Health   Centers for Disease Control and Prevention. https://www.cdc.gov/minorityhealth/racism-disparities/index.html.

Center for Systemic Peace (2021). Polity 5 regime narrative for the United States http://www.systemicpeace.org/index.html.

Chacon, J. M., Johnson, K. R., & Hing, B. O. (2021). *Immigration Law and Social Justice*. Wolters Kluwer.

Chalmers, D. M. (1987). *Hooded Americanism: The History of the Ku Klux Klan*. Duke University Press.

Chambers, H. L. (2013). Slavery, free blacks and citizenship. *Rutgers Law Journal, 43,* 486–513.

Chomsky, N. (2015). *Turning the Tide: U.S. Intervention in Central America and the Struggle for Peace*. Haymarket Books.

Chu, J. (2011). *Rebuilding shattered lives: Treating complex PTSD and dissociative disorders* (2nd ed.). John Wiley.

Churchill, W. (1997). *A little matter of genocide: holocaust and denial in the Americas, 1492 to the present*. City Lights Publishers.

Clifford, J. (2000). Take Identity Politics Seriously: "The Contradictory Stony Ground . . . " In P. Gilroy, L. Grossberg, & A. McRobbie (Eds.), *Without Guarantees: In Honor of Stuart Hall* (94–112). Verso Books.

Comas-Díaz, L. (2021). Sociopolitical trauma: Ethnicity, race, and migration. In P. Tummala-Narra (Ed.), *Trauma and racial minority immigrants: Turmoil, uncertainty, and resistance* (127–46). American Psychological Association. https://doi.org/10.1037/0000214-008.

Comunidad Autónoma de La Rioja. (May 11, 2022). Ley 5/2022, de 25 de abril, para la recuperación de la memoria democrática en La Rioja. Boletín Oficial del Estado 112, BOE-A-2022-7640.

Cordell, K., & Wolf, S. (2010). *Ethnic conflict*. Polity Press.

Cortes Generales de España, VIII Legislatura. (December 27, 2007). Ley 52/2007, de 26 de diciembre, por la que se reconocen y amplían derechos y se establecen medidas en favor de quienes padecieron persecución o violencia durante la guerra civil y la dictadura. *Boletín Oficial del Estado 310, BOE-A-2007–22296.*

Coulmas, F. (2019). *Identity: A Very Short Introduction*. Oxford University Press.

Counter Extremism Project. (n.d.). Hammerskin Nation (a.k.a. Hammerskins). https://www.counterextremism.com/supremacy/hammerskin-nation-aka-hammerskins.

Courtois, C., & Ford, J. (2016). *Treatment of complex trauma: A sequences, relationship-based approach*. Guilford Press.

Crosby, A. (1976). Virgin-Soil Epidemics as a Factor in the Aboriginal Depopulation in America. *William & Mary Quarterly, 33,* 289–99.

Cuison Villazor, R., & Chin, G. J. (Eds.). (2015). *The Immigration and Nationality Act of 1965: Legislating a New America*. Cambridge University Press.

Dalton, A., Huang, L. (2014). Motivated Forgetting in Response to Social Identity Threat, *Journal of Consumer Research*, 40(6), 1017–38, https://doi.org/10.1086/674198.

David, C., & Fischer, M. (2010). Conflict prevention. In Karl Cordell and Stefan Wolff (Eds.), *Routledge Handbook of Ethnic Conflict* (169–86). Routledge Handbooks Online.

Davies, P. (2010). The Front National and Catholicism: from intégrisme to Joan of Arc and Clovis, *Religion Compass*, 4 (9), 576–87.

Davis, N. T., Goidel, K., Lipsmeyer, C. S., Whitten, G. D., & Young, C. (2019). The political consequences of nativism: The impact of nativist sentiment on party support*. *Social Science Quarterly, 100* (2), 466–79. https://scroll.lib.westfield.ma.edu:3150/10.1111/ssqu.12596.

Davis, N. T., Goidel, K., Lipsmeyer, C. S., Whitten, G. D., & Young, C. (2019). Economic vulnerability, cultural decline, and nativism: Contingent and indirect effects. *Social Science Quarterly, 100* (2), 430–46. https://scroll.lib.westfield.ma.edu:3150/10.1111/ssqu.12591.

Dawson, M. C., & Lawrence, D. B. (2009). One year later and the myth of a post-racial society. *Du Bois Review: Social Science Research on Race 6*(2): 247–49.

de Gobineau, J. A. (1853). *Essai sur l'inégalité des races humaines.* n.d.

De Masi, F. (2015). Is the concept of the death drive still useful in the clinical field?, *The International Journal of Psychoanalysis, 96*(2), 445–58, DOI: 10.1111/1745-8315.12308.

De Querold, R. (2020). There was no Reconquest. No military campaign lasts eight centuries. *El Pais.* https://english.elpais.com/arts/2020-02-28/henry-kamen-there-was-no-reconquest-no-military-campaign-lasts-eight-centuries.html.

Declaration of Independence: A Transcription (2023, January 31). National Archives. https://www.archives.gov/founding-docs/declaration-transcript.

Demmers, J. (2012). *Theories of Violent conflict.* Routledge.

Department of Health and Human Services. (2022a, May 31). Monthly Report to Congress on Separated Children | May 2022. HHS.gov. https://www.hhs.gov/sites/default/files/may-2022-monthly-report-on-separated-children.pdf.

Department of Health and Human Services. (2022b, January 31). Monthly Report to Congress on Separated Children | January 2022. HHS.gov. http://www.hhs.gov/sites/default/files/january-2022-monthly-report-on-separated-children.pdf.

Department of Homeland Security. (2021a, April 20). Deportation of Parents of U.S.-Born Children CY 2019 2nd half. Homeland Security. https://www.dhs.gov/sites/default/files/_publications/ice_-_deportation_of_parents_of_u.s.-born_children_first_half_cy_2020.pdf.

Department of Homeland Security. (2021b, October 4). Deportation of Parents CY 2020 1st Half. Homeland Security. https://www.dhs.gov/sites/default/files/2022-01/ice_-_deportation_of_parents_of_u.s.-born_children_second_half_cy_2020_0.pdf.

Derrida, J. (1984). *Margins of Philosophy* (A. Bass, Trans.). The University of Chicago Press.

Derrida, J. (2001). *On Cosmopolitanism and Forgiveness.* Taylor & Francis. https://doi.org/10.4324/9780203165713.

Derrida, J. (2016). *Of Grammatology* (G. C. Spivak, Trans.). Johns Hopkins University Press.

Derrida, J. (2020). *The Politics of Friendship.* Verso Books.

Diamond, S. (1996). Right-Wing Politics and The Anti-Immigration Cause. *Social Justice, 23*(3) (65), 154–68. http://www.jstor.org/stable/29766959.

Díez Gutiérrez, E. (2013). La memoria histórica en los libros de texto escolares. *Didáctica de las Ciencias Experimentales y Sociales.* doi:10.7203/dces.27.2373.

Dijkstra, L., Poelman, H., & Rodríguez-Pose, A. (2020). The geography of EU discontent, *Regional Studies, 54*(6), 737–53, DOI: 10.1080/00343404.2019.1654603.

Dixon, T. (1905). *The Clansman: An historical romance of the Ku Klux Klan.* Doubleday, Page & Company.

Dominian, L. (1917). *The Frontier of Language and Nationality in Europe.* Henry Holt and Company.

Doomernik, J., & Bruquetas-Callejo, M. (2015). National Immigration and Integration Policies in Europe Since 1973. In R. Penninx & B. Garcés-Mascareñas (Eds.), *Integration Processes and Policies in Europe: Contexts, Levels and Actors* (57–76). Springer International Publishing. 10.1007/978-3-319-21674-4.

Doyle, H. D., & Van Young, E. (2013). Independence and Nationalism in the Americas. In *The Oxford Handbook of the History of Nationalism* (1st ed., 97–126). Oxford University Press.

Dreby, J. (2015, May). U.S. immigration policy and family separation: the consequences for children's well-being. PubMed. Retrieved December 14, 2022, from https://pubmed.ncbi.nlm.nih.gov/25228438/.

Du Bois, W. E. B. (1935). *Black Reconstruction in America 1860–1880.* Brace and Company.

Dulić, T. (2015). Rethinking violence, in *The Routledge History of Genocide* ed. Cathie Carmichael and Richard C. Maguire. Routledge.

Duma adopts in first reading ban on putting Soviet Union, Nazi Germany on same footing. (2021, May 25). TASS. https://tass.com/society/1293829.

Dunbar-Ortiz, R. (2015). *An indigenous peoples history of the United States* [Kindle for Mac].

Duschinsky, R., & Foster, S. (2021). Forms of non-mentalizing. In *Mentalising and Epistemic Trust: The work of Peter Fonagy and colleagues at the Anna Freud Centre.* Oxford University Press. https://www.oxfordclinicalpsych.com/view/10.1093/med-psych/9780198871187.001.0001/med-9780198871187-chapter-6.

Duyvendak, J. W., & Kesic, J. (2018, February 1). The Rise of Nativism in Europe. EuropeNow. https://www.europenowjournal.org/2018/01/31/the-rise-of-nativism-in-europe/.

Dyson, Y., Fariña, M., Gurrola, M., & Cross-Denny, B. (2019). Reconciliation as a Framework for Supporting Racial, Ethnic, and Cultural Diversity in Social Work Education. *Social Work & Christianity, 47*(1), 83–95. https://doi.org/10.34043/swc.v47i1.137.

Eberly, J. C., Stock, J. H., & Hunt, J. (2001, November 2). *Retrospective on American Economic Policy in the 1990s.* Brookings Institution. https://www.brookings.edu/research/retrospective-on-american-economic-policy-in-the-1990s/.

Eco, U. (2012). *Inventing the Enemy: And Other Occasional Writings.* Houghton Mifflin.

Eco, U. (2020). *How to Spot a Fascist* (R. Dixon & A. McEwen, Trans.). Penguin Random House.

El Mundo. (2019, April 22). *Un día con Santiago Abascal (Vox) en la Granada 'reconquistada.'* YouTube. https://www.youtube.com/watch?v=BGJuENkPN0I.

Ellyatt, H. (2019, January 28). Mad or miraculous: As the euro turns 20, has monetary union been a good thing? CNBC. https://www.cnbc.com/2019/01/28/euro-turns-20-has-monetary-union-been-a-good-thing.html.

Encarnación, O. G. (2012). Justice in times of transition: Lessons from the Iberian experience. *International Studies Quarterly*, *56*(1), 179–92. http://www.jstor.org/stable/41409830.

Essletzbichler, J., Disslbacher, F., & Moser, M. (2018, March). The victims of neoliberal globalisation and the rise of the populist vote: a comparative analysis of three recent electoral decisions. *Cambridge Journal of Regions, Economy and Society*, *11*(1), 73–94.

Erikson, E. H. (1956). The Problem of Ego Identity. *Journal of the American Psychoanalytic Association*, *4*(1), 56–121. https://doi.org/10.1177/000306515600400104.

Erikson, E. H. (1968). *Identity: Youth and crisis.* Norton.

Erikson, E. H. (1985). *The life cycle completed: A review.* W. W. Norton & Co.

Erikson K. T. (1976). *Everything in its Path.* Simon & Schuster.

Europe and right-wing nationalism: A country-by-country guide. (2019, November 13). BBC. https://www.bbc.com/news/world-europe-36130006.

The European Competition for North America, The British & American Colonial Perspective: A Sampling, 1699–1763. (2009). National Humanities Center. http://nationalhumanitiescenter.org/pds/becomingamer/american/text1/europeancompetition.pdf.

European Union. (n.d.). Euro—history and purpose. European Union. https://european-union.europa.eu/institutions-law-budget/euro/history-and-purpose_en.

Executive Order: Border Security and Immigration Enforcement Improvement. (2017a, January 25). The White House: Office of the Press Secretary. https://www.whitehouse.gov/the-press-office/2017/01/25/executive-order-border-securityand- immigration-enforcement-improvements.

Executive Order: Enhancing Public safety in the Interior of the United States (2017b, January 25). The White House: Office of the Press Secretary. https:/www.whitehouse.gov/the-press-office/2017/01/25/presidential-executive-orderenhancingpublic-safety-interior-united.

Fariña, M. (2013). Failure to mourn white nativism: Impact of deportation on Hispanic American born children and mixed status families. Smith College Studies in Social Work, 83 (2–3), 139–69. doi:10.1080/00377317.2013.803362.

Fariña, M. (2018). *White Nativism, Ethnic Identity and US Immigration Policy Reform: American Citizenship and Children in Mixed Status, Hispanic Families.* Routledge, Taylor & Francis Group.

Fariña, M. (2019). An Integrative Pedagogical Model for the Teaching of Diversity and Social Justice in Social Work Education: The Integrative Sociopolitical and Psychological Analysis Model. *Urban Social Work*, *3*(S1). 10.1891/2474–8684.3.S1.S52.

Fariña, M. (2020). Why can't I be Latina, female, and professional? Clinical Implications of social discourses that render class invisible, *Smith College Studies in Social Work*, *90*(1–2), 54–78. 10.1080/00377317.2020.1706414.

Felice, R. (2011). *Fascismo*. Le Lettere.

Felice, R. (2017). *Fascism: An Informal Introduction to Its Theory and Practice* (M. A. Ledeen, Ed.). Transaction Books.

Ferreira, C. (2019). Vox como representante de la derecha radical en España: un estudio sobre su ideología. *Revista Española de Ciencia Política 51,* 73–98. doi:10.21308/recp.51.03.

Figueras, S. J., & Bazan-Gonzalez, P. (2017). *The Hispanicization of the United States: The Latino Challenge to American Culture*. Edwin Mellen Press.

Finchelstein, F. (2015). *El mito del fascismo: de Freud a Borges*. Capital Intelectual.

Finchelstein, F. (2017). *From Fascism to Populism in history*. University of California Press.

Fix, M., & Zimmermann, W. (1999). All under one roof: Mixed-status families in an era of reform. The Urban Institute. https://www.urban.org/research/publication/all-under-one-roof-mixed-status-families-era-reform.

Fleming, W. L. (1905, June). Immigration to the Southern States. *Political Science Quarterly, 20*(2), 276–97.

Fonagy, P., & Allison, E. (2014). The role of mentalizing and epistemic trust in the therapeutic relationship. *Psychotherapy, 51*(3), 372–80. doi:10.1037/a0036505.

Ford, H. (Ed.). (1920). *The International Jew: The World's Foremost Problem*. n.d.

Freeden, M. (1998). Is Nationalism a Distinct Ideology? *Political Studies, 46*(4), 748–65. https://doi.org/10.1111/1467-9248.00165.

Freire, P. (1970). *Pedagogy of the oppressed*. Seabury Press.

French, D. (2020). *Divided We Fall: America's Secession Threat and How to Restore Our Nation*. St. Martin's Publishing Group.

Freud, S. (1917). Mourning and Melancholia. In J. Strachery (Ed. & Trans.), *The standard edition of the complete psychological works of Sigmund Freud,* (Vol. 14, 237–58). W. W. Norton & Company.

Freud, S. (1921). Group Psychology and the Analysis of the Ego. *The Standard Edition of the Complete Psychological Works of Sigmund Freud, Volume XVIII (1920–1922): Beyond the Pleasure Principle, Group Psychology and Other Works,* 65–144.

Freud, S. (1926d [1925]). Inhibitions, symptoms and anxiety. *SE,* 20, 77–175.

Friedman, U. (2017, April 11). What Is a Nativist? *The Atlantic*. https://www.theatlantic.com/international/archive/2017/04/what-is-nativist-trump/521355/.

Galtung, J. (1996). *Peace by peaceful means: peace and conflict, development and civilization*. Sage.

García, U. J. (2022, November 15). Federal judge blocks U.S. from using Title 42 to expel migrants at border. *Texas Tribune*. https://www.texastribune.org/2022/11/15/border-migrants-title-42-judge-ruling/.

García, U. J., & Schumacher, Y. (2022, April 29). Here's what you need to know about Title 42, the pandemic-era policy that quickly sends migrants to Mexico. *Texas Tribune*. https://www.texastribune.org/2022/04/29/immigration-title-42-biden/.

García-Sanjuán, A. (2018) Rejecting al-Andalus, exalting the Reconquista: historical memory in contemporary Spain, *Journal of Medieval Iberian Studies, 10* (1), 127–45, DOI: 10.1080/17546559.2016.1268263.

Gellner, E. (2006). *Nations and Nationalism*. Blackwell.

Generation of National Identity (2012). A declaration of war from the Generation of National Identity. https://www.youtube.com/watch?v=XA5S5Qrg6CU.

Gentile, E. (2000). The Sacralisation of politics: Definitions, interpretations and reflections on the question of secular religion and totalitarianism. *Totalitarian Movements and Political Religions, 1*(1), 18–55. DOI: 10.1080/14690760008406923.

Ghiles, F. (2019, November 17). *Vox reinvents history to claim 'Reconquista' of Spain. Arab Weekly*. https://thearabweekly.com/vox-reinvents-history-claim -reconquista-spain.

Golash-Boza, T. (2012). Latino Immigrant Men and the Deportation Crisis: A Gendered Racial Removal Program. *Latino Studies, 11*(3), 271–92.

Goncharenko, R. (2022, October 2). *What awaits the people in Russian-annexed Ukraine?* Deutsche Welle. https://www.dw.com/en/what -awaits-the-people-in-russian-annexed-ukraine/a-63308205.

Gonzalez-Barrera, A., & Lopez, M. H. (2020, July 22). Many Hispanics worried about their place in US, faced discrimination before COVID-19. Pew Research Center. https://www.pewresearch.org/short-reads/2020/07/22/before-covid-19 -many-latinos-worried-about-their-place-in-america-and-had-experienced- discrimination.

Gordon, L. (2017). *The Second Coming of the KKK: The Ku Klux Klan of the 1920s and the American Political Tradition*. W.W. Norton.

Gostoli, Y. (2019, May 27). Where do the elections leave Europe's nationalists? Al Jazeera. https://www.aljazeera.com/news/2019/5/27/where-do -the- elections-leave-europes-nationalists.

Gould, R. (2019). Vox España and Alternative für Deutschland: Propagating the crisis of national identity. *Genealogy, 3*(4), 64. https://doi.org/10.3390/ genealogy3040064.

Grandin, G. (2020). *The End of the Myth: From the Frontier to the Border Wall in the Mind of America*. Henry Holt and Company.

Grant, M. (1916). *The Passing of the Great Race*. Charles Scribner's Sons.

Grant, S. M. (2013). State Building and Nationalism in Nineteenth Century USA. In *The Oxford Handbook of the History of Nationalism* (1st ed., 395–413). Oxford University Press.

Green, D. (2016, December 18). Fascism, American Politics, and Merriam-Webster's Word of the Year. *The Atlantic*. https://www.theatlantic.com/politics/archive/2016 /12/fascism-populism-presidential-election/510668/.

Griffin, R. (2006). *The Nature of Fascism*. Taylor & Francis.

Griffin, R. (2019). *Fascismo* (M. Á. Pérez Pérez, Trans.). Alianza Editorial.

Gross, T. (2022, August 11). How the Trump White House misled the world about its family separation policy. NPR. https://www.npr.org/2022/08/11/1116917364/ how-the-trump-white-house-misled-the-world-about-its-family-separation-policy.

Guia, A. (2016). The Concept of Nativism and Anti-Immigrant Sentiments in Europe. MWP. https://www.mwpweb.eu/1/218/resources/publication_2596_1.pdf.

Gumbel, A. (2015, December). Occasional Paper: The Domestic Terrorism Threat in the United States: A Primer. George Washington University: Program on Extremism.

Haaretz and the Associated Press. (2018, July 11). NSU, the neo-Nazi Group That Forced Germany to Confront Its Racist Demons. https://www.haaretz.com/world -news/europe/2018-07-11/ty-article/the-neo-nazi-group-that-forced-germany-to -confront-its-racest-demons/0000017f-e135-d7b2-a77f-e337b8920000.

Habermas, J. (2001, September–October). Why Europe needs a constitution. *New Left Review, 11,* 2001, 5–26.

Hamilton, E. R., Masferrer, C. and Langer, P. (2022), U.S. Citizen Children De Facto Deported to Mexico. *Population and Development Review.* https://doi.org/10.1111 /padr.12521.

Hanke K., Liu J. H., Hilton D. J., Bilewicz M., Garber I., Huang L. L., et al. (2013). When the past haunts the present: intergroup forgiveness and historical closure in post World War II societies in Asia and in Europe. *Int. J. Intercult. Relat.* 37, 287–301. 10.1016/j.ijintrel.2012.05.003.

Hastings, F. (2019, April 26). The New Spanish Islamophobia. New Internationalist. https://newint.org/features/2019/04/26/new-spanish-islamophobia.

Hemmer, N. (2022, September 8). The Man Who Won the Republican Party Before Trump Did. *New York Times.* https://www.nytimes.com/2022/09/08/opinion/pat -buchanan-donald-trump.html.

Hemmerling, A., Hemkentokrax, J., Taßler, J., & Regis, J. (Executive Producers). (2021). *Das geheime Neonazi-Netzwerk* [TV series]. Das Erste.

Henneberger, D. (2022, September 28). *I*taly: Italien hat gewählt—Rechtsbündnis erzielt klare Mehrheit. Friedrich Naumann Foundation. https://www.freiheit.org/ germany/italy-has-voted-right-wing-alliance-achieves-clear-majority.

Herder, J. G. (1774/2010). *Auch Eine Philosophie Der Geschichte Zur Bildung Der Menschheit.* Kessinger Publishing.

Herder, J. G. (1900). *Werke, 1744–1803* (Vol. 5). Union Deutsche Verlagsgese.

Herman, J. L. (2015). *Trauma and recovery: The aftermath of violence—from domestic abuse to political terror.* Hachette.

Heyes, C. (2020). Identity Politics. In Edward N. Zalta (ed.), *The Stanford Encyclopedia of Philosophy.* https://plato.stanford.edu/archives/fall2020/entries/ identity-politics/.

Heywood, A. (2021). *Political Ideologies: An Introduction.* Macmillan Education UK.

Higham, J. (1972). *Strangers in the land: patterns of American nativism, 1860–1925.* Atheneum.

Hing, B. (2004). *Defining America through immigration policy.* Temple University Press.

Hirschberger G. (2018). Collective Trauma and the Social Construction of Meaning. *Frontiers in psychology, 9,* 1441. https://doi.org/10.3389/fpsyg.2018.01441.

Homeland Security. (2022, October 5). Yearbook 2020. Homeland Security. https:// www.dhs.gov/immigration-statistics/yearbook/2020.

Homeland Security. (2023, April 27). Fact Sheet: U.S. Government Announces Sweeping New Actions to Manage Regional Migration. Homeland Security. https:

//www.dhs.gov/news/2023/04/27/fact-sheet-us-government-announces-sweeping -new-actions-manage-regional-migration.

hooks, b. (1990). Marginality as a site of resistance. In R. Ferguson, M. Gever, T. T. Minh-ha,& C. West (Eds.), *Out there: Marginalization and contemporary cultures* (341–43). MIT Press.

Hopper, E., & Weinberg, H. (Eds.). (2015). *The Social Unconscious in Persons, Groups, and Societies: Volume 2: Mainly Foundation Matrices.* Karnac Books.

Hubbard, K. (2021, February 18). Far-Right Extremism Echoes Across Europe, Survey Finds. USNews.com. https://www.usnews.com/news/best-countries/articles /2021-02-18/far-right-extremism-growing-across-europe-survey-finds.

Huddy, L., Sears, D. O., & Levy, J. S. (2013). Introduction: Theoretical foundations of political psychology. In L. Huddy, D. O. Sears, & J. S. Levy (Eds.), *The Oxford handbook of political psychology* (1–19). Oxford University Press.

Human Rights First. (2020, October 30). The Flores Settlement and Family Incarceration: A Brief History and Next Steps. Human Rights First. https: //humanrightsfirst.org/library/the-flores-settlement-and-family-incarceration- a-brief-history-and-next-steps/.

Huntington, S. (2004). *Who are we? The challenges to America's national identity.* Simon & Schuster.

Huntington, S. (2009, October 28). The Hispanic Challenge*Foreign Policy.* https:// foreignpolicy.com/2009/10/28/the-hispanic-challenge/.

Identity and Democracy Party. (n.d.). https://www.id-party.eu/.

Iliyasov, M., & Gutbrod, H. (2022, March 19). Moscow's Manipulated Memory Politics and Attack on Ukraine—PONARS Eurasia. PONARS Eurasia. https: //www.ponarseurasia.org/moscows-manipulated-memory-politics-and-attack-on- ukraine/.

Illegal Immigration Reform and Immigrant Responsibility Act of 1996. Pub. L. No. 104–208, 110 Stat. 30009–546. (1996). https://www.uscis.gov/sites/default /files/ocomm/ilink/0-0-0-10948.html.

Inglehart, R. F., and Norris, P. (July 29, 2016). Trump, Brexit, and the Rise of Populism: Economic Have-Nots and Cultural Backlash. HKS Working Paper No. RWP16-026. https://ssrn.com/abstract=2818659 or http://dx.doi.org/10.2139/ ssrn.2818659.

International Institute for Democracy and Electoral Assistance. (2021). The Global State of Democracy 2021: Building Resilience in a Pandemic Era. International IDEA. https://www.idea.int/gsod-2021/.

Jacobson, M. F. (1998). Introduction: the fabrication of race. In *Whiteness of a different color: European immigrants and the alchemy of race* (1–12). Harvard University Press.

Jacquet-Vaillant, M. (2021, May 24). An Identitarian Europe? Successes and Limits of the Diffusion of the French Identitarian Movement. illiberalism.org. https:// www.illiberalism.org/an-identitarian-europe-successes-and-limits-of-the-diffusion -of-the-french-identitariamovement/.

Jaret, C. (1999, Spring). Troubled by Newcomers: Anti-Immigrant Attitudes and Action during Two Eras of Mass Immigration to the United States. *Journal of American Ethnic History*, *18*(3), 9–39. http://www.jstor.org/stable/27502448.

Johnson, D. (2012). *Right-Wing Resurgence: How a Domestic Terrorist Threat is Being Ignored*. Rowman & Littlefield Publishers.

Johnson, K. (2004). *The "huddled masses" myth: Immigration and civil rights*. Temple University Press.

Jones, D. S. (2004). *Rationalizing epidemics: meanings and uses of American Indian mortality since 1600*. Harvard University Press.

Jones, S. G., Doxsee, C., & Harrington, N. (2020). The Escalating Terrorism Problem in the United States. Center for Strategic and International Studies (CSIS). http://www.jstor.org/stable/resrep25227.

Jones, S. G., Doxsee, C., Hwang, G., & Thompson, J. (2021, April 12). The Military, Police, and the Rise of Terrorism in the United States. CSIS. https://www.csis.org/analysis/military-police-and-rise-terrorism-united-states.

Jones, S. (2022, March 10). Spain's far-right Vox breaks through into regional government. *The Guardian*. https://www.theguardian.com/world/2022/mar/10/spain-far-right-vox-regional-government-castilla-y-leon-peoples-party-deal.

Kakissis, J. (2020, October 7). Golden Dawn: Greek Court Delivers Landmark Verdicts Against Neo-Nazi Party. NPR. https://www.npr.org/2020/10/07/921134005/golden-dawn-greek-court-delivers-landmark-verdicts-against-neo-nazi-party.

Kamedo. (2007, January, 1). The Terror Attacks in Madrid, Spain, 2004 (Issue 90).

Kamen, H. (2020). *La invención de España: Leyendas e ilusiones que han construido la realidad española*. Espasa.

Kaplan, C. (2012). *Identity* Keywords: NYU Press. https://keywords.nyupress.org/american-cultural-studies/essay/identity/.

Kaufmann, E. (2019). *Whiteshift: Populism, Immigration, and the Future of White Majorities*. Abrams Press.

Kauffmann, G. (2016). Les origines du Front national. *Pouvoirs*, 157, 5–15. https://doi.org/10.3917/pouv.157.0005.

Kaufman, S. (2016). Ethnicity as a generator of conflict. In K. Cordell & S. Wolff (Eds.), *The Routledge Handbook of Ethnic Conflict* (2nd ed., 91–101). Routledge.

Kedourie, E. (1960). *Nationalism*. Praeger.

Kepel, G. (2022). *Away from chaos*. Columbia University Press.

Khazanov, A. M. (2008) Whom to Mourn and Whom to Forget? (Re)constructing Collective Memory in Contemporary Russia, *Totalitarian Movements and Political Religions*, 9:2–3, 293–310, DOI: 10.1080/14690760802094917.

Kiernan, B. (2007). *Blood and Soil: A World History of Genocide and Extermination from Sparta to Darfur*. Yale University Press.

Kienpointner, M. (2017). Rhetoric and argumentation. In J. Flowerdew and J. E. Richardson (Eds.), *The Routledge Handbook of Critical Discourse Studies* (228–441). Routledge. https://www.routledgehandbooks.com/doi/10.4324/9781315739342.ch15.

KKK modern white supremacist groups: map: https://www.splcenter.org/hate-map?ideology=neo-nazi.

Klein M. (1932). *The psycho-analysis of children.* Hogarth.

Klein M. (1940). Mourning and its relation to manic-depressive states. *International Journal of Psycho-Analysis, 21*, 125–53.

Klein M. (1948). On the theory of anxiety and guilt. In *Envy and gratitude and other works,* 25–92. Hogarth, 1975.

Knight, B., & Fürstenau, M. (2016, September 6). Bundestag: Neo-Nazi NSU 'had more than three members.'DW. https://www.dw.com/en/bundestag-neo-nazi-nsu -had-more-than-three-members/a-19530129.

Knight, D. M. (1995, August 9). *THE* "HISPANICIZATION" OF THE UNITED STATES IS INEVITABLE AND IRREVERSIBLE. *Greensboro News and Record.* https://greensboro.com/the-hispanicization-of-the-united-states-is-inevitable-and -irreversible/article_da099314-3bb3-58c3-bfec-f4e51d18b65f.html.

Kohen, A. (2009). The personal and the political: Forgiveness and reconcilia-tion in restorative justice. *Critical Review of International Social and Political Philosophy, 12*(3), 339–423. doi:10.1080/13698230903127911.

Kohn, H. (2017). *The Idea of Nationalism: A Study in Its Origins and Background* (C. J. Calhoun, Ed.). Transaction Publishers.

Koposov, N. (2020). Historians, Memory Laws, and the Politics of the Past. *European Papers—A Journal on Law and Integration, 2020 5*(1), 107–17. https://doi.org/10 .15166/2499–8249/390.

Krastev, I., & Leonard, M. (2021). Europe's Invisible Divides: How COVID-19 is Polarising European Politics. European Council on Foreign Relations. http://www .jstor.org/stable/resrep36091.

Kühl, S. (1994). *The Nazi Connection: Eugenics, American Racism, and German National Socialism.* Oxford University Press.

Kurilla, I. (2020, July 06). *Nationalizing Russian (War) Memory Since 2014.* PONARS Eurasia. https://www.ponarseurasia.org/nationalizing-russian-war-memory-since -2014/.

Kurilla, I. (2018, August 06). *"Russia, My History": History as an Ideological Tool.* PONARS Eurasia. https://www.ponarseurasia.org/russia-my-history-history-as-an -ideological-tool/.

La Moncloa. (n.d.). History of Spain. https://www.lamoncloa.gob.es/lang/en/espana/ historyandculture/_history/Paginas/index.aspx.

Laclau, E. (2018). *On Populist Reason.* Verso Books.

Lake, D. & Rothchild, D. (2020). *The International Spread of Ethnic Conflict: Fear, Diffusion, and Escalation.* Princeton: Princeton University Press. https://doi.org/10 .1515/9780691219752.

Largent, M. A. (2011). *Breeding Contempt: The History of Coerced Sterilization in the United States.* Rutgers University Press.

Le Pen, M. (2022a). *Projet pour la France–Marine Le Pen.* Mlafrance.fr. https:// mlafrance.fr/pdfs/22-mesures-pour-2022.pdf.

Le Pen, M. (2022b). *Immigration Control Project.* Mlafrance.fr. https://mlafrance.fr/ pdfs/22-mesures-pour-2022.pdf.

Le Pen, M. (2022c). *Projet-la-Securite—Security Project.* Mlafrance.fr. https:// mlafrance.fr/pdfs/projet-la-securite.pdf.

Leerssen, J. T. (2006). *National Thought in Europe: A Cultural History*. Amsterdam University Press.

Lewy, G. (2004). Were American Indians the Victims of Genocide? History News Network. http://historynewsnetwork.org/article/7302.

Llach, L. (2022, October 11). Outrage in Spain over 'Return to 1936' song at right-wing rally. *Euronews*. https://www.euronews.com/2022/10/11/outrage-in -spain-over-return-to-1936-song-at-right-wing-rally.

LoGiurato, B. (2016, February 1). The long, wild ride to Iowa: How Donald Trump set the presidential campaign on fire. *Business Insider*. https://www.yahoo.com/ entertainment/long-wild-ride-iowa-donald-124700752.html.

Loewenberg, P. (1991). Uses of anxiety. *Partisan Review, 3*, 514–25.

Loewenberg, P. (1995). *Fantasy and Reality in History*. Oxford University Press.

Lopez-Fuentes, J. (2022). A Forgetting for everyone, by everyone? Spain's Memory Laws and the rise of the European Community of Memory, 1977–2007*. *Journal of Modern History, 94(1),* https://doi.org/10.1086/718121.

Luca, E., Rodomontia, M., & Gazzilloa, F. (2017). Psicopatologia e adattamento all'ambiente: il modello di Fonagy e il modello di Weiss a confronto. *Rassegna Di Psicologia, XXXIV*, 37–45.

Lucassen, L. 2005. *The Immigrant Threat: The Integration of Old and New Migrants in Western Europe since 1850*. Urbana: University of Illinois Press.

Lund, M. S. (2009). Conflict Prevention: Theory in Pursuit of Policy and Practice. In J. Bercovitch, V. Kremenyuk, and I. W. Zartman (eds.). *The Sage Handbook of Conflict Resolution* (287–308). Sage.

MacDougall, D. (2022, October 14). Sweden unveils minority government that relies on far-right support. *Euronews*. https://www.euronews.com/2022/10/14/sweden -unveils-minority-government-that-will-rely-on-a-far-right-party.

MacLean, N. (1995). *Behind the Mask of Chivalry: The Making of the Second Ku Klux Klan*. Oxford University Press.

MacLean, N. (2017, March 20). America's Brush With Fascism: The second KKK shared a disquieting kinship with European fascist movements. Why did it fail to take over American politics? Why the second Ku Klux Klan failed to win pervasive American support.https://slate.com/news-and-politics/2017/03/why-the-second-ku -klux-klan-failed-to-win-pervasive-american-support.html.

MacShane, D. (2019, October 2). Why Support for Europe's Far Right Has Peaked. *American Prospect*. https://prospect.org/world/why-support-for-europes-far-right -has-peaked/.

Madley, B. (2017). *An American Genocide: The United States and the California Indian Catastrophe, 1846–1873*. Yale University Press.

Madley, B. (2015) Reexamining the American Genocide Debate: Meaning, Historiography, and New Methods, *American Historical Review*, 120 (1) February 2015, 98–139, https://doi.org/10.1093/ahr/120.1.98.

Mainstreaming Hate: The Anti-Immigrant Movement in the U.S. (2018, November 28). ADL. https://www.adl.org/resources/report/mainstreaming-hate-anti -immigrant-movement-us.

Marples, D. R. (2020, July 5). *Memory Laws: Censorship in Ukraine*. E-International Relations. https://www.e-ir.info/2020/07/05/memory-laws-censorship-in-ukraine/.

Marples, D. R. (2018). Decommunization, Memory Laws, and 'Builders of Ukraine in the 20th Century. *Acta Slavica Iaponica*, 39, 1–22.

Marshall, M. G., & Gurr, T. R. (2005, June). *Peace and Conflict 2005*. Center for International Development and Conflict Management. https://cidcm.umd.edu/publications/peace-and-conflict-2005.

Masferrer, C., Hamilton, E. R., Denier, N. (2019). Immigrants in Their Parental Homeland: Half a Million U.S.-born Minors Settle Throughout Mexico. *Demography 56*(4): 1453–61. doi: https://doi.org/10.1007/s13524-019-00788-0.

Masters, J. (2022, 10 11). Ukraine: Conflict at the Crossroads of Europe and Russia. Council on Foreign Relations. https://www.cfr.org/backgrounder/ukraine-conflict-crossroads-europe-and-russia.

Massey D. S. (2020). Immigration Policy Mismatches and Counterproductive Outcomes: Unauthorized Migration to the U.S. in Two Eras. *Comparative Migration Studies*, 8, 21. https://doi.org/10.1186/s40878-020-00181-6.

Massey, D. S., Durand, J., & Malone, N. J., & (2003). *Beyond Smoke and Mirrors: Mexican Immigration in an Era of Economic Integration*. Russell Sage Foundation.

Massey, D. S., & Pren, K. A. (2012, March). Unintended Consequences of US Immigration Policy: Explaining the Post-1965 Surge from Latin America. *Population and Development Review*, *38*(1), 1–29.

Massey, D. S., Durand, J., & Pren, K. A. (2016). Why Border Enforcement Backfired. *AJS121*(5), 1557–1600. https://doi.org/10.1086/684200.

Matthews, D. (2020, October 23). What is fascism, and is Trump a fascist? 8 experts weigh in. Vox. https://www.vox.com/policy-and-politics/21521958/what-is-fascism-signs-donald-trump.

Mayorkas, A. N. (2021, October 29). Termination of the Migrant Protection Protocols. Homeland Security. https://www.dhs.gov/sites/default/files/2022-01/21_1029_mpp-termination-memo.pdf.

McMahon, R. (2016). *The Races of Europe: Construction of National Identities in the Social Sciences, 1839–1939*. Palgrave Macmillan UK.

Media Education Foundation. (1997). *Bell hooks: cultural criticism & transformation*.

Menéndez Pidal, R. (1929). *La España del Cid*. Editorial Plutarco.

Meyer, M., & Pachico, E. (2018, March 14). Fact Sheet: U.S. Immigration and Central American Asylum Seekers. ReliefWeb. https://reliefweb.int/report/united-states-america/fact-sheet-us-immigration-and-central-american-asylum-seekers.

The "Migrant Protection Protocols." (2022, January 7). American Immigration Council. https://www.americanimmigrationcouncil.org/research/migrant-protection-protocols.

Mihalache, J. (2016). Why always France? The logic behind the surge of islamist terrorist attacks on its territory and possible policy implications. *Centre for Geopolitics & Security in Realism Studies.*

Miller, A. (2017, February 1). *Политика памяти в России. Роль негосударственных агентов*. АИРО-XXI. http://www.airo-xxi.ru/onasgovorjat/2227-2017-02-01-07-20-10.

Mohamed, S. (2015). Of Monsters and Men: Perpetrator Trauma and Mass Atrocity. *Columbia Law Review, 115* (5), 1157–1216. https://ssrn.com/abstract=2640712.

Mora, J. (2016) El populismo de Le Pen es un fascismo disfrazado de democracia, ABC. https://www.abc.es/espana/abci-populismo-fascismo-disfrazado-democracia -201606290918_noticia.html.

Morris, S., & Labonne, V. (2016, February 12). Video: 40 years on, Franco's ghost still haunts Spain—Revisited. France 24. https://www.france24.com/en/20160212 -video-madrid-revisited-franco-ghost-still-haunts-spain-dicatorship-republican -civil-war.

Mossaad, N. (2019, October). Refugees and Asylees: 2018. Homeland Security. https: //www.dhs.gov/sites/default/files/publications/immigration-statistics/yearbook /2018/refugees_asylees_2018.pdf.

Mossaad, N., & Baugh, R. (2018, January). Refugees and Asylees: 2016. Homeland Security. https://www.dhs.gov/sites/default/files/publications/Refugees_Asylees _2016_0.pdf.

Mudde, C. (2004). The Populist Zeitgeist. *Government & Opposition*, 39 (3), 541–63. http://works.bepress.com/cas_mudde/6/.

Mudde, C. (2012). Research: The Relationship Between Immigration and Nativism in Europe and North America. Migration Policy Institute. https://www.migrationpolicy .org/research/relationship-between-immigration-and-nativism-europe-and-north -america.

Mudde, C. (2016a). Europe's Populist Surge: A Long Time in the Making. *Foreign Affairs*, *95*(6), 25–30. http://www.jstor.org/stable/43948378.

Mudde, C. (2016b). *On Extremism and Democracy in Europe*. Routledge.

Mudde, C., & Rovira Kaltwasser, C. (2017). *Populism: A Very Short Introduction*. Oxford University Press.

Muis, J., & Immerzeel, T. (2017). Causes and consequences of the rise of populist radical right parties and movements in Europe. *Current Sociology*, *65*(6), 909–30. https://doi.org/10.1177/0011392117717294.

Mulhall, J., & Khan-Ruf, S. (2020, October 31). Far-right Extremism in Europe 2021. HOPE not hate. https://hopenothate.org.uk/wp-content/uploads/2021/02/ESOH -report-2020-12-v21Oct.pdf.

Murphy, C. (2017). *The Conceptual Foundations of Transitional Justice*. Cambridge: Cambridge University Press. doi:10.1017/9781316084229.

Ngai, M. M. (1999). The architecture of race in American immigration law: A reex-amination of the immigration act of 1924. *Journal of American History, 86(*1*)*, 67–92.

Ngai, M. M. (2014). *Impossible Subjects: Illegal Aliens and the Making of Modern America—Updated Edition*. Princeton University Press.

Nicolas, G., Wheatley, A., & Guillaume, C. (2015). Does one trauma fit all? Exploring the relevance of PTSD across cultures. *International Journal of Culture and Mental Health, 8*(1), 34–45. https://doi.org/10.1080/17542863.2014.892519.

Nissen A. (2020) The Trans-European mobilization of "Generation Identity" In O. Norocel., A. Hellström, M. Jørgensen. (eds.) *Nostalgia and Hope: Intersections between Politics of Culture, Welfare, and Migration in Europe.* IMISCOE Research Series. Springer, Cham. https://doi.org/10.1007/978-3-030-41694-2_6.

Noury, A., & Roland, G. (2020). Identity Politics and Populism in Europe. *Annual Review of Political Science, 23*(1), 421–39.

Nowrasteh, A. (2019, September 16). *Deportation Rates in Historical Perspective | Cato at Liberty Blog.* Cato Institute. Retrieved December 6, 2022, from https://www.cato.org/blog/deportation-rates-historical-perspective.

Olivan Navarro, F., Reglas Escartin, A., Delgado, O., Lionel, S., & Jaziri Arjona, T. (2021). *El toro por los cuernos: Vox, la extrema derecha europea y el voto obrero.* TECNOS.

Olsen, H. (2021, March 18). *Europe is proof that right-wing populism is here to stay. Washington Post.* https://www.washingtonpost.com/opinions/2021/03/18/europe-is-proof-that-right-wing-populism-is-here-stay/.

O'Neill, P., & Farina, M. (2018). Constructing critical conversations in social work supervision: Creating change. *Clinical Social Work Journal*, 46(4), 298–309. doi:10.1007/s10615-018-0681-6.

Ortega, J. (2020, January 2). *Javier ORTEGA SMITH (VOX): "La RECONQUISTA no ha terminado."* YouTube. https://www.youtube.com/watch?v=_sO0zZXA3Oc.

Osborne, D., & Sibley, C. (Eds.). (2022). *The Cambridge Handbook of Political Psychology* (Cambridge Handbooks in Psychology). Cambridge University Press. doi:10.1017/9781108779104.

Ostler, J. Genocide and American Indian History. *Oxford Research Encyclopedia of American History.* https://oxfordre.com/americanhistory/view/10.1093/acrefore/9780199329175.001.0001/acrefore-9780199329175-e-3.

Parker, I. (1992). Discovering discourses, tackling texts. In *Discourse dynamics: Critical analysis for social and individual psychology* (3–22). Routledge.

Passmore, K. (2009). The ideological origins of Fascism before 1914. In Bosworth, R. J. B. ed. *The Oxford Handbook of Fascism.* Oxford Handbooks in History Oxford: Oxford University Press, 11–31.

Paxton, R. O. (2004). *The Anatomy of Fascism.* Knopf Doubleday Publishing Group.

Paxton, R. O. (2009). Comparisons and Definitions. In R. J. B. Bosworth (Ed.), *The Oxford Handbook of Fascism* (547–65). Oxford University Press.

Paxton, R. O. (2021, January 11). I've Hesitated to Call Donald Trump a Fascist. Until Now. *Newsweek.* https://www.newsweek.com/robert-paxton-trump-fascist-1560652.

Pedler, A. (1927, June). Going to the People. The Russian Narodniki in 1874–5. *The Slavonic Review, 6*(16), 130–41. https://www.jstor.org/stable/4202141.

Piereson, J. (2020, January). The idea of an American nation. *New Criterion.* https://newcriterion.com/issues/2020/1/the-idea-of-an-american-nation.

Politico. (2022). POLITICO Poll of Polls—French polls, trends and election news for France. https://www.politico.eu/europe-poll-of-polls/france/.

Preston, P. (2021). *Arquitectos del terror Franco y los artífices del odio*. Penguin Random House Grupo Editorial.

Preston, P. (2020). *A people betrayed: A history of corruption, political incompetence and social division in modern Spain.* Liveright Publishing Corporation.

Putin, V. (2021, July 12). Article by Vladimir Putin "On the Historical Unity of Russians and Ukrainians". http://en.kremlin.ru/events/president/news/66181.

Putnam Weale, B. L. (1910). *The Color of Conflict*. The MacMillan Company.

Quinn, E. (2016). The refugee and migrant crisis: Europe's challenge. *Studies: An Irish Quarterly Review, 105*(419), 275–85. http://www.jstor.org/stable/24871398.

Rahal, M. (2022). The Algerian War: Cause Célèbre of Anticolonialism. *JSTOR Daily*.

Rama, J., Cordero, G., & Zagórski, P. (2021). Three Is a crowd? Podemos, Ciudadanos, and Vox: The End of Bipartisanship in Spain. *Frontiers in Political Science*, 3, https://www.frontiersin.org/article/10.3389/fpos.2021.688130.

Rama, J., Zanotti, L., Turnbull-Dugarte, S., & Santana, A. (2021). *Vox: The rise of the Spanish populist radical right*. Routledge.

Rassemblement National. (2019). *Pour une Europe des Nations*. rn-europeennes.fr.

Reisigl, M., & Wodak, R. (2001). *Discourses and discrimination: Rhetorics of racism and anti-Semitism*. Routledge.

Reisigl, M. (2017). The discourse-historical approach. In J. Flowerdew and J. E. Richardson (Eds.), *The Routledge Handbook of Critical Discourse Studies* (44–59). Routledge. https://www.routledgehandbooks.com/doi/10.4324/9781315739342.ch3.

Renan, E. (1882/2018). *What Is a Nation? And Other Political Writings* (M. F. N. Giglioli, Ed.; M. F. N. Giglioli, Trans.). Columbia University Press.

Riedel, R. (2018). Nativism versus nationalism and populism—bridging the gap. 6 (2), 18–28.

Roberts, K. L. (1922). *Why Europe Leaves Home*. The Bobbs -Merrill Company.

Roediger, D. R. (2006). *Working Toward Whiteness: How America's Immigrants Become White. The Strange Journey from Ellis Island to the Suburbs*. Basic Books.

Rollings, W. H. (2004). Citizenship and suffrage: The Native American struggle for civil rights in the American West, 1830–1965. *Nevada Law Journal, 5*, 126–40. http://scholars.law.unlv.edu/nlj/vol5/iss1/8.

Rosanvallon, P. (2008). *Counter-Democracy: Politics in an Age of Distrust*. Cambridge University Press.

Ross, M. (2007). *Cultural contestation and ethnic conflict*. Cambridge University Press.

Rothman, J. D. (2016, December 4). The Rise and Fall of the Second Ku Klux Klan. *The Atlantic*. https://www.theatlantic.com/politics/archive/2016/12/second-klan/509468/.

Rothstein, R. (2017). *The color of law: A forgotten history of how our government segregated America*. W. W. Norton and Company.

Roush, T. (2022, December 1). UN Requests Record $51 Billion For Humanitarian Relief Efforts. *Forbes*. https://www.forbes.com/sites/tylerroush/2022/12/01/un-requests-record-51-billion-for-humanitarian-relief-efforts/?sh=3b54952a3e01.

Rowley, R. (2018, November 20). Documenting Hate: New American Nazis. *Frontline*. PBS. https://www.pbs.org/wgbh/frontline/documentary/documenting-hate-new-american-nazis/?

Royster, J. (1995). The Legacy of Allotment. *Arizona State Law Journal*, 27, https:// ssrn.com/abstract=1091180.

Royster, J. V., Blumm, M. C., & Kronk Warner, E. A. (2018). *Native American Natural Resources Law: Cases and Materials*. Carolina Academic Press.

RTVE. (1995). *La Transición*. https://www.rtve.es/play/videos/la-transicion/transición -capitulo-1/2066534/.

Rudan, D., Jakovljevic, M., & Marcinko, C. (2016). Manic defences in contemporary society. *The Psychocultural Approach Psychiatria Danubina*, 28 (4), 334–42.

Safran, J. D., & Kraus, J. (2014). Alliance ruptures, impasses, and enactments: A relational perspective. *Psychotherapy, 51*(3), 381–87. doi:10.1037/a0036815.

San Martín, P. (2012). Is Nationalism an Ideology? A critical exploration from the Asturian case. *Dissidences: Hispanic Journal of Theory and Criticism, 3*(4/5), 1–30 https://digitalcommons.bowdoin.edu/dissidences/vol3/iss5/4.

Santana, A., Zanotti, L., Rama, J., & Turnbull, S. (2021, June 18). *The radical right populist Vox and the end of Spain's exceptionalism*. the Loop: ECPR. https://theloop .ecpr.eu/the-radical-right-populist-vox-and-the-end-of-spains-exceptionalism/.

Saul, J. (2022). *Collective Trauma, Collective Healing: Promoting Community Resilience in the Aftermath of Disaster (Routledge Mental Health Classic Editions)*. Routledge.

Schlegel, F. (1988 [1815]). Geschichte der alten und neuen Literatur: Vorlesungen gehalten zu Wien im Jahre 1812. In E. Behler & H. Eichner (Eds.), *Kritische Schriften und Fragmente: Studienausgabe, 6*(4), pp. I-234.

Schnabel, N. (2020). Examining the round table talks from the perspective of the needs-based model of reconciliation: Observations and insights. *Social Psychological Bulletin, 14*(4), 1–11. https://doi.org/10.32872/spb.v14i4.2321.

Schultz, A. P. (1908). *Race or Mongrel*. Colonial Press.

Seeliger, M., & Villa Braslavsky, P.-I. (2022). Reflections on the contemporary public sphere: An interview with Judith Butler. *Theory, Culture & Society*. https://doi.org /10.1177/02632764211066260.

Serwer, A. (2019, April 15). White Nationalism's Deep American Roots. *The Atlantic*. https://www.theatlantic.com/magazine/archive/2019/04/adam-serwer-madison -grant-white-nationalism/583258/.

Shapiro, S., & Benedicte, S. (2003). The French Experience of Counter-terrorism. Brookings Institute.

Siegel, D. J. (2012). *Pocket guide to interpersonal neurobiology: An integrative handbook of the mind*. W.W. Norton & Company.

Silberschatz, G. (2010). Control-mastery perspective: A clinical formulation of David's plan. *Journal of Psychotherapy Integration, 20*(1), 85–88.

Silberschatz, G. (2017). Control-mastery theory. In *Reference Module in Neuroscience and Biobehavioral Psychology, Elsevier,* 1–8. doi: 10.1016/ B978-0-12-809324-5.05280-9.

Silver, L. (2022, October 6). European populist parties' vote share on the rise, especially on right. Pew Research Center. https://www.pewresearch.org/fact-tank/2022 /10/06/populists-in-europe-especially-those-on-the-right-have-increased-their-vote -shares-in-reent-elections/.

Šima, K. (2021). From Identity Politics to the Identitarian Movement: The Europeanisation of Cultural Stereotypes? In J. Barkhoff & J. Leerssen (Eds.), *National Stereotyping, Identity Politics, European Crises* (75–94). Brill.

Simone, R. (2018). Identitäre im Internet: Von Crowdfunding bis Meme Wars. In A. Speit (Ed.), *Das Netzwerk der Identitären: Ideologie und Aktionen der Neuen Rechten* (142–59). Ch. Links Verlag.

Siniver, A. (2017) Managing and settling ethnic conflict. In Karl Cordell and Stefan Wolff (Eds.) *Routledge Handbook of Ethnic Conflict* (187–97). Routledge.

Skey, M., & Antonsich, M. (Eds.). (2017). *Everyday Nationhood: Theorising Culture, Identity and Belonging After Banal Nationalism.* Palgrave Macmillan UK.

Snyder, T. (2017). *On Tyranny: Twenty Lessons from the Twentieth Century.* Crown.

Southern Poverty Law Center. (n.d.). Identity Evropa/American Identity Movement. Southern Poverty Law Center. https://www.splcenter.org/fighting-hate/extremist -files/group/identity-evropaamerican-identity-movement.

Southern Poverty Law Center. (2011, March 1). *Ku Klux Klan: A History of Racism.* (R. Baudouin, Ed.; 6th ed.). https://www.splcenter.org/20110228/ku-klux-klan -history-racism.

Southern Poverty Law Center. (2020). The Year in Hate and Extremism. Southern Poverty Law Center. https://www.splcenter.org/sites/default/files/yih_2020-21 _final.pdf.

Southern Poverty Law Center. (2022, March 23). Family separation—a timeline. Southern Poverty Law Center. https://www.splcenter.org/news/2022/03/23/family -separation-timeline.

Speckhard, D. (2018, May 1). The U.S. helped cause the problems many migrants face in their own countries; we should help fix them. *Baltimore Sun.* https://www.baltimoresun .com/opinion/op-ed/bs-ed-op-0502-caravan-wall-20180501-story.html.

Speit, A. (Ed.). (2018). *Das Netzwerk der Identitären: Ideologie und Aktionen der Neuen Rechten.* Ch. Links Verlag.

Stannard, D. E. (1992). *American holocaust: Columbus and the conquest of the New World.* Oxford University Press, USA.

Statista. (2023, February 28). Italy: election results 2022. https://www.statista.com/ statistics/1335834/italy-election-results/.

Steigmann-Gall, R. (2017). Star-spangled fascism: American interwar political extremism in comparative perspective, *Social History, 42*(1), 94–119, DOI: 10.1080/03071022.2016.1256592.

Steinby, L. (2009, October). The Rehabilitation of Myth: Enlightenment and Romanticism in Johann Gottfried Herder's Vom Geist der Ebräischen Poesie. *1700-tal Nordic Journal for Eighteenth-Century Studies, 6*(54), 54–79. DOI: 10.7557/4.2760.

Stern, A. M. (2020, August 26). Forced sterilization policies in the US targeted minorities and those with disabilities—and lasted into the 21st century. The Conversation. https://theconversation.com/forced-sterilization-policies-in-the-us -targeted-minorities-and-those-with-disabilities-and-lasted-into-the-21st-century -143144.

Stern, D. (2004). *The present moment in psychotherapy and every day life.* W. W. Norton & Company, Inc.

Stern, P. (1995). Why do people sacrifice for their nations? *Political Psychology,16*(2), 217–35. doi:10.2307/3791830.

Stoddard, L. (1920). *The Rising Tide of Color Against White World-supremacy.* Scribner Press.

Stolorow, R. D. (1993). Chapter three: thoughts on the nature and therapeutic action of psycho-analytic interpretation. Progress in Self Psychology, 9, 31–43.

Stolorow, R. D. (2007). *Trauma and human existence: Autobiographical, psychoanalytic, and philosophical reflections.* Routledge.

Stolorow, R. D., & Atwood, G. E. (2018). *The power of phenomenology: Psychoanalytic and philosophical perspectives* (1st ed.). Routledge. https://doi.org/10.4324/9780429448584.

Tajfel, H. (1981). *Human groups & social categories: Studies in social psychology.* Cambridge University press.

Tajfel, H. (1982). Introduction. In H. Tajfel (Ed.), *Social identity and intergroup relations* (1–11). Cambridge University Press.

Thomas, E. (1936). *Nativism in the Old Northwest, 1850–1860.* Catholic University of America.

Thornton, R. (1990). *American Indian Holocaust and Survival: A Population History Since 1492.* University of Oklahoma Press.

Toal, G. (2017). *Near Abroad: Putin, the West and the Contest Over Ukraine and the Caucasus.* Oxford University Press.

TRAC. (2017, November 7). *Secure Communities, Sanctuary Cities and the Role of ICE Detainers.* Transactional Records Access Clearinghouse (TRAC). Retrieved December 6, 2022, from https://trac.syr.edu/immigration/reports/489/.

TRAC. (2016, December 13). Continued Rise in Asylum Denial Rates: Impact of Representation and Nationality. Transactional Records Access Clearinghouse (TRAC). https://trac.syr.edu/immigration/reports/448/.

Tranfaglia, N. (2016). Trump e il populismo fascista, *Articolo 21,* www.articolo21.org/2016/03/trump-e-il-populismo-fascista/.

Trenchard, J., & Peale, C. W. (2019, July 4). The Declaration of Independence: The Twenty-Seven Grievances. *Journal of the American Revolution.* https://allthingsliberty.com/2019/07/the-declaration-of-independence-the-twenty-seven-ievances/.

Trilling, D. (2020, March 3). *Golden Dawn: the rise and fall of Greece's neo-Nazis.* The Guardian. https://www.theguardian.com/news/2020/mar/03/golden-dawn-the-rise-and-fall-of-greece-neo-nazi-trial.

Tsoutsoumpis, S. (2018). The far right in Greece. Paramilitarism, organized crime and the rise of 'Golden Dawn.' *Comparative Southeast European Studies*, 66 (4), 503–31. https://doi.org/10.1515/soeu-2018-0039.

Turnbull-Dugarte, S. J. (2019). Explaining the end of Spanish exceptionalism and electoral support for Vox. *Research & Politics.* https://doi.org/10.1177/2053168019851680.

Turnbull-Dugarte, S., Rama, J., & Santana, A. (2020). The Baskerville's dog suddenly started barking: voting for VOX in the 2019 Spanish general elections, *Political Research Exchange, 2*(1), DOI: 10.1080/2474736X.2020.1781543.

Tutu, D. (1999). *No future without forgiveness.*

Urbinati, N. (2019). *Me the People: How Populism Transforms Democracy.* Harvard University Press.

U.S. Const. pmbl. Preamble of the United States Constitution.

Valencia, L. D. (2018, February 22). *Generation Identity: A Millennial Fascism for the Future?* EuropeNow. https://www.europenowjournal.org/2018/02/22/generation-identity-a-millennial-fascism-for-the-future/.

Van Dijk, T. A. (2015). Critical Discourse Analysis. In D. Tannen, H. E. Hamilton, & D. Schiffrin (Eds.), *The Handbook of Discourse Analysis* (446–85). Wiley.

Van Mol C., de Valk H. (2016) Migration and immigrants in Europe: A historical and demographic perspective. In: Garcés-Mascareñas B., Penninx R. (eds) *Integration Processes and Policies in Europe.* IMISCOE Research Series. Springer, Cham. https://doi.org/10.1007/978-3-319-21674-4_3.

Vasilopoulou, S., & Halikiopoulou, D. (2015). *The Golden Dawn's 'Nationalist Solution': Explaining the Rise of the Far Right in Greece.* Palgrave Macmillan.

Vergara, J. (2007, June). The History of Europe and its constituent Countries: considerations in favour of the new Europe. *Journal of Social Science Education, 6*(1):15–22.

Villarreal, A. (2023, May 15). The US asylum rule replacing Title 42 is strict—here's what we know. *The Guardian.* https://www.theguardian.com/us-news/2023/may/15/explainer-strict-asylum-rules-replacing-title-42.

Villiers Negroponte, D. (2014, July 2). The Surge in Unaccompanied Children from Central America: A Humanitarian Crisis at Our Border. Brookings Institution. https://www.brookings.edu/blog/up-front/2014/07/02/the-surge-in-unaccompanied-children-from-central-america-a-humanitarian-crisis-at-our-border/.

Vollhardt, J., Jeong, H., & Bilali, R. (2022). Reconciliation in the Aftermath of Collective Violence. In D. Osborne & C. Sibley (Eds.), *The Cambridge Handbook of Political Psychology* (582–598). Cambridge University Press. doi:10.1017/9781108779104.039.

Volkan, V. (1988). *The need to have enemies and allies: From clinical practice to international relationships.* Jason Aronson.

Volkan, V. (1998). Ethnicity and nationalism: A psychoanalytic perspective. *Applied Psychology, 47*(1), 45–57.

Volkan, V. (2009). Large-group identity, international relations and psychoanalysis. *International Forum of Psychoanalysis, 18*(4), 206–13, DOI: 10.1080/08037060902727795.

Volkan, V. (2013). *Enemies on the Couch: A Psychopolitical Journey Through War and Peace.* Pitchstone Publishing.

Volkan, V. (2015). *A Nazi legacy: Depositing, transgenerational transmission, dissociation, and remembering through action.* Routledge

Volkan, V. (2017). *Immigrants and Refugees: Trauma, Perennial Mourning, Prejudice, and Border Psychology.* Karnac.

Volkan, V. (2018). *Psychoanalysis, International Relations, and Diplomacy: A Sourcebook on Large-Group Psychology.* Routledge.

Volkan, V. (2020). *Large-group psychology: Racism, Societal Divisions, Narcissistic Leaders and Who We Are Now.* Phoenix Publishing House.

Volkan, V. (2021). Mass traumas, their societal and political consequences and collective healing. *The UNESCO Slave Route Project: Healing the Wounds of Slavery.*

Wachtel, P. L. (2006). Psychoanalysis, science, and hermeneutics: The vicious circles of adversarial discourse. *Journal of European Psychoanalysis, 22,* 25–46.

Wachtel, P. L. (2014). *Cyclical psychodynamics and the contextual self: The inner world, the intimate world, and the world of culture and society.* Routledge.

Wachtel. P. L., & Gagnon, G. (2019). Cyclical Psychodynamics and Integrative Relational Psychotherapy. In Norcross, J. C., & Goldfried, M. R. (Eds.). *Handbook of Psychotherapy Integration* (3rd ed.). Oxford University Press. https://doi.org/10.1093/med-psych/9780190690465.001.0001.

Walicki, A. (1969). Russia. In E. Gellner & G. Ionescu (Eds.), *Populism: Its Meanings and National Characteristics* (62–96). Macmillan.

Wallerstein, I. (2018a). Capitalisme, crise structurelle et mouvements sociaux contemporains. *Revue du MAUSS, 51,* 361–71. https://doi.org/10.3917/rdm.051.0361.

Wallerstein, I. (2018b). *Chaotic Uncertainty: Reflections on Islam the Middle East and the World System* (O. Madi & C. Sisman, Eds.). KOPERNIK Incorporated.

Wallerstein, I. M., Collins, R., Mann, M., Derluguian, G. M., & Calhoun, C. (2013). *Does Capitalism Have a Future?* Oxford University Press.

Walter, B. F. (2022). *How Civil Wars Start: And How to Stop Them.* Crown.

Waltman, M. (2014). *Hate on the Right: Right-Wing Political Groups and Hate Speech.* Peter Lang.

Waltman, M., & Haas, J. (2011). *The communication of hate.* Peter Lang US.

Washington, J., & Brigida, A. (2022, November 21). Biden Is Still Separating Immigrant Kids From Their Families. *Texas Observer.* https://www.texasobserver.org/the-biden-administration-is-still-separating-kids-from-their-families/.

Weiss, J. (2005). Safety. In G. Silberschtz (Ed.), *The transformative relationships: The control-mastery theory of psychotherapy.* Routledge.

White American Resistance. (1985). *WAR 85, 4*(1), 1–16.

White Aryan Resistance. (n.d.).https://resist.com/.

Whitman, J. Q. (2017). *Hitler's American Model: The United States and the Making of Nazi Race Law.* Princeton University Press.

Wilders, G. (2005, March 13). Partij Voor de Vrijheid. https://www.pvv.nl/index.php/component/content/article/30-publicaties/684-onafhankelijkheidsverklaring.

Wilders, G. (2005, May 7). *Onafhankelijkheidsverklaring.* Tweede Kamerfractie: Partij Voor De Vrijheid.https://www.pvv.nl/index.php/%20component/content/article/30-publicaties/684-onafhankelijkheidsverklaring.

Wilders, G. (2021, May 7). *Het gaat om u: Verkiezingsprogramma 2021–2025.* Partij Voor De Vrijheid.https://energeia-binary-external-prod.imgix.net/oqArdrM06kwLNpBgWyU1GoOfmO0.pdf?dl=PVV+Verkiezingsprogram.

Wiles, P. (1969). A syndrome, not a doctrine. In E. Gellner & G. Ionescu (Eds.), *Populism: Its Meanings and National Characteristics* (166–80). Macmillan.

4444

Willinger, M. (1992). *A Europe of Nations*. Arktos Media Limited.

Wilson, J. (2015). Political Discourse. In D. Tannen, H. E. Hamilton, & D. Schiffrin (Eds.), *The Handbook of Discourse Analysis* (775–94). Wiley.

Winnicott, D. (1965). *The maturational process and the facilitating environment: Studies in the theory of emotional development*. In The international psycho-analytical library, series, (Vol. 64). The Hogarth Press and the Institute of Psycho Analysis.

Winnicott, D. (1951). *Transitional Objects and Transitional Phenomena*. Oxford University Press.

Winnicott, D. (1971). *Playing and reality.* Tavistock.

Wodak, R. (2009). *The Discursive Construction of National Identity*. Edinburgh University Press.

Wodak, R. (2017 a). Wie über Integration von Migrantinnen und Flüchtlinge gesprochen wird. In L. Karasz (Ed.), *Migration und die Macht der Forschung: kritische Wissenschaft in der Migrationsgesellschaft* (41–62). Verlag des Österreichischen Gewerkschaftsbundes.

Wodak, R. (2017b). "Strangers in Europe": A Discourse-Historical Approach to the Legitimation of Immigration Control 2015/16. In *Advancing Multimodal and Critical Discourse Studies: Interdisciplinary Research Inspired by Theo Van Leeuwen's Social Semiotics* (31–49). Taylor & Francis. https://doi.org/10.4324/9781315521015.

Wodak, R. (2020). *The Politics of Fear: The Shameless Normalization of Far-Right Discourse*. Second Edition. Routledge.

Wodak, R. (2021). Re/nationalising EU-rope National identities, Right-Wing Populism and Border and Body-Politics. In J. Barkhoff & J. Leerssen (Eds.), *National Stereotyping, Identity Politics, European Crises* (Vol. 27, 95–124). Brill.

Young, J. G. (2017). Making America 1920 Again? Nativism and US Immigration, past and Present. *Journal on Migration and Human Security*, *5*(1), 217–35. https://doi.org/10.1177/233150241700500111.

Zehr, H. (2005). *Changing lenses: Restorative justice for our time.* Herald Press.

Zeldin, W. (2013, March 19). Hungary: Constitutional Amendments Adopted. Library of Congress. https://www.loc.gov/item/global-legal-monitor/2013-03-19/hungary-constitutional-amendments-adopted/.

Zimmer, O. (2013). Nationalism in Europe, 1918–45. In *The Oxford Handbook of the History of Nationalism* (1st ed., pp. 414–34). Oxford University Press.

Index

Abascal Conde, Santiago,
  98–108, 121–30
affective processes: and banal
  nationalism, 14; and identity, 78, 91
Afghanistan War, 43, 150
agrarian populism, 52
Alfonso the Great, king of Spain, 102
American Psychological
  Association, 112
amnesty laws, Spain and, 105–6
annihilatory fear, 111–12, 127; fascism
  and, 57; Rassemblement National
  and, 119–20; VOX and, 121–22,
  130; white power movements and,
  146–47, 157
anocracy, term, 77
anti-Catholicism, 30–31, 38
Anti-Defamation League, 47
anti-Semitism, 38
Antiterrorism and Effective Death
  Penalty Act, 144, 146–47
anxiety. See fear
Arato, A., 51
Arendt, Hannah, 41, 55
armed forces, white power groups and,
  45–47, 152
Articles of Confederation, 22
asylum-seekers: American nativists and,
  149–57; Europe and, 15–16

Austrian Freedom Party, 16
authoritarianism, 13, 54, 77
Axtell, James, 24

banal nationalism, 14–17
Bannon, Steven, 77
Basques, 13, 100, 105
Beam, Louis, 47
Belew, K., 44–45
Bellamy, François-Xavier, 76
Berman, Sheri, 58–59
Biden, Joe, 144–45, 154–55
Billig, M., 14, 75
binary constructions, 3; analysis of,
  89–90; Le Pen and, 97; populism
  and, 53; VOX and, 100, 102, 107
biopolitics, 113
birthright citizenship, 147
Bloc Identitaire, 71
Bloomfield, V., 139
border issues. See immigration issues
Bousquet, Pierre, 92
Bracero Program, 142
Braden, Anne, 36
Brothers of Italy, 59
Brubaker, R., 13
Buchanan, Patrick, 147
Byman, D. L., 47–48

Canovan, M., 52
capitalism, 80–81, 138, 160
caregiver: and externalization, 115; and
    identity formation, 114
Carrillo, Santiago, 123–24
Catalans, 105
Catholicism, and nativism, 30–31, 38
Chandler, Zachariah, 35
Charlottesville rally, 71, 154
children, immigration policy
    and, 144–48
Chirac, Jacques, 71
Chomsky, Noam, 153
chosen trauma. *See* trauma
Christchurch, NZ attack, 74
Christian Identity, 47
civic commitment, 8–9, 14
civic nationalism, 14–15
Clinton, Bill, 143–44, 147–48, 151
collective identity, 113–18
collective mobilization, ISPA model
    and, 78–81
colonization, US and, 23–24
Combat 18, 61
communism: nativism and, 31; Ukraine
    and, 162, 164
conflict intervention plan, 138–39
conflict management/resolution, 135–
    40; ISPA and, 80; nature of, 136–37
conscientization process, 138–39
Constitution, US, 8, 22; 13th-15th
    Amendments, 35
constructive strategies, analysis of, 89
constructivist approaches, and
    identity, 138
containment, 136, 139
Covadonga, Victory of, 102
COVID-19 pandemic, 23, 155;
    populism and, 54–55
Crimea, 162, 164
critical discourse historical analysis
    (CDHA), 88–91
cultural belonging, 8–9
cultural violence, 136
currency, and national identity, 15

curricula: Russia and, 163; Spain
    and, 106, 129
Czechoslovakia, 13

Damigo, Nathan, 71
Declaration of Independence, 22, 26
Demmers, J., 136
democracy: populism and, 55; Spain
    and, 105–6
demographic change: Russia and,
    162–63; South after Civil War,
    36; white power movements and,
    45–46, 48, 146
denial, 124–25, 128, 163
deportations, 144–45, 147–48, 151
deterrence, 143–44
Diamond, Sara, 147
discourse: and banal nationalism, 14;
    Identity Movement and, 74–78;
    importance of, 83–86, 165–66;
    Rassemblement National and, 92–98;
    VOX and, 99, 101–2, 104, 107
disinformation, 77
disintegration fears, 111; VOX
    and, 122–23
dissociation, 124–25; Russia and, 161
domestic terrorism, white power
    movements and, 46–47, 155
Dominian, Leon, 12
Doyle, H. D., 21–22
Dualist worldview, 56;
    analysis of, 88–91
Du Bois, W. E. B., 34
Duey, Randy, 47
Duke, David, 103, 151
Dupont-Aignan, Nicolas, 76

Eco, Umberto, 51
economic issues: and nativism, 37, 40;
    and populism, 60, 65; post-Civil
    War, 34–35
elites: Le Pen and, 97; populism and,
    53; VOX and, 102
El Salvador, 149, 153
Encarnacion, Omar, 123

enemy: Eco on, 51; populism and, 53; reconciliation and, 139; totalitarianism and, 56. *See also* Other
Erikson, E., 126
Estonia, 117
ethnic minorities in other states, 13, 41, 127–28, 162, 164
ethno-geopolitical nationalism, 11–13
ethno-racism: and nativism, 31–32; in US, 23–25
eugenics laws, 42–43
Europe: Identitarian Movement in, 69–81; national identities in, 63; nation-state and nationalism in, 7–8; populism in, 59; World War II and, 62
European Union: Le Pen and, 97–98; versus national identity, 15; PVV and, 84; and Russia/Ukraine war, 163–64
Eurosceptics, 15
externalization, 113, 115–16

family reunification provision, 142
family separations, 144–45
far-right nationalist parties: in Europe, 16–17. *See also specific party*
fascism, 13–14, 40; definition of, 55–57; Ku Klux Klan and, 43; populism and, 49–50, 54–62, 158; stages of, 41–42, 49, 58, 61; VOX and, 104–8
fear: categories of, 111; fascism and, 56–57; identity formation and, 116; of loss of representation, 86; populism and, 65; and US nativism, 28. *See also* annihilatory fear
Felice, Renzo de, 55–57
Fidesz Party, Hungary, 17
Finchelstein, F., 49–50, 57–58, 64
Fischer, Joschka, 16
Florence Settlement, 144
foreign intervention: France and, 120; Spain and, 122; US and, 150, 153, 160

foreign Other. *See* Other
forgetting: France and, 121; Spain and, 105–6; VOX and, 122–24. *See also* memory laws
Fox News, 148
France: Identitarian Movement in, 69–81; Rassemblement National party and, 91–98, 118–21
Franco, Francisco, 102, 104–7, 129
Frank, Leo, 38
Freedom Party, Austria, 5, 17
Freud, Sigmund, 112
Front National, 91–92
Fyssas, Pavlos, 60

Gaetz, Matt, 150
Galtung, J., 136
Gaultier, Léon, 92
Gellner, E., 10, 18–19
Génération Identitaire, 4, 69–72
genocide: Grant and, 27; Indigenous, US and, 23–25
Gentile, Emilio, 56
Ghiles, Francis, 102
globalization, 15; Le Pen on, 93
Global Project Against Hate and Extremism, 72
Gobineau, Arthur de, 11
Goddyn, Sylvie, 76
Golden Dawn Party, 60–62
Gordon, L., 39
government, white power movements and, 44–46
Grandin, G., 151
Grant, Madison, 12, 26–28
Grant, Susan Mary, 23
Greece, 60–62
Griffin, Roger, 55, 57–58
Guatemala, 149, 153
guest worker program, 142
Gulf War, and white nationalism, 43
Gumbel, A., 45
Gurr, Ted Robert, 77

H-2 guest worker program, 142

Hammerskins, 48–49
hardship standard, 146
hate crimes, rates of, 47–48
Herder, Johann Gottfried, 8–9, 11
Higham, J., 23–24, 30–31, 37, 41
high culture, Herder on, 9
historical trauma. *See* trauma
historicity, 9–10; Du Bois on, 34;
    Génération Identitaire and, 73; and
    nativism, 26; PVV and, 84; Russia
    and, 161–65; VOX and, 104
historiography, 87–88
Hitler, Adolf, 27
Honduras, 149
humanitarian crisis. *See*
    immigration issues

Les Identitaires (LI), 71, 74
Identitaren Bewegung, 74
Identitarian Movement (IM), 69–81;
    bans on, effects of, 74–76;
    founding of, 71
identity, 127; analysis of, 89, 91;
    approaches to, 136; fear and, 111;
    ISPA model and, 78–81; new,
    126, 161–65; and populism, 51;
    terminology in, 3–5; trauma and, 117
Identity and Democracy (ID), 5, 97–98
Identity Evropa Movement, 71–72
identity formation, 78, 96; ideology
    and, 63; psychological analysis and,
    113–18; Rassemblement National
    party and, 119–20
identity politics, 62–63, 73;
    national, 3–4
ideology: and identity formation, 63;
    national, 14; and populism, 52
Illegal Immigration Reform and
    Immigrant Responsibility Act,
    141–44, 146–47
IM. *See* Identitarian Movement
Immigration Act of 1924, 29–30
Immigration and Nationality Act, 142;
    Migrant Protection Protocols, 154–55

immigration issues, 3; displacement
    trends, 141; Europe and, 15–16;
    Identitarian Movement and, 72,
    75–76; populism and, 65; PVV and,
    83–85; Rassemblement National and,
    92–96; US and, 25–30, 37–39, 45,
    141–60; VOX and, 101–2
Immigration Reform and Control
    Act, 45, 143
Indigenous genocide, US and, 23–25
inequality, 80
Ingraham, Laura, 150
instrumental approaches, and
    identity, 138
integrated sociopolitical and
    psychological analysis (ISPA)
    model, 5, 78–81; application of,
    142–57, 161–65; and conflict,
    135–40; methodology in, 86–91;
    psychological analysis in, 111–31;
    sociopolitical analysis in, 83–108;
    steps of, 137–40
intergenerational transmission of
    traumas, 116–17, 125
International Institute of Democratic
    Assistance, 76–78
intertextuality, 90
invasion fears, 111; Rassemblement
    National party and, 119; VOX and,
    122; white power movements and,
    149–50, 156–57
Iraq War, 43, 122
Ireland, nationalism in, 13
Islam: PVV and, 84; Rassemblement
    National and, 95–98, 120; VOX
    and, 101–2, 122–23; white power
    movements and, 150
ISPA. *See* integrated sociopolitical and
    psychological analysis model
Italy, 59

January 6, 2021 insurrection, 49–50, 59,
    65, 148, 156, 159
Les Jeunesses Identitaires (JI), 71

Jews, 38
Johnson, Albert, 39
Johnson, D., 45
Johnson-Reed Act, 39, 42

Kamen, Henry, 102, 105
Kedourie, E., 7
Khazanov, A.M., 161, 163
Khrushchev, Nikita, 162
Klein, M., 112
Know Nothing party, 28–29, 32–33
Ku Klux Klan, 32, 149; decline of,
    40–44; and fascism, 43; founding of,
    33–37; rise of, 37–39
Ku Klux Klan Act, 36, 42

Laclau, E., 51–52
lambda symbol, 73–74
language: and culture, 9; Grant on, 12;
    science and, 11
large-group identities: Identitarian
    Movement and, 69–81; Ku Klux
    Klan and, 35–36; psychological
    analysis of, 112–13
law enforcement, white power
    groups and, 150
leaders: fascist, 56; populist, 54;
    totalitarian, 56
Lechevalier, Christelle, 76
Leerssen, J. T., 8, 10, 13, 15
Lega per Salvini Premier, Italy, 5, 59
Le Pen, Jean-Marie, 91–92
Le Pen, Marie, 59, 76, 91–98, 118–21
Luyt, Guillaume, 71

Macron, Emmanuel, 59, 92
Madley, B., 24–25
manic defenses, 128–29, 156, 158
Manichaean worldview, 56;
    analysis of, 88–91
master narratives, 79, 87–88; Abascal
    and, 101, 104, 107; importance of,
    165–66; Le Pen and, 94, 96–97;
    Russia and, 162–63; white power
    movements and, 146–47

McVeigh, Timothy, 46
media: VOX and, 99–100; white power
    movements and, 150, 157
mediation, ISPA and, 135–40
Meggs, Kelly, 147
Meloni, Giorgia, 59, 131
memory laws: ISPA and, 140; Russia
    and, 162; VOX and, 103–4,
    106–7, 129–30
Menendez Pidal, Ramon, 105
mentalization, 124, 129, 139
Mexico, and immigration issues, 141–60
Mezinger, Tom, 45–46
Minutemen Project, 151–52
miscegenation, fears of, 11; American
    nativists and, 28, 37, 146; VOX
    and, 101–2
mobilization: ISPA model and, 78–81;
    Le Pen and, 98
monogenism, 11
Morano, Nadine, 76
Morawiecki, Mateusz, 131
Morocco, 122
mourning, 113, 126–27, 139, 160;
    Russia and, 161–65
Mudde, C., 52–53
music festivals, white power
    movements and, 49

narratives. *See* discourse; master
    narratives; rhetoric
nation, definition of, 7
national identity, 10; definitional
    issues, 14–15
national identity politics, 3–4
national ideology, 14
nationalism, 7–19; banal, 14–17;
    definitional issues in, 7, 18; ethno-
    geopolitical, 11–13; in Europe, 7–8,
    11–14; psychological borders and,
    96; and racial paradigm, 10–11; rise
    of, 131, 135; Russia and, 161–65;
    term, 3–6; VOX and, 99
National Origins Quota Act, 29

National Rally. *See* Rassemblement
    National party
National Sozialistischer
    Underground, 49
nation-state: in Europe, 7–8; formation
    of, 23–25; nativism and, 30–32;
    US as, 22–23
nativism, 21–32; definitional issues,
    21, 23–25; and resistance to
    transformation, 157–60; rise of, 135,
    145–48; term, 3–6; war and, 33–50
NATO, Russia and, 161
Nazism, 56. *See also* fascism
neoliberalism, 18, 80–81, 138, 160
neo-nationalism, 18
neo-Nazis, 48–49. *See also* fascism
Northern Triangle Countries, 149, 153
nostalgia, Russia and, 163

Oath Keepers, 148–49, 152–53
Obama, Barack, 143–45, 152
object relations theory, 113
Oklahoma bombing, 46
100 percent Americanism, 37–39
Onfran, Michel, 76
Orbán, Viktor Mihály, 53, 131
The Order, 47
Ordre Nouveau, 91–92
Ortega Smith, Javier, 102
Ortego Lara, Jose Luis, 98
Other, 113, 159; populism and, 53; PVV
    and, 85; Rassemblement National
    and, 96–97, 120; reconciliation and,
    139; totalitarianism and, 56; US and,
    143; VOX and, 122–23

paramilitary groups, 44–48; France and,
    121; and immigration issues, 148–57;
    transnational, 48–50
Partido Popular, 98–100, 103
Party for Freedom,
    Netherlands, 4, 83–85
Patriot movement, 45
Paxton, R. O., 41–42, 57–58
People's Party, Austria, 16

"people"/true people: defining, 30–32;
    populism and, 52–53
personality, psychology and, 113
perspective taking, 129
Pitcavage, M., 47–48
Poland, 13, 77
polarization, 3, 77, 153; psychological
    analysis of, 118
political nativism, 31
political populism, 52
political psychology, 112–13
politics: Identitarian Movement and,
    75–81; sacralization of, 56
polygenism, 11
popular culture, Herder on, 9
populism, 51–66; definition of, 51–52;
    and fascism, 49–50, 54–62, 160; and
    resistance to transformation, 157–60;
    rise of, 131, 135; term, 3–6
postwar period: nationalism in, 13–14;
    populism in, 63–65
preservative strategies: analysis of,
    89; Le Pen and, 93, 96, 98; VOX
    and, 99, 107
Prichard, J. C., 11
projection, 115, 128
propaganda, fascism and, 56
Proud Boys, 148
psychological analysis, in ISPA model,
    79, 111–31; application of, 118–30;
    in conflict management/resolution,
    138; definition of, 112
psychological borders, 96, 113–18;
    VOX and, 108
Public and Health Act, Title 42, 155–57
public opinion: disinformation and, 77;
    Identitarian Movement and, 75
purity: populism and, 53;
    Rassemblement National
    party and, 119
Putin, Vladimir, 163–64

quotas, racial, 29, 140

race issues: ethno-racism, 23–25, 31–32; post-Civil War, 34–37; in US, 21–32. *See also* white power movements
racial paradigm, nationalism and, 10–11
radicalism, nativism and, 31
Rajoy, Mariano, 100
Rassemblement National party (National Rally), 17, 59; and Génération Identitaire, 76; psychological analysis of, 118–21; sociopolitical analysis of, 91–98
rational choice, 113
Reagan, Ronald, 45
recommitment, and conflict resolution, 140
reconciliation, versus amnesty, 105–6
Reconquista, 73, 101–5, 121–23
Reconstruction, 34–36
recontextualization, 73, 90, 104–5, 154, 165
recruitment, white power movements and, 146, 152
Reed, David, 39
refugee crisis. *See* immigration issues
religion: Le Pen and, 94–96; and nativism, 30–31; VOX and, 102, 104
remigration: Identitarian Movement and, 72; PVV and, 85
Renaissance Coalition, 97
representation: fears of loss of, 86; importance of, 83–86
repression, 124–25, 128, 163
Republican Party, 153–54, 160
resistance, 126, 140, 157–60; Russia and, 161–65
rhetoric, 3, 111; Génération Identitaire and, 69–70; importance of, 83–86; Putin and, 163–64; Rassemblement National and, 92–98; VOX and, 99, 101–2; white power movements and, 146, 150
Rhodes, Stewart, 148–49
Robert, Fabrice, 71
Roberts, K. L., 28–29

Romanticism, 8–9, 88, 95
Rosanvallon, P., 55
Ross, M., 91
Rousseau, Jean-Jacques, 8, 53
Rovira Kaltwasser, C., 52
Rubinstein, William, 24
Russia: and Estonia, 117; and Ukraine, 161–65

sacralization of politics, 56
Saul, J., 125
Schlegel, Frieder, 9
Schultz, A. P., 27–28
self-preservation behaviors, 116; Rassemblement National party and, 119
Sellner, Martin, 72, 75
Serwer, A., 27
Sforza Italia, 59
Simmons, William J., 38
slavery: Know Nothing party and, 33; US and, 23, 35
Smith, Barbara, 73
social contract, 9, 78
socialism, nativism and, 31
social media, Identity Movement and, 72, 74
social reconciliation, 137–38
sociopolitical analysis, in ISPA model, 79, 83–108; application of, 91–98; in conflict management/resolution, 137–38
Soviet Union, collapse of, 161–63
Spain: and fascism, 104–8; VOX, 59–60, 98–108, 121–30
Speckhard, D., 153
Steigmann-Gall, R., 43
Stoddard, Lothrop, 27–28
stories: importance of, 165–66. *See also* discourse; master narratives; rhetoric
strategies, analysis of, 89–90
structural violence, 136
Sweden Democrats party, 131
symbols: bans on, 129; lambda, 73–74; types of, 115

Tarrant, Brenton, 74
Taylor, Jared, 76
Telegram, 74
terminology, 3–7; importance of, 83–86
territorial borders: and identity, 113–18; and nation, 10
terrorism: Identitarian Movement and, 74; Islamic, 120, 122; white power movements in US, 46–47, 155
Thomas, E., 32
time collapse, 118, 124
Title 42, Public and Health Act, 155–57
totalitarianism: fascism and, 55; US and, 42
transformative strategies, analysis of, 89
transitional objects, 114
transitional space, 114
trauma, 116–18, 125–26; in Europe, 86; France and, 121; ISPA and, 80, 135–40; Rassemblement National and, 120; treatment of, timing of, 124; US and, 158; VOX and, 105, 122–23
Trump, Donald, 4, 53, 131; and border issues, 144–45, 155–56; and disinformation, 77; and fascism, 54, 58–59; and white power movements, 148, 150, 154
Trumpism, 65
trust issues: Europe and, 16; polarization and, 77; in US, 65
Tsitselikis, Konstantinos, 61

Ukraine, 161–65
Une Autre Jeunesse (UAJ), 71
United Nations, 141
United Nations High Commissioner for Refugees, 157
United States: authoritarianism in, 77; nativism in, 21–50; populism in, 53–54, 58–59, 64–65; white power movements in, 141–60; World War II and, 62
Unité Radicale, 71
Unite the Right Rally, Charlottesville VA, 71, 154

Urbinati, N., 53
Utley, Robert, 24

Van Young, E., 21–22
Vardon, Philippe, 71
Verstrynge, Jorge, 60
veterans: Identity Evropa and, 71; white power groups and, 45, 152
victim stance: VOX and, 100; white power movements and, 152
Vidal-Quadras, Aleix, 98–99
Vietnam War, and white nationalism, 43, 45
violence, 136–37; American nativists and, 38–39; fascism and, 55; populism and, 58, 60; psychological analysis of, 118; Trump and, 59, 65; white power movements and, 46–48
Viva22 rally, 129, 131
Volkan, Vamik, 79, 112–13, 116–17, 120
voluntaristic will *(volonté générale)*, 8, 53
VOX, 59–60; psychological analysis of, 121–30; sociopolitical analysis of, 98–108

Wachtel, P. L., 118
Walters, Barbara, 77
war, and nativism, 33–50
Weale, B. L. Putnam, 29
Weaver, Randy, 47
White Aryan Resistance (WAR), 45–46, 146
white nationalism, in US, 21–32
white power movements: in Europe, 69–81, 121; and immigration issues, 146–57; and political parties, 90; and resistance to transformation, 157–60; transnational, 48–50; in US, 33, 44–48
Wilders, Geert, 4, 83–86
Wiles, P., 51
Willinger, Markus, 4
Winnicott, D., 112–14
Wodak, R., 88

World War I, 11–13, 37–39
World War II, 40–44, 62

Yanukovych, Viktor, 164
youth, white power movements and, 146

Zapatero, Jose Luis, 106
Zeldin, W., 17
Zemmour, Eric, 76

About the Author

Maria del Mar Fariña, PhD, is an associate professor in the Westfield State University Graduate Social Work Program, adjunct professor at Smith College School for Social Work, adjunct associate professor at Columbia School of Social Work, and course facilitator at Boston University School of Social Work. Her research in political psychology pertains to American immigration policy, immigrant integration, and contemporary rising socio-political ideologies in Europe and the United States, with a primary focus on nationalism, nativism, populism, and white power groups discourse. Her work has been presented in Europe, the United States, and Canada, including at the International Society of Political Psychology (ISPP), and Processes Influencing Democratic Ownership and Participation (PIDOP), part of the European Commission, under the Seventh Framework Programme. She is the author of *White Nativism, Ethnic Identity* and *US Immigration Policy Reforms: American Citizenship and Children in Mixed Status, Hispanic Families*. Her work has also been published in the *Clinical Social Work Journal, Journal of Social Work Education, Smith Studies in Social Work,* and *Urban Social Work Journal*.

www.ingramcontent.com/pod-product-compliance
Lightning Source LLC
Chambersburg PA
CBHW050709280326
41926CB00088B/2882